# • CLAUDE BELLONI

Claude (Boy) Belloni, about 1970

Family Claude (Boy) Belloni; Claude, Anita, Louise, Renée,
Hollandia Harbour, New Guinea, about 1960

RENÉE BELLONI * THE SUN IN HIS EYES

Renée Belloni

# The Sun In His Eyes

Claude (Boy) Belloni

(Batavia, 1922-The Hague, 1995)

An incredible life

His life's journey

through

The Dutch East Indies, Japan, New Guinea and the Netherlands

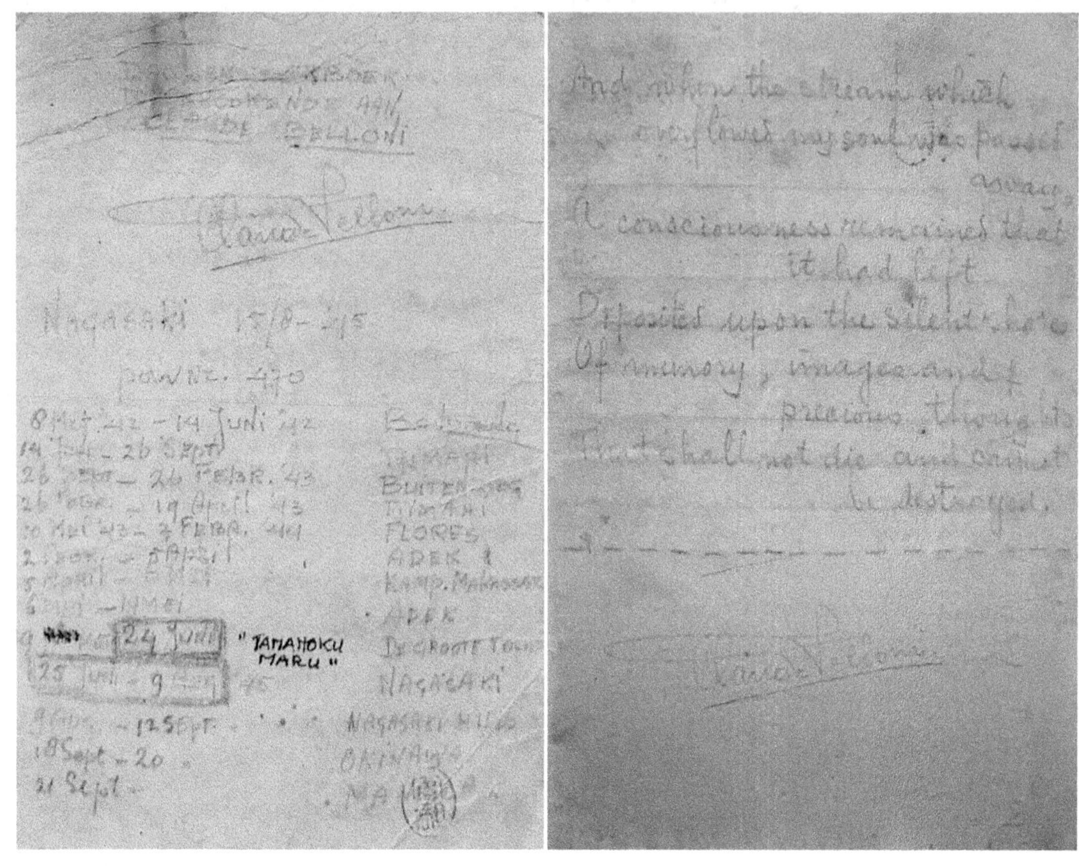

In honour of my father. The first two pages of Claude's well kept diary

# FOR ELLA, PHOENIX AND KAI

# Contents

Claude (Boy)

# INTRODUCTION

*My* search for Claude's past often gave me an oppressive feeling. When I read new passages from his diary, I thought, how will he get through this?

I'm pulling the curtain back on 'The Sun In His Eyes.' It's a bit of my heart spilt across pages, telling my father Claude's story against the backdrop of the Dutch East Indies and Japan during the war. It's a mix of the real tough life he went through and a bit of storytelling to connect the dots.

## Dedication

This one's for hoping we can all find some peace, starting with ourselves. If we can get there, maybe there's hope for the rest of the world too.

Anne Frank's been on my mind a lot. Through her diary, she showed us bravery and hope in the face of the unimaginable. – a young, hopeful voice tragically silenced in a Nazi concentration camp, yet her message of peace and resilience endures.

"When you find peace within yourself, you become the kind of person who can live at peace with others."

I'm handing this story over to my grandniece Ella and my grandnephews, Phoenix and Kai. It's a bridge to their great-grandparents' world — a world of love, loss, and the stories that stick to your soul. It's about holding onto our roots and passing on the torch of their stories.

My parents, Claude and Anita, they've been through the wringer — surviving the war, the camps, and all that came after. But instead of letting it turn them bitter, they chose forgiveness. They taught me that hanging onto anger doesn't lead to peace. It's about letting go or holding it differently, and looking forward.

Writing this book? It's been a road to healing for me. Diving into their lives, I got to see their courage, their love, and yeah, their pain, in a whole

Fred and Nettie Belloni, both 15 years old

new light. It's been tough, emotional, but also a kind of healing. Sharing their journey, I hope it brings some understanding, maybe even a bit of peace, your way too.


## My search

The search for Claude's past always felt like walking through a thick fog. Every new line I read in his diary was a step deeper into his world, and I kept asking myself, "How did he get through all of this?"

Claude was born into the Belloni family on 9 July, 1922, in the middle as the second of three kids. His parents, Frederik Hendrik Belloni and Charlotte Antoinette Belloni-Strengnaerts, first welcomed his older brother, René, and then his younger sister, Desirée, joined the crew. Friends and family knew him as 'Boy' — a name that stuck all his life, a familiar call among those who were close to him.

Before Claude, there was Margot Leonie, the daughter Charlotte was expecting, with her first husband, Gérard Rohart. But fate had its plans, and Gérard never got to meet his daughter, leaving Charlotte a widow before Claude's chapter even began.

In 2019, my sister Louise and I decided it was time to dive into Claude's life story. We found ourselves sitting on the floor in a cozy spot of her Mooloolaba atrium, the Australian sun filling the space with a warm, easy light. Right there with us was this big cardboard box, waiting to be opened. It was like a time capsule from our parents' house in Leidschendam, a quiet place not too far from The Hague, the Netherlands. These memories had been sitting in a cupboard, out of sight but not forgotten, until we were finally ready to sift through them.

Opening the box felt like stepping back in time. Inside, we found folders stuffed with photos — big ones, tiny ones, mostly in black and white — and some other things like newspaper clippings, letters, journals and more, each with its own piece of our family's puzzle. Back in the Netherlands, we still had boxes full of slides and old films, from the small 8mm ones to the slightly larger super 8. Claude, ever the journalist and photography enthusiast, had collected all these as a way to tell his story. He'd show these slides and films at family gatherings, turning each viewing into a mini history lesson. We always thought we knew all these stories because Dad could remember every little detail like it was yesterday.

Starting this project, Louise and I felt a mix of excitement and respect for what our parents went through. This book is built around the photos from our family's collection, snapshots that are about seventy years old now. They're not just old pictures; they're gateways to the stories and dreams of the past. Sure, some of the photos got a bit blurry when we turned them into digital images, but they still capture our family's spirit and the adventures they lived through. These memories, even if they're a bit faded, are our link to a legacy that's as rich and detailed as any family's could be.

As I sit down to bring these memories to life, I'm fully aware that my take on things might be coloured by my own feelings and maybe a bit idealised. It's a bit like trying to paint a portrait from what you remember; no matter how hard you try, your feelings and personal views are going to influence the picture you end up with. I'm not saying this to cover my tracks but rather to invite you into this story, to see it not just as a series of events but as a human story, shaped by the way we hold onto our past.

The starting point for all this is Claude's diary. It's a treasure trove of insights, even though the earliest parts were lost when he was a prisoner in the East Indies and the Japanese forces found and destroyed his first diary. That loss cuts a big hole in our family's story. But Claude kept going, starting a second diary from 1943 to 1948 that shows just how tough he was. This diary stayed with my mum until she passed away in 2011, and now it's with Louise and me. The thoughts and experiences he wrote down, which we've included here, are raw and real, his personal truth captured in words, his words.

My main goal in telling this story has been to show how big, sweeping events — like wars — can completely change a person's life. My father's life was shaped by the harsh realities of war, a truth he and my mum lived through from the day they got married. I think a lot of Dutch Indos will see parts of their own family stories in Claude's journey. But more than that, I hope this story reaches people who might not have any direct ties to the Dutch East Indies, New Guinea, or the Pacific wars of 1942-1949. I want to bridge the gap between different times and places, to bring people into Claude's world, hoping they will find something in his story that resonates with them, something that makes them feel connected to a larger human story.


## Explanation

To provide context and clarity, here is a brief explanation of several terms related to the Dutch East Indies, which are used throughout the book:

In this book, quotes from the diary or from Claude's articles do not have inverted commas, but have a different font and two blank lines before the beginning of a quote and after a quote. The same applies to his journals about the expeditions in New Guinea, which have another font and two blank lines before and after.

The language and spelling are as they were in those days. We might think and write about it differently now. The same applies to the description of the culture and life of the people living on New Guinea Island at that time and the treatment of their diseases.

- My father was called Claude or Boy and I use these two names interchangeably.
- Regarding the 'u/oe' writing, I have chosen to write all the words which should have a 'oe' or 'u', with a 'u'. In the English language, using the 'u' is more common.
- 'Dutch Indos' are ethnic Dutch people with a family history in the former Dutch East Indies (the present Indonesia). They are therefore not Indonesians.
- We can roughly divide the Dutch East Indies into Indo-Europeans and 'Totoks' also called 'Belandas'.
- Totoks are full-blooded Europeans who were born in the Dutch East Indies or who had lived there for a considerable time.

- Indo-Europeans, sometimes called 'Indos', are the descendants of people from Europe who married indigenous people in the Dutch East Indies at that time. You could also say that they are people of mixed blood of Asian-European descent. The word 'Indo' is not derived from the Indonesian or Indian language.
- "Indisch" in Dutch is used by the Indo-Europeans and is not translated in this book. So an Indisch cuisine means traditional food of the Dutch East Indies.
- 'Native' is the word that was used for the original, indigenous inhabitants of the former Dutch East Indies and New Guinea.
- "POW" = Prisoner/s of war
- "KNIL" = Koninklijk Nederlands Indisch Leger, The Royal Dutch East Indies Army

Nettie Belloni, in the Netherlands, about 1936

# Claude's Bloodline

The roots of Claude's family tree stretch back to 1811 with the birth of Jean Baptiste Belloni Jr. in Leuven, Belgium.

He's Claude's great-grandfather, a man who, in 1835, set out far from home to the island of Java in the Dutch East Indies. He was part of the *'Korps Jagers van Cleerens,'* (Corps Hunters of Cleerens), a group of hunters and adventurers. His journey didn't stop there; he later made his way to Padang on the island of Sumatra.

Jean Baptiste's life took a turn when he met Nasari, a local woman. They shared their lives for many years, and along the way, they welcomed six children into their world. It was only after these years of companionship and family life that Jean Baptiste asked Nasari to marry him.

## A Belgian soldier in Sumatra

*J*ean found his world linked with Nasari, a local woman with indigenous roots as deep as the history of the land itself. Their love story wasn't loud or flashy; it was a quiet stand against the world's expectations, proving that love doesn't care about borders or backgrounds. Prior to making any formal commitments, they had already established themselves as a family, navigating the ups and downs of raising six children. When Nasari became Maria Magdalena through baptism, it wasn't just a name change — it was a new chapter for them, expanding their family to seven kids, with a few following in their father's military footsteps. In reality, Jean Belloni's household included eight children. Among them was a foster child, Johannes Hendrikus Cress, tied to them by fate's unseen threads and a shared past with Jean's comrade. Johannes' father had died when he was four years old and his mother was an indigenous woman. Jean had known Johannes' father because he was his comrade in the KNIL. Therefore, there was a strong bond between them. Johannes always considered Maria and Jean Belloni as his 'parents'.

The final chapter of Jean Baptiste's journey wrapped up in Harderwijk, the Netherlands, in 1874, and Maria's story ended in Semarang, Central Java, in 1893. They left behind more than just memories; they left a legacy that's still part of us today.

Petrus Lavenus, born in 1860 before his parents officially tied the knot, carried on the family tradition. Like his father, he too found love with a local woman, Norana. They got married in 1893 in Fort de Kock, Bukittinggi, West Sumatra. Following her baptism, Norana took on the name Christina Josephina. Together, they had a house full of kids — ten in total, with half of them born before the wedding bells rang. Christina's life, bustling with the energy of ten little ones – and even more, some of whom sadly never saw the fullness of life – was a relentless cycle of pregnancy and childbirth, a common rhythm of life back then.

Petrus Lavenus Belloni, grandfather of Claude, about 1900

Claude's lineage is a rich shade of cultures. Looking back through the Belloni family tree, I've found roots stretching from Italy and Belgium to the Netherlands, France, and even distant ties in China.

Christina Josephina (Norana), with grandchild and children

## The Fred Belloni family

In Claude's family, music wasn't just background noise; it was like a natural gift. My granddad, Fred, turned out to be a wonderful musician, which was something else, considering back in his day, making a career out of music was almost a fantasy. It's a bit of a shame, though, that Claude's grandpa, Petrus Lavenus Belloni, couldn't see past music being just a hobby, never realising the depth of this family talent.

Flipping back through my memory album to the sixties — that's when we ended up in Holland, leaving Dutch New Guinea behind. My head's filled with snapshots of that time: bundling up in winter coats, the artistry of ice flowers on windows, the thrill of skates on frozen ponds, mornings wrapped in fog, the fearless hippies, and the never-before tunes of The Beatles and The Stones. It was an era of disorder and colour, of wild hearts and fresh ideas. Among these vivid recollections, one stands out:

the day I met my grandparents Belloni, Nettie and Fred, in The Hague on *'Kerkstraat'*, known as Church Street. To me, they were Oma and Opa Bell, my dear Grandma and Grandpa Bell — figures of warmth and love in my childhood.


## The musician Opa Bell

Opa Bell was more than just a man who knew his way around a violin. He was a full-on maestro. Many visits were like a private concert; he'd just grab his violin and let it sing, playing by heart and making it up as he went. My father always said that when Opa played, it was like he wrapped the entire room in his love for music. It was as if he'd drift off to another place, totally caught up in the music. On stage, everyone knew him as Fred Belloni, but to us, he was born to make music, picking up the violin on his own and making it look easy.

Fred Belloni wasn't just a name at home; he was known far and wide, in the East and the West, for his skills with a violin, his compositions, and his leadership in orchestras. He had this amazing ability to bridge worlds with his music, dabbling in everything from the tuneful strains of Kroncong and the beat of Gamelan to marching tunes, dance tracks, jazz, and the sophisticated world of classical music.

I remember learning the ropes of Kroncong and Gamelan music from him was like opening a door to different worlds. Kroncong has this vibe that pulls from Portugal and Spain, with guitars and tambourines leading the charge, and sometimes you'd find violins, flutes, cellos, ukuleles, banjos, and double basses joining the mix. Gamelan, on the other hand, is this whole other scene — pure traditional tunes with oriental scales, a collection of Javanese percussion, and instruments like the 'rebab' and flutes adding layers to the sound.

Newspaper article. Columbia records. Fred Belloni, 1930

Opa Belloni's love for music went way beyond just playing tunes; he was a creator, crafting and conducting his own pieces with a joy that was contagious. His music had this Kroncong vibe — catchy, bittersweet, and always with a deep, passionate pulse. He had this talent for blending those laid-back, Portuguese-inspired tunes with his own unique twist, making something really special.

What started as simple do-re-mi's jotted down in his teens turned into full-blown scores, leading to grand pieces played by big orchestras in all sorts of places. His work made it onto over fifty records in the '20s and '30s, all under the big-time label Columbia Records Company.

Fred's big win was mixing East and West in his music, getting those traditional Eastern sounds to hit just right for Western listeners. His piece, '*Langs Java's Stranden*' (Along Java's Beaches), is a classic example, blending Western styles with Gamelan flair.

Growing up, Fred was just one of many in a musically charged family of ten siblings, plus a few half-brothers and sisters. Pretty much everyone, even their father Petrus, played something, turning their home into a non-stop music festival. Music was the glue that kept the family tight, especially when times got tough.

My dad and his half-sister would talk about how, even when money was tight because of how many of them there were, music was their escape. It was their real treasure, with everyone's voices blending with clarinets, flutes, cellos, pianos, and violins to lift them out of their struggles.

What would his child do, anyway, with a career in the unstable world of entertainment? Playing with staves was more of a leisure activity, according to Petrus, who spoke from his own experience.

But Fred didn't let that hold him back. He used his gift, composing for anyone who'd asked, like the appealing 'K.W.S. March' he wrote for the Queen Wilhelmina School for Trade and Shipping, where he dipped his toes into architecture. Fred was the life of many parties and jubilees, bringing his compositions to life with his ensemble or even leading a thirty-man orchestra at the K.W.S. festival in Batavia when he was just in his twenties.

Fred Belloni in London. Conductor of Columbia Symphony Orchestra, 1936

## The musical Fred Belloni family

In 1936, while in the Netherlands, Fred received an invitation from Columbia Records to record and conduct in London, an honour extended to his entire family as well. For this special occasion, he composed two overtures: *'Kembang Ramping'* (Slender Flower) and *'Een Tocht Door Insulinde'* (A Journey Through 'Insulinde', a term of endearment for the Dutch East Indies).

In London, Fred recorded these instrumental pieces, along with other arrangements. There, he also took the baton to lead the 80-member Columbia Symphony Orchestra. For Claude, seeing his father at the helm of such a massive ensemble was nothing short of magical.

In Fred's home, music was like the air they breathed, setting the rhythm for their daily lives. So, it's no surprise his kids were steeped in it from the get-go. René and Claude, his boys, were practically glued to the violin as soon as they could hold one, and Désirée, or Dési as everyone called her, took her skills to the next level at the conservatory in The Hague. Aunt Dési wasn't just any musician; she had a soprano voice that could make you stop and listen, and she was pretty slick on the piano too. When she teamed up with Opa Fred for performances, they were unbeatable. Their music, a blend of her powerful vocals and his emotive violin play, often-brought tears to the eyes of those, especially repatriates, touching something deep inside them.


## Indisch cabaret evenings

Tjalie Robinson, or Jan Boon to those who knew him before he became 'the voice of the East Indies in the Netherlands', was a big deal in our community. He was the man behind *'Onze Brug'* (Our Bridge), a magazine that later turned into 'Tong Tong' and then *'Moesson'* (Monsoon). In 1958, Tjalie's foundation, Tong Tong, pulled off something special — they set up three nights of Indisch cabaret at the Royal Tropical Institute in Amsterdam. These nights were extremely popular, tickets sold out rapidly, and Queen Juliana

Her Royal Highness Juliana with composer and violinist Fred Belloni.
On the right Tjalie Robinson

made a special appearance on the final night, making it a highly regarded occasion. The mix of plays, dances, and music had everyone talking.

Fred Belloni, was one star of those nights, sharing his Indisch tunes with everyone. There was this one break when Queen Juliana met the performers, and Opa got to shake her hand. That instant got snapped in a photo that he cherished, framed and sitting on the black marble mantelpiece in their house in The Hague for all his years.

Since 1959, the Tong Tong foundation has kept the spirit alive with a huge annual festival in The Hague, starting as the Pasar Malam Besar and now known as the Tong Tong Fair. It's this massive celebration of Indisch culture, mixing an international fair vibe with foodie heaven and a cultural fest, all rolled into one. There are different pavilions and stages, each showing off a piece of our heritage. And get this — there's a spot they still call 'Belloni Square' or 'Belloni Street,' named after my Opa, a nod to the mark he left on our community's culture.

Tong Tong Fair 2023

Fred Belloni. Bandung, 1932

## Opa Bell is no more

It was a regular day turned into an unforgettable one, when we lost Frederik Hendrik Belloni, our Opa Bell, to a heart attack on 25 April, 1969, in The Hague. He was 77, a full life behind him. Despite that, it felt too soon. Right up to the end, Opa was all about the music, sharing tunes on his violin with Nettie, his partner through everything, and with kids and his grandkids. His music, a constant in our lives, just stopped.

Losing Opa shook our world to its core. Oma Bell, suddenly alone without her other half, moved in with us into our tight-fit three-bedroom flat in Leidschendam. Space was tight, but I didn't think twice before offering my room to her. That meant my new spot was a camp bed in my parents' room. Those thirteen months, all of us squeezed together but closer for it, are locked in my heart. It wasn't until we found a bigger place, still in Leidschendam, that we could give Oma a bigger room again. Charlotte Antoinette Belloni, our dear Oma Bell, left us peacefully on January 6, 1979, at 89. The love and warmth of my grandparents, that's something that'll stay with me forever.

Nettie and Fred, The Hague, 1938

"

You can hide your memories

But

You cannot erase your past

*With thanks to:*
*Author: Haruki Murakami*
*Book: Colorless*
*Publisher: Penguin Random House LLC (US)*

Family Fred Belloni. From left to right. On top: Claude, Nettie, Désirée.
Underneath: Fred, René

# MORE ABOUT CLAUDE

Raised in two worlds and yet growing up as a true Indo, he was a man of two cultures.

Claude was a perfect mix of different worlds, a true Indo through and through. Raised between two cultures, he wasn't just caught in the middle — he fully embraced his Indo-European roots with pride and loyalty. To me, Claude was the epitome of what it means to be Indo: proud of who he was, never wavering in his commitment to his cultural heritage and traditions, right up to the end.

His tastes were as eclectic as his background. Claude loved his Indo food, could never get enough of rice and the variety of Indo snacks. But then he'd turn around and demolish a pack of wine gums in one sitting. His sweet tooth was legendary; he'd drive for an hour just to get his hands on some nougat or Turkish delight.

Every morning started the same way for Claude: with a cup of '*kopi tubruk*', sweet and heavy with sugar, always leaving those telltale coffee grounds at the bottom of the cup. His conversations were something else — full of life, hands moving, often adding a splash of humour to any family get-together.

When it came to music, Claude's tastes were all over the map. He loved the gypsy jazz of Django Reinhardt and Stéphane Grappelli, the classic swing of Glenn Miller's Orchestra, not to mention his love for country & western, rock and roll, and classical music. His hobbies were just as varied: from reading to tennis, ten-pin bowling, hunting, fishing, and getting hooked on his favourite TV shows. Each interest, each hobby, painted a part of the picture of Claude — a man who grabbed life with both hands and lived it to the fullest.

## Claude's nature

Growing up straddling the East and West, Claude was a blend of the best of both worlds. To outsiders, he might appear reserved. He was the quiet type, modest, sometimes shy, deeply feeling, and could even seem a bit timid. But there was so much more to him beneath the surface — a straightforward, tender but tough individual. He valued making his home a home of warmth and safety, yet his essence was anything but simple.

I remember Dad for his kindness and warmth, unwavering loyalty, and incredible empathy, especially towards those he loved. He had this unique ability to really get what others were feeling, a skill that was golden in his journalism career. Those traits — his focus, drive, ambition, intuition, creativity, and the ability to inspire — didn't just help him in his work; they were his support system through all kinds of adventures and challenges.

Claude's imagination was another layer of his complex personality. Sometimes, he seemed to live in a world all his own, a characteristic that must have been a source of comfort during the tough times of his captivity. When the going got tough, he'd dive into a better, more hopeful place in his mind, a testament to his ability to rise above the grimness of his surroundings.

Claude had the gift of the gab. His wit was sharp, and he knew how to use words, fluent in multiple languages. This skill made him a hit at public events. He'd stand up to speak with just a slip of paper with bullet points, yet he'd captivate everyone with his relaxed confidence and eloquent speech.

At more laid-back gatherings, like parties or birthdays, you'd find Claude at the centre of it all. He had a talent for storytelling and timing his jokes just right, always gathering a crowd around him. He was the spark of any celebration, often setting the tone for the entire event.

But Claude was human, with his own set of quirks. He could be messy and mischievous, adding to the tapestry of who he was. These traits, while perhaps not as polished, were part of the charm that made him the unique and unforgettable character we cherished.

Looking back now, I see just how lucky I was to have a father like Claude, who didn't hang on to anger. Sure, he carried a bit of sadness with him, but who doesn't? That side of him was a gift, especially during my teenage years, when I was testing the waters and stepping out of line more than a few times. His calm nature made those rebellious moments a lot smoother for both of us.

During my time in secondary school, Dad's gift for languages really came into play. He'd sit with me for hours, walking me through the intricacies of English, German, and French. With his help, I went from middling grades to scoring A's and B's. His patience and dedication didn't just boost my report card; they left a lasting mark on me. Thanks to him, I still use those languages today.

Thinking about Dad, I picture a man who stood firm on his values and ethics, a person with an enormous heart, endless patience, and a gentle touch, yet he was also tough and knew how to have fun. He had this playful side to him, a bit of a flirt even, which was all part of his charm. To me, Claude wasn't just my dad; he was my hero. He was someone I loved deeply and whose memory I keep alive and dear to my heart, just like my mum.

Claude and Renée

Nettie Belloni with her three youngest children. Left to right: René, Désirée, Nettie, Claude, about 1928

With Dutch clogs through Holland, Public domain

# Overture
## Part I
## Before World War II
## 1. From the Dutch East Indies and back

A *babu* (nanny),

a rascal,

and a new adventure

Claude as a four year old boy

# 1.1 Claude's childhood, 1922-1940

Claude grew up in pleasant neighbourhoods of the cities of Batavia and Bandung. He had a pleasant Indo-European childhood.
As free as a bird!

*H*is older brother, René, was the first child of Fred and Nettie, born in 1918, with Claude arriving four years later. Their birthplace was *'Weltevreden'*, a suburb that lived up to its name, meaning "satisfied" in English, sitting comfortably about ten kilometres southeast of Batavia's city centre (known today as Jakarta) and a good 150 kilometres northwest of Bandung. Weltevreden was a spot favoured by Europeans, named after an estate in the area. Nettie and Fred, originally from Bandung in West Java — a city celebrated for its European flair, set in the middle of the volcanic mountains, rice fields, and tea plantations — had moved to the capital, Batavia, in search of better job opportunities. Bandung was designed as a garden city, filled with parks and green spaces that made it a picturesque place to live.

However, after spending five years in Batavia, Fred and Charlotte decided it was time to move back to Bandung with René and Claude, where Fred took up a new role as a deputy qualified technical officer at the *'P.T.T.'*, the postal, telegraphy, and telephony service. It was in Bandung, surrounded by its natural beauty and garden city charm, where their third child, Désirée, was born on 15 November 1924.

## Baby and stories

Back when Claude was just a little lad, everyone called him Boy, and he had this amazing babysitter, his babu, who took care of him like no other. She'd wrap him up in a *'slendang'* sling, kind of like those baby wraps people use today, but it was a special thing from back in the East Indies. His family says he was always snuggled up in there, pretty much his first little safe spot.

By the time Boy was four and ready for kindergarten in Bandung, he was all set to go, always with his babu by his side. School for him wasn't just about ABCs and 123s; it was where all the fun was at — playing, making new friends, and honestly, he'd rather hang out there than stick around with his cousins. But the best part? Story time. It was like the stories his mum used to tell him at home, all about Teddy, the bear's adventures, or the cool stuff they'd see through the Magic Lantern. They'd even sing together, with Boy chiming in softly.

Every night, they followed the same sweet routine: kissing him goodnight, tucking him in tight with his bear, and then quietly closing the door, leaving him to dream about all those stories they shared. That's pretty much how Boy, started loving stories so much.

## Nice teacher and siesta

At six, Claude's journey to school took on a new form. No longer accompanied by the babu. Now, he walked with a sense of pride next to his older brother, René, making their way to the primary school a half-hour's journey from home. Stepping into the 'big' school at 7:30 a.m., Claude was a mix of bravery and nerves. Decked out in short dark trousers and a light shirt with short sleeves, topped with a light-coloured tie and knee-high socks — all hand-me-downs from René — he was ready to take on the world. There was a sparkle of excitement in starting fresh, part of which surely came from his liking for the kind teacher at school. He enjoyed staying longer after classes wrapped up at 1 p.m. to help clean up the room, even though René would often wait, tapping his foot, ready to head home for lunch and the much-needed siesta to escape the midday heat.

From two to four, the house would quiet down for siesta time. On days when sleep seemed miles away, Claude would quietly slip out the bedroom window for some secret playtime, always careful to stay close for a swift return. After the quiet hours, Claude, ever the conscientious student, would settle down to go over his schoolwork. And when tricky math problems proved a challenge, René was there to lend a hand.

At eight, a significant moment came into Claude's life when his dad offered him the choice of picking a musical instrument. Echoing his father and brother, Claude chose the violin, embracing an instrument that sang in harmony with the Belloni family's musical legacy.

## An old bicycle and the bow

With René moving up to secondary school, Claude got his brother's old bike, a tad too big but a treasure in his eyes. The bike was his ticket to freedom, letting him dart to playgrounds or drop by friends in the nearby *'kampongs'* (villages). It was among these village friends that Claude soaked up lessons on nature and survival, figuring out which wild edibles were safe and learning home remedies for common sicknesses.

Riding high on this newfound liberty, Claude's days were a blur of visits and races, always zipping back home as dusk approached. This freedom, this slice of adventure, painted his childhood in strokes of unbridled joy.

Yet, at ten, the shift from optional violin practice to a must-do wasn't exactly thrilling for Claude.

One afternoon, driven by a mix of rebellion and a craving for the open air, he devised a plan. Coming home from school, he grabbed his violin bow and, without a second thought, thrust it into his bicycle wheel in a moment of defiance. The aftermath was a loud bang, a broken bow, and a fleeting sense of victory.

Claude thought he'd outsmarted his obligations, pedalling away in bliss. However, the intact bike wheel was the only win of the day. His dad, Fred, who usually steered clear of physical punishment, decided this was a teachable moment. The broken bow didn't just mark the end of Claude's escape plan; it also left a distinct mark on him, one that stayed both on his skin and in his memory. Years down the line, Claude would share this tale, the mischief, the consequences, and all the details still vivid in his memory.

Claude around 12 years old, the Netherlands

# 1.2 Departure

During his teenage years, Claude wasn't just known for his cheeky antics; he was also bursting with the spirit of an adventurer, always on the lookout for new experiences and eager to step beyond the confines of his familiar surroundings.

Working in the tropical climate of the Dutch East Indies was no joke — the heat was just one part of it. So, people who worked for the Dutch government or in business often got a break. They could head back to the Netherlands for a bit, anywhere from six months to a year, just to cool off and recharge. That's exactly what Fred, Claude's dad, did in May 1933. Claude was just ten years old then and got his first taste of a real culture shock landing in the chilly Netherlands. But it wasn't all about the shock; it was a door to new adventures and making friends in a totally different setting, with new weather and new ways of doing things.

When it was time to get back, Fred was supposed to move to Borneo for his job. But he wasn't having any of it. Borneo was going to be way too hot, especially compared to the cool, comfy climate of Bandung, sitting pretty on its high plateau. Plus, Fred had bigger plans for his kids — he wanted them to get an excellent education. So, he stretched their Netherlands stay far beyond the initial plan, ending up there for almost seven years longer than expected. After a while, he went from being on leave to getting redundancy pay, until finally, in 1936, Opa was officially retired.

## The Belloni Family in The Hague

When the Belloni family arrived in The Hague, they settled into the Flower district, a place that buzzed with the same vibrancy its name suggested. The move wasn't smooth sailing, especially for Fred, who quickly realised that living off a musician's income was tougher here than expected.

Fred was never one to sit back. He dived into art photography with the same passion he poured into his music. Without the luxury of online tutorials, Fred learned the old-fashioned way — through persistence and a fair share of mistakes. His determination bore fruit when he earned a diploma in portrait photography, eventually opening "Charlotte," his studio, in the bustling *'Goudenregenstraat'*, Laburnum street. The whole family pitched in, the kids turning their bathroom into a makeshift darkroom and assembling photo frames in the studio.

Yet, music remained Fred's true calling. He even studied harmony and counterpoint to a Czech professor, keen on honing his musical talents. Fred's intellectual curiosity didn't end there; he took up radio courses in English and Esperanto, driven more by a love of learning than practical necessity. These endeavours were all part of Fred's commitment to his art and to making a life for his family in this new land.

For Dési and Claude, adapting to Dutch schools was an adventure. Claude thrived in the local primary school, showing a resilience that surprised everyone. René, after high school, toyed with studying medicine in Leiden but ultimately followed his passion for aviation, earning his pilot's wings at Soesterberg Air Base.

During Claude's teenage years in The Hague, he engaged in the typical pursuits of youth — making new friends, experiencing first loves, and taking part in popular pastimes of the era such as dancing, skating, and fishing. School, initially daunting, became a place of belonging.

Fishing, in particular, became Claude's hobby of choice. He and his friends would cycle to quiet fishing spots, more for the camaraderie than the catch. The fish they brought home never quite lived up to the tales they spun, but those stories grew with each telling. This love for fishing and the art of storytelling stuck with Claude into adulthood, weaving itself into the fabric of his personality.

Claude (left) with his friends and their 'big' catch, the Netherlands

Music of Fred Belloni and his 'boys'. Citizen internment camp, Bandung, 1942

# 1.3 Fear of War

As the skies over Europe grew heavy with the threat of war, Fred couldn't shake off a gnawing worry.

*T*he headlines screamed of conflict in England, France, and Germany, and Fred felt it in his bones — the Netherlands wouldn't be far behind. With a heart heavy with foresight, he made a bold choice: it was time to pack up and head back to the East Indies, a place he deemed safer than their current home.

Boy, the family's young adventurer, was more than ready for this next chapter. Holland had been an adventure, but Insulinde — that was home. He longed for the friends and the life he'd left behind, excited to jump back into his studies and pick up where he'd left off.

Aunt Dési would often recount with a twinkle in her eye how Fred had seen the storm coming long before others did, convincing them to make their escape just in the nick of time. Their journey to safety was an adventure in itself — leaving from Naples on one of the last ships to the Dutch East Indies, avoiding the rumoured mined waters of the North Sea. They travelled by night train through Germany and Northern Italy, a silent, tense journey to Naples, where the M.S. *Sibajak* awaited them. René, with his pilot's license freshly in his hand, had already set off ahead of them to join the military forces waiting in the East Indies.

Their voyage was anything but calm. The M.S. *Sibajak*, escorted by the powerful tugboat *Zwarte Zee*, Black sea, zigzagged through dangerous waters, narrowly avoiding mines. A heart-stopping moment occurred when a British destroyer halted them near Gibraltar, but luckily, they received permission to proceed without significant delay.

Landing back in the East Indies felt like a sigh of relief. Fred discovered they wouldn't need to move to Borneo as he'd feared. They settled back into life in Bandung, where Fred dreamt of a peaceful retirement filled with music. He poured his heart into building a new home on '*Wajanglaan*', naming it Shadow Lane, a place where shadows danced gently in the peace of their backyard.

For Boy, being back on familiar ground meant diving back into his studies with gusto. He enrolled in a business course at the P.T.T., ready to tackle his education with the same adventurous spirit he'd applied to everything else. But just as he was finding his rhythm, the war in Southeast Asia erupted, throwing yet another curveball his way.


## Captured

Fred's life turned upside down when the Japanese troops stormed into Bandung. One day, he was living his normal life, and the next, he was being herded like cattle into '*Maria Sterre der Zee*', a makeshift internment camp set up in a convent. The place, run by nuns, felt ironic to Fred. The walls, meant to offer peace, now trapped him in. Even the priests, usually a source of comfort, were just as stuck and helpless as he was.

Fred's violin, an old, trusty thing he'd had for years, became his escape in the camp. It wasn't much to look at, but when he played, it felt like he was somewhere else, if only for a moment. He wasn't alone in his love for music. A couple of other prisoners, who knew their way around a melody, joined him. They'd play together whenever they could, their music a mix of sad and lively tunes that seemed to lift everyone's spirits, if only just a bit.

After Fred left the convent, they moved him to '*Sukamiskin*' prison, and then to a place called '*Land-Opvoedings-Gesticht*', also called the Upbringing Institute, on Daendelsweg. It was a grim, old youth prison with walls so high they blocked out most of the sky and topped with broken glass that glinted menacingly in the sun. Here, his violin wasn't just for escape; it was his only friend, helping him keep his head above the waves of despair with every note he played.

Meanwhile, the Wajanglaan quarter, where Oma and aunt Dési used to live, had changed completely. Their neighbourhood, once full of friendly faces and familiar sights, had transformed into a women's camp. The two of them had to leave their home, carrying whatever they could and wandering in search of a safe place. They ended up in a small pavilion near someone they knew. It wasn't much, but it was something.

But then Joke and her son André, René's wife and son, got caught up in the mess. Because they were Dutch, the authorities arrested them and sent them to a camp. André, just a little kid of not even two years old, did not make it; he died from dysentery. It hit the family hard, showing just how cruel and senseless the war was.

Oma Bell and Dési had barely started feeling safe in the pavilion when they got evicted. Japanese soldiers took over the place with no warning, and they were back to square one, homeless again. Every day was a reminder that nothing was certain anymore.

They eventually found a small place in Naripan, a little south of Bandung. It was a cramped three-room house, but it was a roof over their heads. To afford it, though, they had to sell almost everything they owned. It was tough, but it gave them a place to call home, something they managed to keep even after the war was over.

After getting out of the camp, Fred had only one thing on his mind: finding his eldest son, René. He disguised himself, trying to blend in with the locals, and spoke Sundanese as best he could. He went from village to village, always looking, always hoping. But being obvious not from around there made it hard. He kept asking himself, would he ever find René? Was he even still alive?


**Rosary**


In the Belloni household, Roman Catholicism was not just a religion; it was a way of life that bound the family together. My grandparents Belloni, along with their children, including my mother, Louise, and I, were devout followers of this faith. Sundays found the Fred Belloni family in church, an image of devotion, as they knelt, prayed, and clutched their rosaries, each bead a symbol of their commitment to their beliefs.

Perhaps Fred fortified this steadfast faith during the trying times he faced in the internment camp. Opa Fred often recounted how his time in the Maria Sterre der Zee camp, alongside learned priests also held captive, deepened his understanding and devotion. Through many and profound discussions about faith, he not only gained knowledge but also found a renewed strength in his beliefs. This period of his life was transformative, turning him into a fervent advocate for his faith, unafraid to engage in debates and deeply committed to the lay apostolate.

Fred's faith wasn't passive; it was active and giving. Fred donated a significant portion of his pension to support the mission. Warmth and a deep-seated belief in its principles marked his advocacy for the lay apostolate. This aspect of his life left a lasting impression on those around him, that much so that when Fred passed on, a member of my grandparents' senior club remarked to Claude, "We don't really need to pray for Fred; he has already secured his place in heaven."

Opa Belloni, around 1967

René ready for departure

# Part II
# Before and during the Japanese occupation
## 2. Claude and the second world war

Pleasure,

a samurai sword

and a booted foot

Fred Belloni in piano trio

# 2.1 Claude's experiences

# The years 1940 - 1941

1940 wasn't just the start of Claude's studies; it was a blast of a year, full of fun.

Claude kicked off his training with the P.T.T. as a business official right in Bandung, not too far from where he lived. Study time aside, he had loads of chances to chill, have fun, and hit the town. The movies were a big hit — everyone was crazy about the wave of Hollywood films, jazz, swing music, and dance nights. It felt like everyone was living in a bubble of fun, convinced that with the mighty American and British fleets around, Japan wouldn't dare come anywhere near the Dutch East Indies. But when the mobilisation call came, it hit everyone hard.

Even the Indo-European newspapers were all over it with headlines like, "DO WE REALISE?"

"Tarakan has been attacked and they are fighting to the death and we know that at that moment Dutch and Indo-European blood are flowing. We know that the war, with all its horror, has come to our country. But this cannot interrupt, even for a moment, the desire for pleasure. The jazz music rages on. The dancing goes on. And our brothers and sons are giving their lives on Dutch East Indies soil for the freedom of the country. But it does not penetrate." *"Djongos bawa pait lagi!"*, or "Boys, bring me another pint!" "Kassi beer!", and "Miss, may I have this dance? Hey, did you hear the latest joke?"... "We still do not realise that we are a country at war."

It was like everyone was in denial, not ready to face the fact that we were now a country at war.

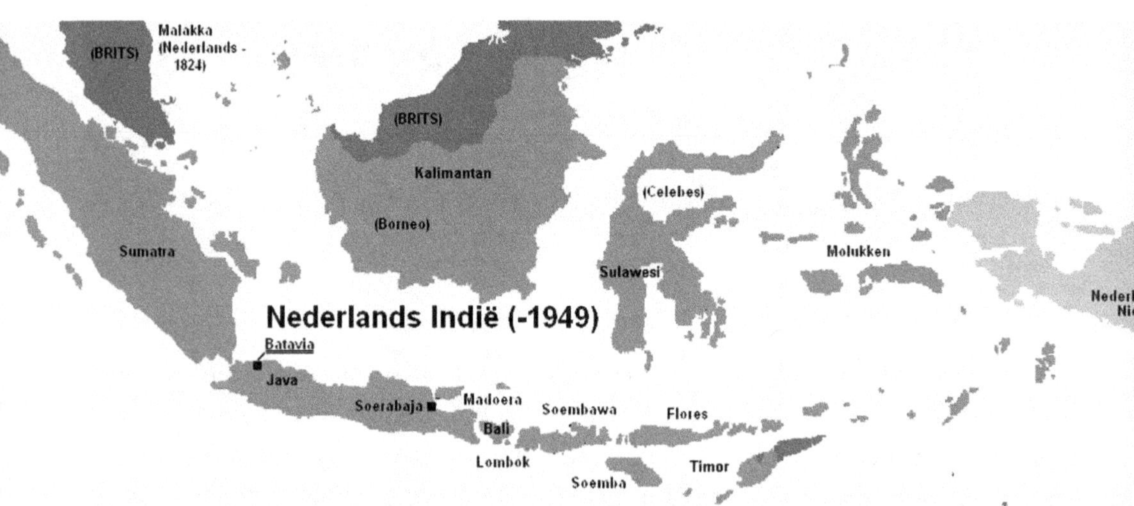


Map of the Dutch East Indies

# 2.2 JAPAN FORGES ITS PLAN

In the early 1940s, the world was on the edge, with conflicts brewing everywhere, and Japan was no exception.

Japan was on a mission to build 'Dai Nippon', or the Empire of the Rising Sun, dreaming big like Europe's vision of 'Gross Deutschland'. But this wasn't just about politics. The Japanese firmly believed that it was their destiny to lead an Asian order under the guidance of the Japanese Emperor.

1941, the Year of the Snake, seemed to echo the growing tensions between the United States and Japan. These issues weren't new; they were the result of long-standing diplomatic disagreements that had been simmering for years. Japan's eye on China wasn't just for show. It was driven by a mix of needing more space for their growing population and wanting to dominate the Chinese market. The desire to dominate the Chinese market was not just a strategy; it was seen as a necessity for Japan's survival and growth.

There was a strong feeling in Japan that their culture was sacred, that their traditions and values were not just unique but superior, and meant to be shared across Asia. This belief in their cultural dominance was what pushed them towards expansion.

When Japan declared war on China in 1937, it was more than a political move — it was them saying they believed they had a rightful place in the world. This move, however, didn't sit well with the United States, which saw Japan's aggression as a threat to global balance and peace.

The United States didn't want to jump straight into conflict, so they hit Japan with what they had — economic sanctions and trade embargoes. These weren't just economic strategies; they were a clear message of disapproval from America. But these actions only pushed the two countries closer to an inevitable clash that would drag the entire world into war.

By 1940, the trade relationship between the United States and Japan was falling apart. The end of the 1911 trade treaty was a big deal, a sign of trust breaking down and alliances weakening. The American embargo that followed, which started with aviation materials and soon included oil, iron, and steel, was like a warning of the storm to come.

Then, Britain, Australia, and the Dutch joined the United States, making the embargo even bigger. This wasn't just a few countries acting on their own; it was a united front, a group of nations coming together to say they weren't okay with Japan's push for more territory.

For Japan, the stakes couldn't have been higher. Japan was facing a future where their military strength would suffer greatly due to the lack of critical resources like oil. Even more alarming was the prediction of an economic crash within two years if things didn't change. Backing out of China and stopping their push for more land seemed like obvious exits, but those moves felt like admitting defeat, a hit to Japan's national pride and goals that was too hard to swallow.

As talks between Tokyo and Washington kept going with little progress, any hopes for sorting things out peacefully were fading fast. These drawn-out negotiations were tense, each side sticking firmly to their guns, making it feel like everyone was walking a tightrope over a deep chasm. With every day that went by without a deal, the worry of a looming crisis grew, leaving folks in Japan, the U.S., and their Allies all on edge, wondering not if but when things would boil over into outright war.

Then, on 6 September, 1941, a meeting in Japan's Cabinet laid down a choice that would change the world forever. Admiral Yamamoto got the green light for a plan that would push Japan from playing it safe to taking bold, aggressive moves.

Japan laid out two big strategies: the Eastern Plan and the Southern Plan. The Eastern Plan was all about making a bold move to Pearl Harbor and taking over the Philippines, which was under American control back then. The Southern Plan was the major goal, aiming to grab Malaysia (then a British territory), Borneo, Java, Sumatra, and more. These weren't just battle tactics; they were part of a bigger plan on the world stage.

7 December, 1941, became a day that would forever be remembered. The attack on Pearl Harbor, on the Hawaiian island of Oahu, was so precise that it caught the U.S. completely by surprise. The sight of American battleships, the pride of the U.S. navy, being sunk or badly damaged, would stick in the minds of people for generations.

Following the surprise and catastrophic strike on Pearl Harbor, along with simultaneous attacks on other territories, the United States, joined by Britain and the Netherlands, officially entered the war against Japan. This alliance signalled a critical turn in World War II, as these countries rallied together to push back against Japan's bold moves.

Just days later, on 10 December 1941, the Allies faced a stark reality check about the strength of Japan's military might. Japanese aircraft took the British battleships H.M.S. *Repulse* and H.M.S. *Prince of Wales*, central to 'Force Z' down. These ships, sent to guard Malaysia, were caught off guard without the support of air defence. The Japanese attack was relentless and well-coordinated, with a barrage of bombs and torpedoes that the British fleet couldn't withstand.

## Japanese declaration of war

In a twist of fate, despite being initially exempt from military service because of his brother René's enlistment, Claude found himself drafted into the military as the global situation intensified. On 2 August 1941, he received orders to join the military as a soldier in the 1st Department Battalion, gearing up for training with the 14th Battalion Infantry. This abrupt call to service marked a significant detour from the future Claude had imagined for himself.

Claude's talent for radiotelegraphy quickly led to his reassignment to the Engineer Troops of the KNIL in Tjimahi. There, as a radio operator or 'Tik', he played a vital role in transmitting and receiving messages through Morse code. The challenging tropical climate often made radio communication tough, with signal reception proving to be unreliable and difficult.

Just a few months into his service, Claude, like many others of his generation, found himself caught in the wave of general mobilisation. The wave of general mobilisation pulled young men away from their civilian lives, jobs, or studies and sent them to serve at military bases far from home, drastically changing their life paths.

On 10 January 1942, Japan officially declared war on the Dutch East Indies, motivated by a mix of strategic and economic ambitions. Their primary goal was to dismantle the Dutch's long-standing economic stronghold in the region. For Japan, taking over wasn't just about expanding territory; it was a very much needed move to boost their economy.

The Dutch East Indies were rich in natural resources, especially the oil fields in Sumatra, which were particularly attractive to Japan. Securing these resources was essential for powering Japan's Navy and Air Force. Therefore, the invasion aimed not just to achieve a military victory but to seize economic control, redirecting the wealth that had benefited the Dutch for centuries into Japanese hands.

Claude is ready to go

Claude in uniform

# 2.3 Attack to the Dutch East Indies cities

These attacks, too, were part of Japan's detailed plans.

*R*ight after Pearl Harbor, Japan didn't waste any time. They charged straight for the East Indies, bringing their whole military might — ships, planes, you name it. One by one, islands just started falling under Japanese control. By 11 January, 1942, they hit Celebes first, and then they were all over Borneo's key spots by the end of the month. They were after the airfields and the oil — big time. The Dutch forces, KNIL, tried their best but were just no match for the Japanese; they were outclassed and outgunned.

In mid-January 1942, America, Britain, Australia, and the Dutch teamed up under the short-lived supreme command for allied forces, called ABDACOM, with British General Wavell calling the shots. The idea was to gang up and stop Japan from steamrolling over Southeast Asia and protect their own turf. But after Japan nailed the Philippines, Singapore, and the Dutch East Indies, that alliance kind of fell apart. What was left of the team hunkered down to defend Java as best they could.

This Dutch admiral, Karel Doorman, was in charge of this mix-and-match fleet from all those countries, trying to block Japan's move into the region. Come the end of February 1942, they all faced off in the Java Sea. It was a tough fight, but Japan had the upper hand and won. It was brutal — over two thousand of the Allied side didn't make it. Among the ships that went down were the HNLMS *Java* and HNLMS *De Ruyter*, both under Doorman's lead. It was a real low point, showing just how tough it was going to be to stop Japan's push through the East Indies.

So René, who had already got his pilot's license, was now a Second Lieutenant Pilot with the KNIL's Military Aviation, stationed in Andir, Bandung. He was part of the 1-VL GI division, flying Glenn Martin Bombers. On this crucial day, 28 February 1942, he and his squadron took to the skies to hit the Japanese fleet over the Java Sea. Luckily, they all made it back without a scratch.

The way was now open for Japan to conquer Java. On 1 March, 1942, they went all in. They targeted big cities like Batavia and Buitenzorg, where the big boss of the Dutch East Indies, Dr H.J. van Mook, lived. They also aimed for the Kalidjati airfield north of Bandung and Surabaya's naval base. Taking Kalidjati meant Japan could control the skies over Java. Despite the KNIL and the Allies throwing everything they had at them, Batavia was wide open for the taking, with Buitenzorg quickly following.

By 4 March, 1942, it was Bandung's turn — Claude's hometown. Japanese bombers hit the Andir airbase first, then their ground troops moved in, and the city was under heavy fire for four days straight. Soldiers and civilians alike were running south, trying to escape the disarray.

Bandung's center, especially the Chinese quarter, was hit hard. Walking down those streets, you'd crunch glass under your feet, dodge rubble, and, sadly, see blood splattered everywhere — on the ground, on the walls. The KNIL did their best to fight back, but in just three months, Japan had taken control of the key spots across the Indo archipelago.

The 8th of March turned out to be an important day. That's when the Dutch Governor-General, Alidius Tjarda van Starkenborgh Stachouwer, and the top man for the KNIL and Allied ground forces, Lieutenant-General Hein ter Poorten, had to sit down with Japanese General Imamura Hitoshi at Kalidjati airfield for a chat. Ter Poorten got the word from the Dutch government back in London to only agree to Bandung's surrender. But Hitoshi, he wasn't having any of that — he wanted the Dutch to throw in the towel, no conditions.

Looks like there was a bit of a split on what to do among the Dutch leaders. The Japanese general was pretty clear, though; he only wanted to deal with the military personnel, including Ter Poorten. And he laid it out: if the Dutch didn't agree to surrender, Japan was just going to keep bombing Bandung.

Ter Poorten had just ten minutes to make up his mind. With that kind of pressure, he ended up caving to the Japanese demands. And the spot they picked to have this showdown, the Kalidjati air base, wasn't just some random choice. The Japanese had a forceful presence there, with plenty of fighters and bombers ready to go if the Dutch tried to stall. So, the Dutch had no option but to go along with what Japan wanted, leading to the Dutch waving the white flag right there at Kalidjati air base.

On that same day, 8 March, 1942, at 10 p.m., the British got a surprise phone call saying the Dutch had agreed to Japan's terms for an unconditional surrender of the Dutch East Indies, KNIL included. They also wanted all the other allied forces to give up. The British commander was stuck; he had to go along with it.

Then, on 9 March, the whole surrender deal was inked and broadcast by Governor-General Tjarda van Starkenborgh Stachouwer over the Bandung radio station NIROM, making it official.

Once Java was in Japanese hands, it was basically game over for the Dutch East Indies. Now Japan ruled the entire area. This was an enormous blow to the Dutch and marked the end of their colonial reign there. To the Indonesian people, this defeat made the Dutch look a lot less powerful.

The Japanese takeover was rough. Harbours got wrecked, crops were ruined, leading to a massive food shortage, especially rice. Things got really tough for everyone, especially those of Dutch and mixed heritage. Japan wanted everything Japanese — no speaking Dutch, no Dutch radio, newspapers, or schools. Everyone had to learn Japanese, and you'd see Japanese flags flying over government buildings. Dutch people who used to be in charge, like military officers, business leaders, and government officials, ended up in Japanese camps. These camps, where both civilians and military were held, were known as *Jappenkampen* or 'Jap camps'.

Second World War Camp in the Dutch East Indies. Public Domain

# 2.4 Inside and outside the Japanese camps

The Japanese authorities quickly established civilian and prisoner of war camps.

*T*he Japanese began by sorting out everyone who wasn't native to the region, marking a clear line between those who were fully European and those of mixed ancestry. At first, the mixed-race Dutch-Indos weren't thrown into camps. The Japanese were on the fence about where their loyalties stood, so they got a pass, at least for a little while.

But by 1943, the Japanese went for round two, getting even more detailed in their sorting process. They'd judge by the way you walked, the colour of your eyes, and even required a '*asal usul*', basically a family tree document. This was how they decided who you were and where you stood. Despite the pressure, the Indo-Europeans wouldn't side with the Japanese. So, lots of them, along with many Dutch Indisch, ended up in Japanese prison camps.

It wasn't just the Dutch getting locked up. KNIL soldiers, allied civilians, men, women, and even kids were sent off to camps spread across the East Indies, Thailand, Japan, and Singapore.

Those who weren't carted off to camps, often women and children left behind when the men were taken, were known as '*buitenkampers*' or 'outer campers'. This group, a mix of Ambonese, Menadonese, Timorese, Moluccans, Chinese, Japanese, and Dutch-speaking Indonesians, lived under tight restrictions. They were pretty much confined to their houses, forbidden from even stepping into their own yards, meant to stay out of sight for their safety. House searches were common, often ending in mistreatment or worse. They were even forced to witness public executions by the Japanese, who were infamous for their brutal methods of torture, from hanging by limbs to beatings, and other unspeakable acts of cruelty. The Japanese used these terror tactics believing it was the way to maintain control, leaving much to the whims and cruelty of the moment.

Civilians living under Japanese rule were pretty much left without rights. The Japanese soldiers could take over their homes whenever they felt like it. Women, sometimes given just a few minutes, had to grab whatever they could carry by hand. Mums with little ones often had to squeeze into smaller spaces or bunk with other families, quickly finding themselves broke. Bank accounts were locked up, and no one was getting paid anymore. Women with older kids were sent off to women's camps where, right at the gate, their stuff would be rummaged through, and anything valuable got swiped. Everyone was tagged with a band and a number on it. Conditions were harsh — sitting and sleeping on the ground without food, water, or a chance to clean up. The women tried to keep each other's spirits up by sharing stories, teaching, and making up songs, but keeping a diary was off-limits.

Life in the camps was tough, with roll calls twice a day and chores that had to be done. "*Keirei!*»—that was the command for bowing deeply as a sign of respect to Emperor Hirohito. This ritual was no small deal. You had to stand just so, with everything precise — from where you looked to how your arms and hands were positioned. And the Japanese were serious about this bow. You'd see them bowing all the time, even to people they'd run into multiple times a day, sometimes even while biking.

The prisoners had a hard time paying respect to the then Japanese Emperor. The bow had to be quick, deep, and done just right. Mess it up — too slow, not deep enough, or just wrong — and the Japanese guards would see it as a major disrespect, and then things would really get bad.

The Japanese didn't waste any time; they rounded up all non-Japanese soldiers and tossed them into internment camps. This meant the KNIL commanders couldn't even get a word out or make any official moves. Pretty quickly, the whole structure of the KNIL just collapsed. The Japanese took everything — supplies, clothes, shoes — leaving the KNIL soldiers with nothing.

Not just the soldiers, but prisoners of war from the army and navy, including Dutch, KNIL troops from Ambon and Menado, and Allies like Americans, Brits, and Aussies, were all put to work. Even civilians pulled from other camps were forced into labour. They were put to work on railroads, like the infamous Burma and Pakanbaru lines, as well as airfields, bridges, and roads, not to mention factories, mines, and ports. It was brutal slave labour, with folks working in terrible conditions, often without enough food or medicine.

Those working on the railway lines had it especially tough. They built the tracks by hand, which meant clearing forests, digging up the ground, breaking rocks, laying down sleepers and rails, and building dams — all while dealing with snakes, disease-carrying bugs, crocodiles, and floods. Their shelters, like tents and barracks, would get flooded out regularly. Many didn't make it, dying right there from overwork, diseases, beatings, or epidemics like cholera and dysentery.

The Japanese also roped in thousands of Javanese, called *'romushas'*, for work in coal mines and on railroads both in the Dutch East Indies and places like Burma. These romushas were drawn in with promises of volunteer work to rebuild the country, with hints at future independence. But really, they were trapped between volunteering and being forced into labour, often taken prisoner. These men had next to nothing in terms of clothes or personal stuff.

In May 1944, the first prisoners and labourers arrived in Pakanbaru to build a railway line through the Sumatran jungle for the Japanese. As the war progressed, the Japanese used more and more coercion. In the final phase of the war, thousands of romushas were shipped to places outside the Dutch East Indies, without warning. They had to work for the Japanese under conditions bordering on slavery. The romushas were treated badly, hardly given any food and were beaten or mistreated. They often died alone, far from their homes. Their chances of survival under these conditions were extremely poor. They died from hunger and disease by the hundred. Surviving romusha prisoners described their horrible treatments which left them with very deep psychological wounds.

Besides these poor Javanese workers, there were also thousands of

Indonesians who volunteered as auxiliary soldiers the *'heihos'* in the Japanese army. There were special regiments of well trained Indonesian soldiers, PETA, formed by the Japanese Imperial Army. These Indonesians were treated much better than the romushas.

## Suffering in the prisoner of war camps

To the Japanese during World War II, being captured as a POW was a sign of cowardice and failure.

The Japanese held a firm belief that a loyal soldier would never surrender. As a result, the Japanese often punished entire POW camps for any perceived wrongdoing, including starvation or even more brutal group punishments.

Claude found out firsthand how harsh these punishments could be for what the Japanese saw as serious offences. For instance, he tried to keep a diary, which was against Japanese rules. Unfortunately, he was caught in the act. The Japanese soldiers didn't just take his diary and pencil; they physically assaulted him as they took him away. Claude was then locked in a cage for several days without food or water as punishment, and he never saw his diary again.

If the POWs didn't meet the Japanese's standards for hard work, or if they broke any of the camp rules, severe punishments or torture were guaranteed. Some of the punishments involved being locked in an open-topped cage for days, exposed to the elements, sometimes without clothes, food, or water, under the blazing sun. POWs could lose their balance from standing in one spot for so long, becoming disoriented and weak.

Other forms of torture included being forced to kneel with a bamboo stick wedged behind the knees, being made to exercise in extreme heat, staring into the sun, or having one's food ration set on fire. Minor infractions could lead to beatings with sticks, whips, clubs, the sheath of a samurai sword, or kicks from booted feet.

The *"samurai"* sword, a symbol of honour and service in Japanese culture, was especially revered. Only Japanese were allowed to carry it, and unauthorised touching or use was considered a grave insult, punishable by death. These swords were crafted with extreme care, sometimes taking a year to complete, making them not just weapons but works of art and symbols of the samurai's duty and privilege.

To make sure everyone was thoroughly scared, the Japanese would often make other prisoners watch as they dished out public punishments. If anyone tried to escape, they'd almost always be killed. Many times, people who were punished would just vanish, and no one would know where they were taken or what happened to them. This kind of uncertainty and fear really messed with the prisoners' heads. Claude told me it got to a point where grown adults were so scared, they acted more like frightened animals than people.

The Japanese had a way of keeping you alive on the bare minimum, making you work even though there was hardly any food, water, basic hygiene supplies, or medicine around.

I've read other survivors' camp diaries, and they all say the same thing about how terrible the living conditions were. The latrines were a nightmare — just a small ditch that was always overflowing, turning the place into a breeding ground for diseases. Just going to the bathroom could be deadly, with dysentery and cholera spreading super fast. Malaria was also a constant threat. The sleeping areas were infested with bedbugs, leaving everyone with itchy welts. And, of course, there were flies, rats, mice, cockroaches, ants, and all sorts of pests everywhere — in the beds and all over the living quarters.

Like I mentioned earlier, in the eyes of the Japanese soldier, being a POW meant you were a coward and a failure because you got captured. They were taught to fight to the death or, in the worst-case scenario, take their own lives rather than surrender. So, to them, a prisoner wasn't even seen as a full human being anymore.

Claude, along with many others, was trapped behind the 'kawat', the barbed wire that marked the boundaries of their prison. He wrote in his diary, unable to foresee the full extent of the harshness he would face during his time in captivity.

His own ordeal as a prisoner of war stretched out for three and a half long years, which he later recounted as the most gruelling period of his life.

Camp in the Dutch East Indies, 1943, Public domain

# 2.5 CLAUDE'S CAPTIVITY,

# 1942 - 1943

The cruel Japanese treatments prevented the prisoners of war, including Claude, from escaping as they held them captive behind the *'kawat'* (barbed wire). That is what he wrote in his diary. He could not imagine what was in store for him during his captivity.


*I*t all started on 8 March, 1942, in Bandung, when he, just a 19-year-old radio operator for the Battalion Engineer Troops of the KNIL in Tjimahi, was told to report in uniform. No reason was given, and he arrived with nothing to his name, not even a toothbrush.

He found himself among approximately ten thousand soldiers, as well as unarmed women and children in Bandung, all confined behind the kawat in makeshift 'pre-camps'. Claude shared these memories with me when I was about twenty, during a conversation about my parents' upcoming trip to Japan, which seemed to bring all these memories flooding back.

He recounted his experiences under the Japanese with such clarity and detail. One incident he vividly remembered happened around 10 a.m., when a Japanese NCO, a non-commissioned officer, caught him exchanging items for food at the camp shop and eating it secretly under a tree. The guard struck Claude with a thin, sharp bamboo stick, whipping him so hard that Claude could hear the stick whistling through the air before it painfully struck his back. Despite the relentless beating, Claude didn't make a sound, trying to relax his muscles to absorb the blows.

But the caning wasn't deemed enough of a punishment by the Japanese NCO, so Claude was forced to stand in the roll call area for the rest of the day without food or water, the sun glaring in his eyes, trying to maintain his composure despite the welts marking his back.

Claude took a moment to say a quick prayer and thought about his family. He wanted to be strong for them, especially his parents, whom he loved dearly and always wished to shield from harm. He felt a deep regret that the war had impacted his family, and there was nothing he could do to protect them from its reach.

I think Claude's resilience, even in the face of such adversity, was fuelled by his faith and his deep love for his family — his parents, siblings, and his half-sister Margot. It was this love and faith that helped him keep his composure under the harsh conditions imposed by the Japanese.

For any minor mistake, punishment was swift and severe. And if someone was caught trying to escape the camp, it was made into a spectacle. All the POWs were gathered to watch the execution, where escapees' bodies were often hung or thrown to the ground. Witnessing such brutality was designed to crush any thoughts of escape or rebellion among the prisoners. This fear and control tactic was precisely what the Japanese aimed for, to keep the POWs in line.

The broader strategy of the Japanese army in Asia was to eliminate all Western influence, under the belief that Asia belonged to Asians, and they were particularly anti-white. They saw themselves as the rightful leaders of Asia, pushing a narrative that Asia was for Asians, aiming to push out Western powers and their cultural impact.

Claude picks up his story.

In this internment camp in Bandung we got evidence of the brutality of the Japanese. I was confronted by my first gruesome event. In the evening, it was almost chaotic, even outside our camp, with so many military vehicles. A roll call in the middle of the night, not to mention the rumours that were going around. It made me nervous and of course I could not sleep. We all couldn't sleep. In the morning, we had to line up in the large roll call area.

The Japanese camp commander shouted at the guards in such a way that they also became nervous. We were surrounded and herded to the scene of the calamity by dozens of Japs with loaded rifles and bayonets. Our sleeping quarters were searched for one straggler. The 'Nips', executed three boys because they had gone home in the evening to escape millimetre trimming of their hair. Unfortunately, they were discovered. Their hands and feet were tied. They tied the boys separately to three poles. There was a shout of commands. We were all silent. My heart was racing. I was quite scared. I didn't know what was going to happen. Some Japs, about six of them, stepped forward. They bayoneted these three lads until they were dead. You could hear a pin drop. We were all forced to watch, including the wounded and the sick. The Japs then stuck and twisted their razor-sharp bayonets into the stomach, chest, neck and heart of the three. Some of the boys watching fainted. And a few gaged. It was horrible to watch. Indescribable. I myself was also almost gagging.

For two days, the three condemned young men hung dead from the posts by the hedge as a terrifying example. That constant pressure every day. That daily humiliation. That dog-like obedience. Making sure you were not punished if you accidentally looked a Jap in the eye. We were not allowed to show any emotions, no fear and no anger. They were not allowed to read anything in our eyes. Couldn't make anything out of our body language. It was a time of violence, inhumanity and oppression. We were always on our guard. Every day the Japs were stricter and even more cruel. Every day we had to be tougher. Stronger. At least on the outside. My heart cried inside. Crying about what they were doing to my fellow men and myself.

From what I've pieced together through various diaries and POW stories, and something Claude himself confirmed, the real agony of those times wasn't so much about the physical pain from beatings, as brutal as they were. It was witnessing your friends suffer, hearing them cry out for their mothers under the torment — that's what really tore you apart inside. This kind of mental anguish sticks with you, gnawing away inside, something Claude knew all too well and never could shake off.

Fred and Nettie, 1965, Claude loved them both

By mid-June 1942, Claude's journey took him to the Tjimahi camp, located to the west of Bandung. This place, set in the northern part of the city, served as both a collection point and a transit camp where he spent the next four months.

The march to Tjimahi kicked off early, with around four thousand men, loaded up and on foot, making their way through the city streets. As they moved, people lined the streets watching them — some were laughing, while others were crying. Every now and then, someone in the crowd would raise a hand or wave, a small gesture of connection.

They were heading to the Tjimahi camp 4, which used to house the 4th and 9th garrison battalions. Now, it was set to accommodate prisoners of war from various backgrounds: British, Australian, Dutch, Indo-European, Moluccan, and Menadonese. Spread over roughly two thousand square meters, the camp had twenty-seven barracks built without windows, just large doors and cement floors, all arranged around a stark, treeless square, making the place look desolate. Enclosed by a bamboo fence, this part of the camp earned the nickname "bamboo camp." Although these barracks were initially intended for twenty-five hundred men, they were now packed with about four thousand.

Claude just arrived in the Tjimahi camp, 1942

In 1942, the food situation in the camp was relatively okay in terms of quantity and quality. Prisoners could still collect their meals from the *'Bergartillerie'*, a Japanese Mountain artillery warehouse. If you had a little money, you could buy extra food at the camp store. Privacy was non-existent, with everyone crammed together, regardless of health status. The overcrowding made personal hygiene a challenge, and sleep was nearly impossible. Any form of communication with the outside world was strictly prohibited, though risk-takers managed to smuggle notes in and out, facing severe repercussions if discovered.

Bribing the Japanese guards was a risky strategy that sometimes paid off, especially since they had a thing for watches. Claude managed to barter his watch for a pile of English books. By the time he left Tjimahi camp, he was without his watch and had a shaved head.

In the camp, life had its small escapes. You could lose yourself in a book passed from hand to hand, or get caught up in the drama of theatre shows. Debates sparked up now and then, and music still found its way to their ears through a makeshift orchestra. They'd collect a bit of cash from these shows, enough to chip in for some extra grub. But that was just a brief break from the tough reality they were living in.

Later on, Claude got moved to a place near Buitenzorg, a good bit away from Batavia. This place had him spending his days training horses for the Japanese army. According to my dad, winding up there was a bit of luck, even if calling it 'lucky' feels a bit weird. It wasn't exactly a vacation spot. Just like before, the Japanese were calling all the shots, leaving him and everyone else just to follow orders without any say in what went on.

Boy on the horse I.P.K. in prisoner of war camp Buitenzorg, December 1942

Claude continues.

I had a limited amount of freedom. Worked in the open and rode horses. The food was not too bad, and I even earned a little money each day. The work was hard, though, as I worked eighteen hours a day and even longer on night watch. I looked like a scraggly thing on the outside, black as a cricket, but I became tough, hardened. Here I lived in a small world far away from the real world.

Boy had a way with horses that really stood out. He'd talk to them gently, really focusing on them, offering encouragement, and getting them ready for their role with the Japanese field artillery. He was pretty much the go-to guy for the animals, especially the older ones that were skin and bones. He'd head into a nearby forest with either some local Indonesians or Japanese soldiers to scrounge up food for them and made sure they were fed every day. A lot of these horses weren't doing too well, beaten down and full of sores from too many whippings, and there wasn't any medicine around for them. Heck, there was barely enough medicine for the people, let alone horses. Claude did his best to ease their pain and keep them as comfortable as possible, even during training.

After his time with the horses in Buitenzorg, things took a turn for the worse. By the end of February 1943, he found himself back in the Tjimahi camp. But this time, it wasn't just four thousand of them; it was crammed with about thirty thousand POWs.

Life in the camp had gone downhill fast. The food was even worse than before, and now everyone was feeling the pinch of hunger. Meals were down to scraps of rice, beans, and bone, with not a bit of meat in sight. With stomachs swelling from malnutrition, Claude saw the writing on the wall — ; his odds of making it through were getting slimmer. The numbers of dead rose every day.

Tanjung Perak. Near the harbour of Surabaya. Public domain

# 2.6 In the jungle

By May 1943, Claude's journey took another turn. He, along with about two thousand other POWs, landed on Flores, which is part of the Lesser Sunda Islands, just east of Bali. The way Claude put it, *"they went straight from the water and onto the sand"*.

From Claude's diary, May 1943.

I left Tjimahi in mid-April, about nine kilos lighter than when I first came in. I was one of the soldiers from the selected group of POWs, who left by train via Batavia for Surabaya. We hardly had any food or water during the ten hour train journey.

In Surabaya, the Korean soldiers were ready to transport us to a camp, while screaming and kicking us. We stayed in this camp for a few days with little or bad food.

Again we took the train this time to Tanjung Perak, Silver Cape, Surabaya's harbour and we were transported to Flores by ship. On the way, near Timor, we were attacked by our own air force stationed in Australia, who did not know that there were prisoners of war on board.

When we arrived on Flores, we had to take the ship's goods ashore. It was terrible on Flores. The people there died of dysentery in large numbers. They had to be burned immediately because of the danger of contamination. Of course, the Japanese left this task to the POWs. Near Maumere, in the Eastern part of the North coast of Flores, we started to build an airstrip in the jungle, specifically for the Japanese

'Zero' fighter planes. The airstrip was to serve as a base for the Japanese air attacks on Australia.

The ordeals we had to endure on this island were unbelievable. We were just dumped on the beach. There were no barracks, nothing, not even any medication. An appendectomy was done with a pocketknife. The first thing we had to do was to take care of the sick, who had contracted bacillary dysentery along the way because of the terrible conditions on board. The sick and we were literally kicked onto the beach. If you fell, the soldiers were ready with their sticks to hit you.

We were forced to find a place to sleep in the open on the bare ground under coconut trees, among snakes and scorpions. We built the barracks in the two labour camps and the sick camp, the Wulff camp. We used bamboo and 'atap', palm leaves roofing, surrounded by barbed wire. I ended up in the Blom camp. Of course, we had no electricity and there was hardly any water to drink. Here it was slavery and forced labour of the worst kind. Aircraft bombarded us repeatedly. You could not hear them coming. They let themselves slide down over the mountains with the engines turned off. They scared the hell out of us.

Besides a tear, a laugh was necessary, so a camp cabaret was set up at the beginning. One time, a captain held a lecture on the great usefulness of the coconut tree. The man told us very seriously that such a tree had the kindness not to drop fruits when people walked under it. A little later, he received a cluster of three on his head and became unconscious.

Swimming in the sea was one of the few forms of recreation. With Rudy Rosier, my buddy and best friend, I practised underwater swimming. That skill became very useful to me later on.

The regime was harsh and cruel. The Korean guards naturalised Japanese, rattled you for the slightest thing. The Japs did not consider them worthy of their position. Many of them therefore wanted to prove their loyalty by acting cruelly. We suffered heavy mental blows in Maumere. Especially from the physical and cruel Koreans, we nicknamed 'Bloempotje', 'Flowerpot', 'de Bolle', 'The Gobbler'.

On Flores I became ill. I reached the point of almost total exhaustion due to dysentery and malaria. I had daily hallucinations about good food. In full consciousness, I saw delicious meals hanging in the coconut trees. This must have happened during my delirium brought on by the high fever, when I was intensely cold and shivering, suffering terrible headaches and diarrhoea.

Once the work on the airstrip was done, Claude and the survivors, all of them really thin by then, left Flores. They headed back via Surabaya to Batavia. A lot of the POWs didn't make it due to severe dysentery, malaria, malnutrition, sheer exhaustion, or harsh treatment. Claude and his buddy Rudy managed to keep each other going, offering support to stay strong. They didn't know what the future held, feeling down about losing mates and always wondering if their turn was next. Somehow, they made it through better than some, even though Claude picked up chronic dysentery there, which stuck with him for much of his time as a POW.

After the Military Tribunal, 'Bloempotje' and 'de Bolle' ended up being executed.

Back in Java, Claude was sent to the ADEK camp, which stood for '*Algemeen Delisch Emigratie Kantoor*', or General Delisch Emigration Office. This place used to recruit labourers, or '*coolies*', for work on the tobacco plantations in Deli, Sumatra. The camp had family barracks fenced in by high double barriers topped with barbed wire and '*gedek*', a kind of woven bamboo wall, making it impossible to see outside. Guards kept watch from high towers at the camp's corners, guns at the ready for any trouble or escape attempts.

Originally, these barracks were meant for Javanese contract workers and their families waiting to head to or return from Deli. The ADEK camp turned into a jack-of-all-trades – a civilian camp, a POW camp, and from mid-August 1945 to '46, even a reception camp. As more prisoners were crammed in, everyone had to squeeze tighter, space per person shrinking from fifty centimetres down to about thirty. You couldn't even roll over. The latrines were a nightmare – just holes in the ground with footrests and low dividers, filthy and hardly ever cleaned, making privacy and cleanliness a distant dream.

Every morning and evening, there was roll call in the big field, and part of the routine was singing the Japanese national anthem. The rule was simple: no work, no food. So, you had to keep going no matter what. Working too slow? You risked a beating. Got caught looking around? That could get you beaten too.

Cut off from the outside world, the prisoners were starved for information. They were desperate to hear any news, to know what was happening beyond the camp's fences. Sure, rumours would float around now and then, but after a while, you learned not to get your hopes up. Most rumours turned out to be just that — unconfirmed whispers that only added to the anxiety. Every so often, there'd be talk that the war was over, "*war done*" they'd whisper. But those were just false hopes, especially hard on those who were quick to grab onto any bit of optimism.

Reading through the camp diaries of those who made it out, I saw that many POWs, Claude included, talked a lot about being constantly hungry. That hunger pushed them to do whatever it took to survive. Despite the constant hunger, the diseases, and their weakened state, both physically and mentally, their will to keep living was incredibly strong.

Even though those false rumours sometimes gave some hope, for some, the constant letdowns were too much, and they just gave up, resigned to their fate. How each person kept their spirit alive varied wildly. Some were fuelled by the thought of reuniting with their loved ones — spouses, families, parents, friends — while others found solace in their faith. Claude, I think, just took it one day at a time, focusing on finding small ways to keep going. He might have also escaped into his imagination, dreaming of hope and freedom, which gave him the strength he needed. He had a knack for that, retreating into his own little world to keep his spirits up.

By April 1944, Claude found himself in Kampong Makassar transit camp in southeast Batavia, just for a month. From January 1943 until 1945, this place served as a stopover for POWs heading elsewhere, shipped out from Tanjung Priok, Batavia's port. The Japanese called it Bunsho 1, Camp 9 in their records.

Around this time, the mental toll on the POWs ramped up with the increased bombings by Dutch B-25 Mitchell bombers from Australia. Everyone was on edge, scared that the next bomb might drop on their camp, especially as MacArthur's forces kept bombing island after island.

After Kampong Makassar, Claude was back in the overcrowded ADEK camp for a few weeks before being moved to Tanjung Priok. His journey, filled with trials, was far from over. More challenges lay ahead.

On 19 May, 1944, Claude left the Dutch East Indies, starting a journey that would prove deadly for many.

The main entrance of the ADEK camp. November 1945. Public domain

Drawing of the sinking ship *Tamahoko Maru*

# Transport by ship to Japan
## Claude (Boy) 1944 – 1945

A torpedo and

an atomic bomb

Tanjung Priok quay. Harbour of Batavia. Public domain

# 2.7 THE 'GREAT JOURNEY', 1944

Claude's 'Great Journey' started when he was packed on a ship from Tanjung Priok to Japan.

*T*his journey was nothing short of a nightmare for him, pushing him to his limits and testing his will to survive like never before. The only thing that kept him going was daydreaming about starting over, about a life far away from all this. But dreaming was one thing; the hard reality was that he had no idea where he was headed or if he'd even make it alive.

Then, Claude and the rest of the prisoners were shipped off to Singapore on the *Kiska Maru*. Surprisingly, things on this ship were okay — food was decent, and they even had doctors looking after them. But there was a twist: the Japanese were filming them for a propaganda piece. So, while they got treated alright on camera, it was a whole different story off-screen, and definitely not what most POWs had to go through on other ships.

From Claude's diary May 1944.

We were filmed extensively for propaganda purposes and we prisoners soon understood that it was a kind of model transport. There were thirty-five doctors, a huge staff of nurses and sulphur medications on board. Something usually unheard of. We were even given the same food as the Japanese. Nevertheless, the days for us prisoners of war below deck seemed endless.

Via the Banka Strait we arrived in Singapore, in Keppel Harbour, on 22 May 1944. Where I, with my fellow prisoners, were transported in trucks to 'Havelock Road Camp'.

From Claude's diary June 1944.

On the morning of the 2nd of June, hundreds of us marched from the camp to the harbour where we were transported by barges to the ship moored in the 'Roads'. The ship the Miyo Maru left Singapore on 3 June in a convoy of eleven ships, three of which were transporting POWs. The convoy was escorted by four 'frigates', warships for anti-submarine warfare and protecting convoys and continued on to Manila Bay. The sequel turned out to be a journey to Nagasaki in Japan. That did not bode well and was also a dangerous journey. Allied submarines were everywhere. In the beginning, everything went well; the convoy was even protected by Japanese frigates and whalers converted to warships.

By the time Claude was shipped off, he was just 21. Going through something like that had to have left its mark on him. Even though he sticks to just the facts when he talks about it, you can bet it scared him to his core, time and time again.

Claude's continues.

We sat and slept with about seven hundred men in the hold. The hold was in the front part of the ship, under hatches numbers 2 and 3. Another part of the crew slept on deck.

After the departure from Singapore we noticed some activity, such as a forced gathering of all prisoners. Under threat of machine guns and with sirens blaring, we were pushed down into the bowels of the ship. Bombs were thrown, followed by a deafening explosion, pressure wave and echo. Needless to say, we were all terrified. This feeling was accentuated when the lead frigate was torpedoed during the night of 6 - 7 June and disappeared into the ocean.

Kapok lifebelts were on board but were not issued. It was not until 8 June that Major Morris, our leader, managed to distribute them to the prisoners. On 11 June, the convoy arrived in Manila Bay for a short stay. On 14 June, the convoy continued on its way to the then port city of Takao on Formosa, now Taiwan. For this part of the journey, a mine-layer and a whaler were added to the convoy.
If a submarine attack started and we thought the ship had been hit, we all ran to the one steel staircase that led upwards.

We soon ran into a typhoon, which lasted four days. As a result, our holds were closed for those four days. No food and nobody was allowed on deck, so also no use of the 'benjo', the outboard toilet. The hurricane caused much damage to the Miyo Maru that further sailing to Japan was impossible.

In Takao we changed ships and continued our journey. On 20 June 1944 with another, larger passenger freighter, the M.S. Tamahoko Maru we arrived at the Japanese port of Moji, on the island of Kyushu, one of the larger islands to the south of Japan.

The convoy consisted of 12 ships this time, escorted by two frigates, a minelayer, destroyer and a converted whaler, which was just as dangerous as a torpedo boat. The convoy also included a bauxite ship of the 'Rotterdamsche Lloyd', a passenger ship with Japanese civilians evacuated from Formosa on board. The ship, the Tamahoko Maru, which partly carried rice and mainly icing sugar, was in the convoy that transported the prisoners of war to Japan. On board were not only Dutch, but also Australian, British and American prisoners of war. In the back of the ship were hundreds of Japanese soldiers.

We, the prisoners, were above the sugar holds on the intermediate deck at the front of the ship, under the deckhouse with the ship's bridge and under the large wooden shutters numbered 1 and 2. Some 300 men slept on the front deck again.

Access to the hold was via the wooden ladders under each hatch. A wooden ladder led to the main deck where there were also prisoners of war. There was also a steel escape ladder to the hatchway. This hatchway led to the upper deck and an air shaft.

Just imagine how it feels when you are with hundreds of men and you hear the bombs exploding under water. Those sounds travelled through and vibrated in thunderous ways through the steel ship's walls. You know that if you got hit, that was the end.

At night, it was pitch black in the filthy hold. We were in the hold most of the time, 'jongkok', squatting with feet flat on the ground, with little air, food or drinking water. There was no ventilation, as the system did not work. The food was bad. Many prisoners became ill because of this.

Once a day we were ventilated for fifteen minutes. We had to use the outside toilet during those fifteen minutes, or using just one bucket. When the bucket was full, it had to be raised with a rope. One unstable pull and the contents would spill on the floor of the hold. Infectious diseases were unavoidable.

Again, lifebelts were present, but despite protests, not handed out. They were piled up against the front of the ship, close to the guards. The ship approached Nagasaki Bay on a pitch-dark night as the coastline came into view. Safety was not guaranteed.

The captain stopped the zigzagging that was intended to make the task of the anti-submarine boats more difficult but he reduced our speed. He obviously felt safe in the waters so close to home. He was probably unaware of what was happening around him in the deep waters.

We were to arrive the next day, on 25 June. And I can remember some of the prisoners of war singing some songs together. Only six hours to go. We are safe now, they thought. A few of us put on their uniforms before going to sleep, because they imagined what the next morning would be like. We kept hearing 'hayaku, hayaku' - shouts from the Japanese to hurry up.

On that night before arrival, 24 June 1944, a submarine grazed one of the escort ships. In our big four-master, which sailed nearby, we could feel the hit, after the explosion. We were shaking with fear. It did not stop there. A few seconds later, our ship came under fire. The torpedoes almost blew the Tamahoko Maru apart, piercing the front hold and then the middle hold of the ship. The prisoners were showered with icing sugar. There was a loud, intense bang and a blaze of fire. Seawater gushed in, causing our ship, with hundreds of people on board, to sink rapidly in the high waves.

'TORPEDEERING', TORPEDOING: what a terrible word, heightened in its horror by the fact that an allied hand caused it and with one hand movement sent hundreds of prisoners of war and dozens of crew members and others to their death.

We left with 772 POWs. A number of fellow-POWs were stowed away in the forward hold. They were terrified. Their deadly fear was that they were only separated from the deep water by an inch of steel. Bombs exploded all around us. The water is as much the carrier of sound as the air.

The cries of friend to friend in the icy water and Rudy, Rudy, sounded like a leitmotif in this symphony of horror.


It is unclear which bombs Claude meant, perhaps they were depth charges detonated by American or Japanese bombers.

Diary; Torpedoing

# Torpedoing

From Claude's diary, on the night of 24-25 June 1944.

I was dozing on a hatch covering the lower hold, which held sugar and was awakened by the sound of a violent explosion. In the middle of the noise, the voice of an Aussie, who was apparently sitting on the outboard toilet, suddenly yelled, "Torpedo coming in". Lots of bubbles had given its position away. I rolled off the hatch, leapt to my feet and immediately jumped on the edge of the hatch. I looked at the bridge where the crew was trying to see what was going on. My thoughts were that our escorting destroyer had spotted a submarine and was now pursuing and attacking her. And then it happened!

A tremendous, intense and indescribable explosion was accompanied by waves of water and falling beams. Bodies seemed to fall everywhere.

I was in the upper hold, the explosion pushed away the heavy planks of the hatch and I fell one hold lower, fortunately already in the swirling sea water that was rushing in. I was buried under the planks so that they forced me under water and I tried desperately to free myself. Strangely enough I then thought, while still under water and already starting to swallow some water, that drowning is a gentle death after all. Fortunately, I was able to free myself and survived. I had just taken a few breaths of fresh air when I was sucked down again by the suction of the rapidly sinking ship. This time, I was sure I went pretty deep, because my nose was bleeding and my eardrums seemed to burst.

But here God's rescuing hand saved me. When I went down I reached around me and got hold of a rope. This rope was attached to a piece of wood of at least one or two square metres. This God-sent raft took me to the surface. I looked around and saw no sign of the ship I had been on.

What a miracle! On the way up, all my clothes had been pulled off my body. Perhaps by people grabbing onto one another. I was left with scraps of my trousers held on by my belt.

I heard the soft voice of my 'slapie', bunk-mate Rudy, "Boy, Boy!" But I could not see him anywhere. I called out to him too, "Rudy, Rudy, Rudy!" I couldn't hear his voice anymore nor could I see him anywhere.

At that time, Claude saw that not everyone was as fortunate as he was. It looked like luck, or that guardian angel, just wasn't there for some of the other POWs, especially those who had been sleeping on the hatch covers. In hindsight, only one of those men, a fellow prisoner named Rien, managed to survive what came next.

Suddenly, there was this massive explosion — a huge blast of fire and a loud bang that blew the hatches wide open. The explosion ripped two big holes in the deck right into the sugar hold. Many of the men tried running for the ladders to escape, but the ladders were gone. Instead, they found themselves falling through the hole into the lower hold, landing on top of hard bags of sugar. Some tried to make it to the life jackets, but they either got trapped or were swept away by the freezing cold sea water that rushed in. With the ship going down, many had no choice but to jump into the sea, their screams and desperate splashing filling the air. Survival in those moments came down to being able to swim, grabbing a life jacket, or finding some piece of wood to float on. Anyone who couldn't manage that didn't make it.

It wasn't just their ship; a Dutch vessel loaded with bauxite got hit too. It snapped in half and went down, along with another ship and a passenger ship that had been evacuating people from Formosa.

## In the freezing water

Being out in the ocean, no clothes on, in the dead of night with the rain and sleet coming down, and the sea all churned up — it wasn't just cold on the outside. It got right into your bones, the kind of cold you feel deep inside. But somehow, you kept going.

For Claude, this part was like living through his worst fear. He really thought he was going to die out there. But, as luck would have it, he made it through — his buddy Rudy wasn't so lucky, though. Claude said one of the scariest parts was feeling like he was about to drown. Even worse was hearing people screaming for help all around him and then watching them just vanish into the freezing water. Those terrible moments, those sounds and sights, stuck with Claude for a really long time.

Claude's diary continued about the night 24-25 June 1944.

It was a moonless dark night in which the ocean swell pulled the drowned from the tops of the waves into deep valleys. You just cannot imagine this awful nightmare.

Another group of people, or their silhouettes appeared high above you. Then they were below you again. It was pitch dark. It was terrifying.

I looked around and I could no longer see anything of the ship. Not even any bubbles. I felt an enormous pressure on my body and suddenly heard the boilers exploding in the depths.

That night the sea was rough, it rained hard and there was still some sleet. The hours that followed were the coldest I have ever experienced. Even in Holland, where I experienced temperatures of -19 degrees Celsius, I never felt so cold.

I called repeatedly for Rudy Rosier, my dearest friend and bunkmate, with whom I had been through so much on Flores and afterwards.

Unfortunately, Rudy must have died and I, I was lucky enough to fight the waves. It was not easy to stay on the piece of wood and I fell countless times into the ice-cold water. I also helped others, without letting go of the rope. No matter how difficult it was because of my ice-cold hands, I did not let the rope attached to the raft slip from my hands.

Practising underwater swimming on Flores helped me with this. I did not want to think about the sharks that swam in these waters. It was a cacophony of sounds. People were screaming, crying and praying, 'Our Father' and 'Avé Maria'. The Japanese sang war songs and mothers cried for their children. Others cried out for help. Probably, because they could not swim. All nationalities helped each other. I was glad to be able to help and give a drowning man a place on my raft. Together we picked up a floating piece of bacon out of the sea and rubbed each other with it against the cold. By now we had been sitting on the wooden raft for hours or were lying in the water because of the high waves.

Suddenly, we heard some Japanese close by. He had a samurai sword in his hand and tried to swing us off the raft. Another prisoner dived deep into the water and somehow managed to kill the Japanese with his own samurai sword. When he surfaced, he just said: 'There, that's done'.

## Drowning victims

From Claude's diary 25 June 1944.

A few unmanned lifeboats were deployed. Most of the surviving prisoners managed to get hold of a raft or other wreckage and, together with the Japanese survivors they waited for dawn.

By morning the sea calmed down a little though it was still raining. The lifeboats deployed picked up only Japanese. Later that morning still freezing cold, we were able to hoist ourselves into one of those unmanned boats. I sat down on the oars to get warm. A passing frigate, a three-master, took us along and placed us on the foredeck. This ship was specialised in picking up prisoners, so the whole process was efficient and reasonably quick. There were also two aircraft that provided assistance. It felt like a lifetime floating around in the freezing cold sea in the rain and wind. The image of people in the water crying out for help never left me. The image of my mates drowning before my eyes remained forever in my mind.

Some people were lucky enough to get picked up by converted whalers in the commotion. But then, the Japanese captain of one of these whalers made a cruel call — he separated out the non-Japanese survivors and chucked them back into the freezing water. They were told to swim to another whaler, but not everyone could swim; some who had been rescued ended up drowning anyway. Women and children got priority, but only after the Japanese, leaving the POWs to be saved last.

The whole ordeal was a constant state of fear for Claude. From the instant he was trapped in the dark hold, hearing bombs go off and people desperately trying to escape up the only staircase, many not making it and falling back. Despite being a strong swimmer, he was convinced he'd drown in the dark sea. The night was a blur of trying to save others, the heartbreak of losing his friend Rudy, and just the sheer terror of it all. This stayed with Claude for the rest of his life, sharply contrasting with the peaceful propaganda film the Japanese shot as they left Batavia. Four ships were lost, and the submarine that attacked them disappeared without a trace. Claude was among the few POWs who made it through, battered, freezing, and in some cases, severely injured or like Claude, with nothing on at all. The ordeal was far from over.

Claude wrote in his diary, in a tribute to Rudy Rosier, "I MISS YOU MY DEAR FRIEND RUDY."

These haunting memories drove Dad to look into the shipwreck later on, and I followed suit. We found out it was the U.S.S. *Tang* (SS306) along with two other American subs that snuck into the convoy on 24 June. The U.S.S. *Tang* surprised one of the escort Japanese ships and didn't stop there. It also launched torpedoes at the large ship they were on, hitting the front and then the middle, causing catastrophic damage before making a quick escape.

# Prisoners of war in Nagasaki

## 2.8 Camp Mitsubishi-Fukuoka 14b, 1944-September 1945

The ship Claude was on, a three-masted frigate, made it to Nagasaki, Japan, by 12:30 p.m. on June 25, 1944. When the dust settled, they found out that 211 POWs survived the ordeal. Sadly, about 560 of their fellow POWs didn't make it. But arriving in Nagasaki brought up a big question: what was next for them there?

*I*nitially, those who survived from the *Tamahoko Maru* were pretty much in the dark about what awaited them in Japan. They had no clue where they were being taken, how they'd be treated, or how long they'd be stuck there. Claude found himself in a place called camp Mitsubishi, landing there on the same day they arrived in Nagasaki. It was only later he found out the camp's official name was Fukuoka 14.

From Claude's diary 25 June 1944.

Cold, exhausted, hungry and skinny we arrived at the port of Nagasaki in southern Japan. On the quay we were hosed down and counted and counted again. The counting simply did not stop. Then I changed into a sort of pair of trousers which must have been a doctor's polo shirt. Among the Tamahoko Maru victims were several doctors. I hoisted myself up through the armholes and fastened the shirt around my waist with my old belt.

The prisoners of war were formed into four groups. For a while I thought I was safe here, not knowing what was in store for me. At the end of the afternoon my fellow prisoners and I were lifted into trucks and transported to the camp near the Mitsubishi factories. There, around 18.00 hrs., we were given a hot meal of rice, seaweed and a few soy beans.

We were given some tropical clothing, which unfortunately was not suitable for the cold. Sleeping mats were also distributed. Japan has severe winters. The prisoners only had thin rags to wear in that bitterly cold Winter.

In camp Fukuoka 14 we had no real external information. We heard rumours which turned out not to be true. It was difficult to find out the truth. One of our guys who could speak and read Japanese kept us somewhat informed of the latest news.

Claude shared that a couple of days after they got to the camp, another Dutchman from the *Tamahoko Maru* was brought in. This was Dr. H.P.L. van Doornum, and he turned out to be the 212th survivor. The doc had managed to grab a gangway during the tumult and strapped some life jackets to it, which helped him float far away from where the ship went down. Later on, a Japanese fishing boat found him passed out on his makeshift raft and rescued him. At first, they took him to a hospital, but once they figured out he was a POW, they sent him over to join the rest of them at Fukuoka 14.

Claude's diary July 1944.

We learned that during the Winter of 1943-44 prisoners in Fukuoka camp 14 had died due to the terrible cold, malnutrition or pneumonia.

My group of prisoner of wars who had survived the Tamahoko Maru disaster were separated from the prisoners already there and provisionally housed in the infirmary of the existing building, a factory shed, which had been built for 300 prisoners and was now too small to accommodate the more than 200 extra men. In this section were the prisoners who had been held in Fukuoka Camp 14 for more than a year. Besides the Dutch there were also British and Australian prisoners.

The Japanese had set up eleven Fukuoka camps across southern Japan. At the beginning, Claude didn't realise that these camps were numbered, and that he had landed in what was officially called Fukuoka 14. He came up with the name Camp Mitsubishi because he and the other POWs were put to work in the Mitsubishi factory area. This place was in the middle of the Saiwamachi factory district, right by the Urukami River and about a kilometre away from Nagasaki's central train station. A few wooden houses separated the campsite from the road, which led to a bridge crossing the river.

The Dutch lieutenant Aalders was in charge of the prisoners there. He was the kind of guy who took his responsibility seriously, always looking out for his men. He made it a point to meet with the Japanese commanders regularly, pushing for more food and better conditions for his people.

The new lads at Fukuoka 14, including Claude, were given numbers ranging from 329 to 541, and these numbers were marked on their caps. Claude's number was 470. This way, the last lot of them were identified as the survivors from the *Tamahoko Maru* disaster.

After a while, the newcomers, including Claude, were roped into working on a new project: constructing a second living quarters right behind the original building and the factory shed. Their job was mainly to clean up old wood, pulling out nails and getting it ready for the Japanese carpenters to work their magic on.

The design of this new section, dubbed 14B, was pretty straightforward.

About six weeks into the work, by August 1944, the fresh batch of prisoners moved into five long wooden barracks, all linked by corridors along the front and back. The sixth barrack was set aside partly as a medical treatment area for those who were seriously sick.

Right next to the railway and along the connecting corridor, they set up toilets, three workshops, an open space, a laundry area with a couple of baths and water basins, the boiler room, and the kitchen zone that also had an office attached. There was a spot for polishing rice to make it white, and a secure food storage area. They even managed to squeeze in a vegetable garden.

Instead of one big roll call space, they had a smaller one out in the open, between the toilets and the garden. There was a guardroom at the exit to the outer yard, which led to a second exit out towards the Mitsubishi factory area. Outside the camp fence, there was a tiny spot where they kept some pigs. And, between the camp and a row of houses near the kitchen, there was another yard with a lockable shed for rice storage.

Here's a picture showing a scale model of Residence Building 2, Fukuoka 14B, with its six wooden barracks laid out.

Scale model Fukuoka 14B. Thanks to © Indischhistorisch.nl

In the new setup, the two different groups of POWs were thrown together. The front side of the barracks ended up housing about a dozen Japanese officers and some doctors. The original POWs from the first arrival were placed in the second and third barracks, while the fourth barrack, specifically rooms 16 to 20, was reserved for the Dutch newcomers. English-speaking prisoners got rooms 23 through 27 in the fifth barrack. Those who were seriously sick were put in the sixth barrack.

Over time, some of the prisoners shifted around to different rooms. The way it worked, a room and your work crew kinda became your social circle. Most guys only really opened up to one or two close pals or the person they shared a bunk with.

Later on, Claude ended up in room 11, which was set up with bunk beds lined up on both sides, stacked five high. He snagged the second bunk on the left, which was one level up from the floor. Each room squeezed in twenty beds.

Sleeping was tough. They had these thin mattresses topped with wicker mats, which were a real pain to lie on, especially for the prisoners who were already skin and bones. Life in the Fukuoka camps could be pretty rough, and a lot depended on the mood swings of the camp bosses and guards. They all looked down on the POWs for surrendering to Japan back in the Dutch East Indies.

Camp 14B wasn't much different from the other Fukuoka places. The food was scarce and lacking in nutrition, there was hardly any drinking water, medical supplies were either extremely limited or nonexistent, warm clothes were a luxury, soap was rare, and pests like fleas, bed bugs, and lice were everywhere. The prisoners had to endure constant harsh and often sadistic treatment, with barely any downtime. The guards, if they had their way, seemed to get a kick out of making the prisoners' lives miserable, often leaving them with next to nothing and just watching them suffer.

From Claude's diary April 1945.

The Japanese did not show any compassion. They did not know what it was. For the slightest offence they would beat and cane us. They hit us with pieces of bamboo on the back and on the buttocks. You could defend yourself against that by tying Japanese newspapers to your body and putting them in your trousers. When we were beaten, we squealed like pigs, even though we didn't feel a thing. They also had other punishments, holding your arms up for 48 hours and so on. Being beaten was not as bad as the continuous humiliation. However, just when you hadn't counted on it, the bamboo stick suddenly appeared and was used to beat you for the slightest reason or when the guards just didn't like something you did. You did not try to escape because the Japs said five men would be beheaded, the one who slept on your left or right and five who slept in front or behind you.

They told us this regularly and indeed, they were really capable of carrying out something so barbaric. Also, the guards had told us several times that in case of an American invasion, they would kill us. This had a negative effect on our peace of mind and made us very restless.

The food was scarce and monotonous. It consisted of rice balls, soup, sometimes a piece of bland whale meat and seaweed, which was the Japanese staple food.

The Japanese war rules in the camps were simple. Not working meant no food, even if the food was awful, you still got something into your stomach. We made time to remove the hundreds of fleas from our wicker-sleeping mat in Summer and Winter. We used our free time to wash our clothes. We had a work jacket and long work trousers. If it rained, you had to keep your wet clothes on, even in Winter when it was really freezing. Moreover, you were punished if you warmed yourself up somewhere in the factory. If you did so and were discovered, you got a severe beating. Sometimes you had to work twelve or thirteen days at a stretch and on the fourteenth day you could do your laundry. Of course, you then stank, even if you had washed yourself.

I came across stories from families of the men locked up in Fukuoka 14B. Turns out, those who were there the longest got sent off to work at the Mitsubishi shipyard, which was a bit of a hike, like three kilometres, from where they were staying.

The majority from the *Tamahoko Maru* ended up in factory jobs right near the camp, churning out parts for ships like propellers and engine bits. After a bit, even the ones initially sent to the shipyard had to join in on the factory work. This shift was a bit of a break for them because walking back and forth was getting tougher by the day due to how worn out and weak they were getting. Claude's crew was among those sweating it out in the Mitsubishi iron foundry.

They were all too aware of the horror stories from the Burma railway — loads of men didn't make it because of the brutal forced labour. In Singapore, on their way to Japan, they'd bumped into some who survived that hell, but those survivors were shipped off to work in mines across Japan, not Nagasaki. Stuck in camp 14B, thoughts of their loved ones back home — be it their family, partners, or kids — were constant. Worry for their families was a heavy load, and sometimes, out of nowhere, the stress and fear just poured out.

Claude's diary July 1945.

I often thought about my dear parents, my sisters Dési and Margot, and my brother René, who must have aged rapidly in the Japanese camps. I prayed that they would remain healthy and suffer little pain.

The Japanese tried to break down people's resistance. Or rather, they wanted to break the prisoners. In some cases they succeeded because the men in Fukuoka 14B did the craziest things. Like animals, they fished out maggots from a cesspit and ate them to get some fat or they caught mice or rats and ate them too. It was disgusting and terrible to see how mentally broken people could become.

Camp life in the new second building proved to be more varied than in the old building, the factory shed. The new group recounted their latest traumatic experiences of the shipwreck or they told about the slave driver, whom they called 'Oortje', because of his shrivelled ear. The Japanese became more cautious as the Americans approached Japan, although some continued to put death and national honour above the lives of the people.

In 1945 some Japanese began to believe that they might come out of the war as losers. The Americans were approaching Japan mainly from the air. This gave us courage and, at the same time, fear of a miserable end, for we knew what the code of honour meant. It prescribed that the Japanese soldier should prefer death to surrender. Our hopes rose, but so did our despair. With my English friend Ben Drewery, I had to shovel sand and carry it in wheelbarrows. As we worked, we would softly sing a duet from the Pearl Fishers with our own freedom-loving English lyrics. For us, this was like an escape from our labour.

Listening to Claude's tales, along with stories from families of the Fukuoka 14B men, it's clear life got progressively tougher for the POWs. They were wasting away, getting sicker as diseases like diarrhoea, dysentery, malaria, bronchitis, and beriberi took hold. Beriberi was nasty because it came from not getting enough vitamins and led to all sorts of health problems. By the Summer of 1944, pneumonia even broke out in the camp. Japanese summers were brutal — hot, wet, and prime time for cyclones.

Meanwhile, American bombings ramped up. One bomb scored a direct hit on the train station, and the residential stretch between there and the factory didn't escape damage either, leading to civilian casualties.

By mid-1945, the camp itself wasn't spared from the air raids. They had these concrete bamboo shelters to run to, but they were often flooded, which made some POWs question their worth. They were cramped, wet, and didn't really offer much protection. Some guys figured they were better off hiding in the top bunk of their beds during raids, since the guards tended to only swing at the lower bunks with their rifles.

For those initially working at the shipyard, the constant air threats and a shortage of materials forced a shift back to factory work. Turns out, the factories were just as risky as the shipyard when bombs were falling.

The bomb shelters were in such bad shape that Commander Aalders had to ask for permission to dig out new ones — safer, drier trenches away from danger. They got the green light on 4 August, and the very next day, they started carving them out from the rock at the base of the hills, right behind the new barracks, in the vegetable garden. It was back-breaking work, hacking away in shifts, but it still felt like forever before they were done.

Through all this, Claude always had high praise for one of the men he was locked up with, Louis Seydel.


From Claude's diary 30 July 1945.


> To avoid collective punishment, Louis sacrificed himself and gave himself up as the perpetrator of a break-in at the Red Cross depot. In all that time, we had only received one thing from the relief packages, so 'Wietje', as we called Louis, went to get food from that depot and shared it with his mates. For twenty hours they made him stand with the pack above his head. If he lowered his arms, he was beaten, but he kept it up. Three days after that punishment, he broke in again. To me, he was a real hero.


From my perspective, as Claude's daughter, Louis Seydel was nothing short of heroic. The courage it took for him to consistently put himself on the line for others is beyond what most can even imagine. He took the fall, endured severe punishments, all to protect his fellow campmates. Thanks to Louis, or *Wietje*, Claude and his friends managed to get a bit more food. My respect for Louis is boundless. He was a real hero in every sense of the word.

## Oh most dreadful day of days

One of Claude's campmates shared in his camp story some of the darkest moments and fears that haunted the prisoners. One campmate had a nightmare about finding ground glass in their food. Another dreamt he was digging a trench for cover, only to imagine it filling with gas, believing he was about to be gassed right there. And there was a story about a fellow prisoner dreaming that American soldiers stormed into the camp and took out the Japanese guards — a glimpse of hope twisted into a terrifying scenario.

There was a chilling situation when a Japanese guard made a grim promise to a prisoner, saying, "If the Americans land here, it will go like this." He gestured from the prisoners to the guns, implying the machine guns would mow them down if the Americans invaded, following the Japanese code of honour to the bitter end.

They were also warned about an approaching cyclone, with instructions to alert the sick in the infirmary. The ill had to take cover under blankets to shield themselves from debris and glass. When the cyclone hit, glass shattered and flew across the infirmary, but miraculously, the patients remained unharmed, while the Japanese guardhouse got tossed about a hundred metres away.

From July, American B-29 bombers started targeting Nagasaki and even Fukuoka 14B. This was part of General Douglas MacArthur, the Commander-in-Chief of the Allied Forces in the South-West Pacific's, larger strategy to push Japan towards surrender.

Claude's diary 9 August 1945.

On 1 August, a heavy bombardment of Nagasaki was carried out. The factory district in which we were located, was one of the bombers' main targets.

We were waiting in the old dugout trenches made of reinforced concrete and bamboo stakes. You could hear the bombs coming closer. We were being hit closer and closer. There was a lad in the trench with us who could see where the bombs were landing. At one point he shouted, "They're going to land here". We quickly lay flat on the ground and some of us in the groundwater. The bombs fell in a cluster of five around us, without actually hitting us. Except for one bomb, which fell more or less on the edge of one of our dugout trenches. It collapsed and several of our boys were buried under heavy concrete blocks. We prayed and pulled like mad to get them out while bombs rained around us. Fortunately, we were able to free almost all of them. One friend we could not dislodge, his head was stuck between blocks. A few were wounded and in shock and unfortunately one campmate was killed.

It was an infernal racket. The clatter of bullets from fighters' guns on the zinc roofs of the barracks was unbearable. The groundwater poured into our trench because of that bombardment. After this day the air raids became so intense that we were seldom sent to the foundry. The trenches became our second home. In addition, debris had to be cleared from the factory around the first few factory halls. The debris was shovelled into wheelbarrows and these were taken to specified places.

Japan refused to capitulate. A few prisoners were able to tell us something about the bomb that fell on Hiroshima on 8 August. They had heard from a guard, who in turn had heard it from a Japanese commander.

On... 9 August.......

At about 7.00 hrs. there was another air raid and we had to go back to our trenches. A plane circled above our heads for almost an hour but nothing happened. Around 8.00 hrs. we got the all clear signal and left the shelters.

A squadron of aircraft flew over us. One group went back to work in the wood factory behind our camp. The foundry group had to stay inside the camp, perhaps because the foundry was further away. My British friend Ben and I worked in our hideout. We had to drain the remaining groundwater and dry it out with blankets. Finally we were finished. Ben stayed in the shelter to secretly smoke a cigarette, which he lit with a pair of glasses. I crawled through the kitchen to my bunk, using the unexpected free time to get some rest, which was absolutely forbidden.

I did not see the explosion of the bomb itself, which happened around eleven o'clock but I was caught in the middle of everything which happened immediately afterwards. There was no air alert this time. Apparently the Japanese knew nothing about it and were completely taken by surprise.

A huge explosion caused me to roll off my mattress and I fell on the ground and part of the asbestos sheets from the roof fell on top of me. All kind of materials such as pieces of wood and metal flew through the air. Fortunately, I was protected by a 'tatami', a reed mat on which I slept. Other tatamis from the bunks above fell on top of me. Finally I came out from under the rubble. Miraculously still in one piece. Under the debris of our barracks lay a few of my comrades. My mates and I helped them get out from under it.

Some shouted, "incendiary bombs"! That was the moment I tried to get my bearings, which I couldn't do, the world around me had changed. Everything looked different. Everything was gone, the fence of the camp, everything around me had been flattened, the environment as I knew it had disappeared. The two big gas cylinders and the guardhouse were no longer there.

Nagasaki lies in a valley with rows of hills on either side and a river running through the town. The sky was clear blue. I looked around me and I could see straight into the hills. The valley was completely empty. On both sides I saw many houses on fire. I thought, my goodness, what kind of bomb had caused this? I could hardly see anything. I tried to run in one direction. I saw Sergeant 'small bamboo' coming towards me. This time without a bamboo in his hand, but with a drawn samurai sword. I immediately turned around and ran in the opposite direction.

The boys working outside told me that at first they thought the three parachutes were weather balloons, because they looked like weather balloons. Suddenly flashes of light appeared in the sky. A blinding light appeared and suddenly disappeared, followed by a dark red sky and intense heat. A roar like a hurricane caused intense pressure resulting in an explosion. No one understood the darkness just after the explosion. What was it?

It was later explained that they were all temporarily blinded. Only after some minutes did they regain their sight. The air pressure was so great that the entire factory district, several kilometres long, was totally destroyed and even houses on the surrounding hills, built high up against it, were crushed like matchboxes and some were hit and burned by that terrible blast. This blast started fires which, because Nagasaki is built entirely of wood, spread rapidly. God, my God, how thankful I am to You that, except for a few cuts, You left me unharmed. Again You held Your helping Hand over my head and spared me.

After helping my friends I ran into the hills. From the hill I looked down on a sea of flames, roaring and crackling, devouring everything. We could only flee from the conflagration. On my way out of the camp, I met some campmates. We walked past the latrines. There I heard someone crying. "Help, help". I pushed open the half collapsed door and saw an American who must have sat on the toilet when the bomb fell. The man was unharmed, however he was covered from head to foot in muck. Despite the seriousness of the situation, we laughed. We, the prisoners and wounded and the guards walked together further up the hills to find shelter, to cool down. First of all we walked along paths and then up through prickly bamboo groves. The hills, 300 to 400 metres high, lay like a horseshoe around the densely populated centre of Nagasaki. From here we also had a good view of the burning wooden houses. The suburbs, the factory district along the river and the St. Franciscus Cathedral were totally destroyed. All that was left was a bare plain.

The wounded men who had looked at the light of the bomb had almost all been affected. Many suffered horrific burns on all or parts of their bodies. Huge water blisters appeared where the skin was uncovered. Large areas of skin just hung from their swollen bodies. From the hills there used to be a view of the city. What city? It seemed as if a giant hand had bent all the chimneys and everything that had stood upright to the left and to the right. Nagasaki was on fire and was one immense conflagration. Nagasaki was no more.

Claude continued writing in his diary, 9 August.

The bomb had exploded at a height of about 500 metres. Towards the centre of the impact, the bomb had caused an implosion and destroyed all buildings in the city centre, the sports stadium, the cathedral, the hospital and the two Mitsubishi factory complexes. Near the epicentre of the explosion there were no more flowers, no trees, no grass. Only concrete and molten iron and steel remained. Within a minute, thousands of houses were on fire. We saw black rain, which turned out to be ash. We heard cries of the dying amidst the roaring, crackling, devouring flames. The stench was incredible. The guy next to me said "it smells like roast beef". The penetrating stench was indescribable, an awfully foul smell of burnt flesh of thousands upon thousands of bodies.

Claude found out something pretty intense later on.

The person in charge of dropping the atomic bomb that took out Nagasaki, Commander Sweeny, actually did a test run with a dummy bomb over the Pacific before the real deal, which was nicknamed 'Fat Man.' They were initially aiming for Kokura, but bad weather made them change plans and delay their departure. On 9 August, around 11 a.m., under Charles Sweeney's command, they dropped the actual plutonium bomb from the B-29 called 'Bockscar'. It ended up landing about three kilometres off their intended target but still wiped Nagasaki off the map.

Claude also heard this bizarre story about the bomb's radiation effects. A work crew, about a kilometre from the camp, was taking turns between working with pneumatic drills and resting in the sun. Oddly, the men who were working didn't get hurt, but those chilling in the sun ended up with third-degree burns. How does that even happen? Claude ended up writing about it for '*Life*' magazine. They had a science expert suggest that maybe the bomb's radiation hitched a ride on the sunlight. The scale of the Nagasaki disaster was beyond what anyone could really wrap their head around. Claude got off with just a few scratches. He was dazed but overwhelmingly grateful to be alive, thinking to himself, "I'M ALIVE! I've made it through again." Despite the horror of the bomb, he didn't see the "destructive light" directly. Once more, he felt like his guardian angel had his back.

Even though the Fukuoka 14B camp was torched, being so close to where the bomb hit — only 1,850 metres from the centre — it's nothing short of a miracle that most of its people made it through. Claude mentioned hearing rumours that swirled around, saying if the Americans ever invaded, the Japanese planned to take out all the POWs first, as a twisted form of payback for the Allied bombings. This left everyone on edge, running scared of what might come next.

Mushroom cloud, 9 August 1945, 11.02 a.m.

Aerial photograph Fukuoka 14B after the blast. Thanks to © US National Archives And Records Administration

## Inferno

From Claude's diary; August 1945

I walked a little ahead. There was not much wind. I was thirsty and struggled through the trees and plants towards the bamboo forest. As we walked there, someone called out, "Another bomb has exploded." We looked up and saw a reddish-orange ball tumbling down. It was close to us. We crawled under the broad leaves of watermelon plants on the ground and we were scared and we were absolutely terrified. Suddenly someone started laughing. It was a hysterical, almost inhuman laughter that said: "It's nothing, it's the sun." And indeed it was the sun in our eyes. The enormous smoke curtains of the burning houses in Nagasaki drifted like a thick layer over the hills. What we saw was an optical illusion, the sun through the huge layers of clouds above us.

Before we left the camp it appeared that one of our boys, 'Megens', had become trapped under a heavy steel and wooden beam in the timber factory. Some mates had to give up trying to free him despite several heroic rescue attempts. The flames and smoke in the burning factory came closer and closer. He was conscious. He still whispered, "Are my legs still there? I can't feel them. Let me lie down. You guys go." The boys had to leave him, feeling very guilty. The roof collapsed almost over their heads. He was burned alive. Later we found his ashes and bone remains and put them in an urn. God have mercy on his soul!

Nagasaki after the blast. Thanks to © heirs Roger Mansell

## Plague of flies

Claude continues writing, August 1945.

At first we stayed in an abandoned camp in the mountains. After a few days we went to another makeshift camp, near the destroyed barracks of our old camp 14B. If there was any suffering, it was here. Maggots were crawling all over the men's wounds. The camp orderlies tried their best to stop the wounded from scratching their wounds. The wounded had to endure the terrible pain. Body fluids accumulated under the skin, causing huge blisters. The plague of flies quickly found their way to the blisters, laid eggs there and drove the men crazy with itching. Of course, you could not kill the flies on their burnt spots. They even laid eggs on the bandages, through which the pus oozed. After a few hours, the eggs hatched and people perished due to the insufferable pain and itching.

Can you imagine the suffering? There was only burn ointment. There were no other medication. What the nurses and attendants did among us was to remove the thick maggots from the flesh every day, early in the morning. I could hear those men screaming in pain. The young and small maggots were left in the wounds which kept the wounds clean, for they ate all the pus. When the bandages were taken off, you could see that the wounds, which were so dirty at first, had now been eaten clean by the maggots. That is how my wounded mates survived. They lived to see the end of the war.

## Overwhelmed by emotions

'I saw the trams with the passengers still in them. Black skeletons like thin charred dolls.'

Claude's diary continues. August 1945.

In the camp, our assignments were also frightful and in another way painful. The next day and days after, we, the healthy men, returned to the severely damaged and devastated city Nagasaki. We wandered around in the radioactive area for days without realising it. With a small group, we helped with the cleaning up. First near our camp and later in the city. We helped to pick up the bodies, remove bodies from under the rubble and cremate them on pyres. The last thing we could do for the dead. We were even able to rescue a single wounded, trapped Japanese person from the inferno and transported him on a door which served as a makeshift stretcher. Another group was looking for wood for the pyres.

We returned to the city to help where we could, nothing remained except for dark imprints on charred bricks. People just melted in the heat. The trams, with passengers like charred dolls still in them were seen on the street.

In the days following the destruction of Nagasaki, we returned again and again to the hard-hit city, helping the wounded, burning countless corpses, digging in the rubble. We just walked around among the ruins, often lying on pavements to pull people out of the debris. We even dug up food and ate it without having any idea of the possible consequences. The Japanese ex-guards were a bit more amiable when they saw us working like this and especially when we performed the respectful cremations.

On 14 August our camp commander Lieutenant Aalders died, a good man was lost. In total we now mourned the death of five friends. That there weren't more was another miracle. God help us.

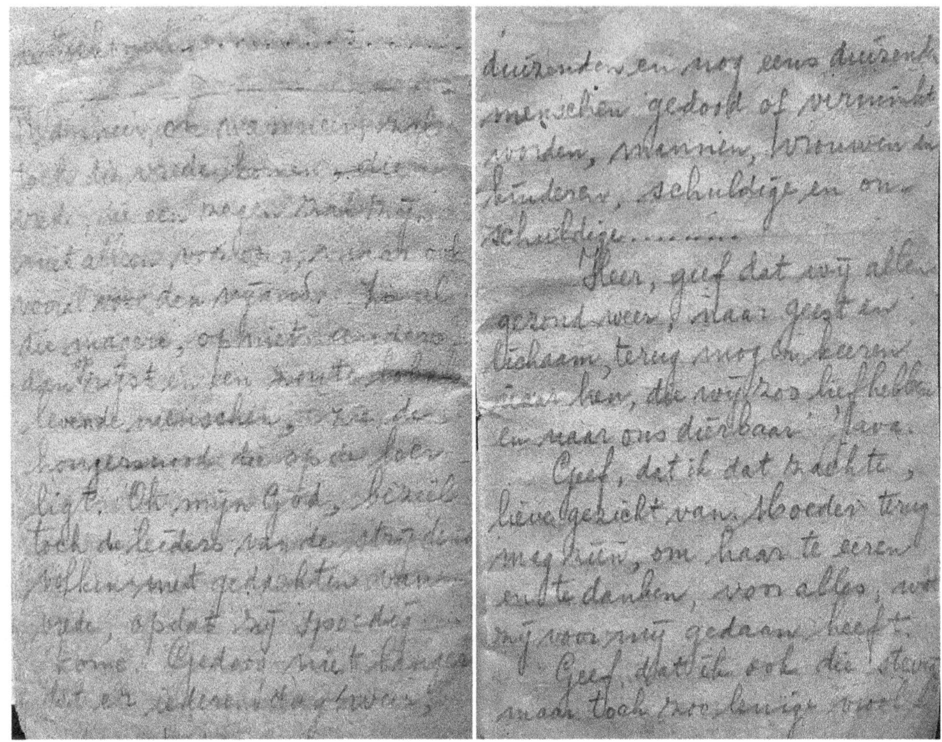

Diary, after the atomic bomb, August 1945

## Claude continues in his diary with emotion, August 1945.

My heart is crying for all these poor Japanese people. When, oh when, will peace come, this peace, which will be a blessing, not only for us, but also especially for the enemy. Look at all those skinny people, living on nothing but rice and salty 'lobak', fish.

Oh, my God, I prayed, inspire the leaders with thoughts of peace. Do not allow thousands and thousands of men, women and children to be killed or injured every day. Please spare the guilty and the innocent. Lord, grant that we may all return to our homes healthy in mind and body, to those we love and to our beloved Java. Grant that I may see the soft, sweet face of my mother again, to honour and thank her for all she had done for me. Grant that I may also hold father's firm yet supple violin fingers and may his talents be passed onto me. Oh father, how often in silent moments I still see and hear you playing your gypsy violin. How I long, now that I feel capable, that I am older and more mature, to ask you to teach me about composition, harmony and counterpoint. I do not doubt father, that you have also used your talents in captivity, where you have or had more free time, in order to create perhaps wonderful compositions. Please grant that I may also see my sisters again, Lord. Now matured into women, not only through years, but also especially through the distressing circumstances that they have endured or still have to endure. I also pray that I may see my brother René again.

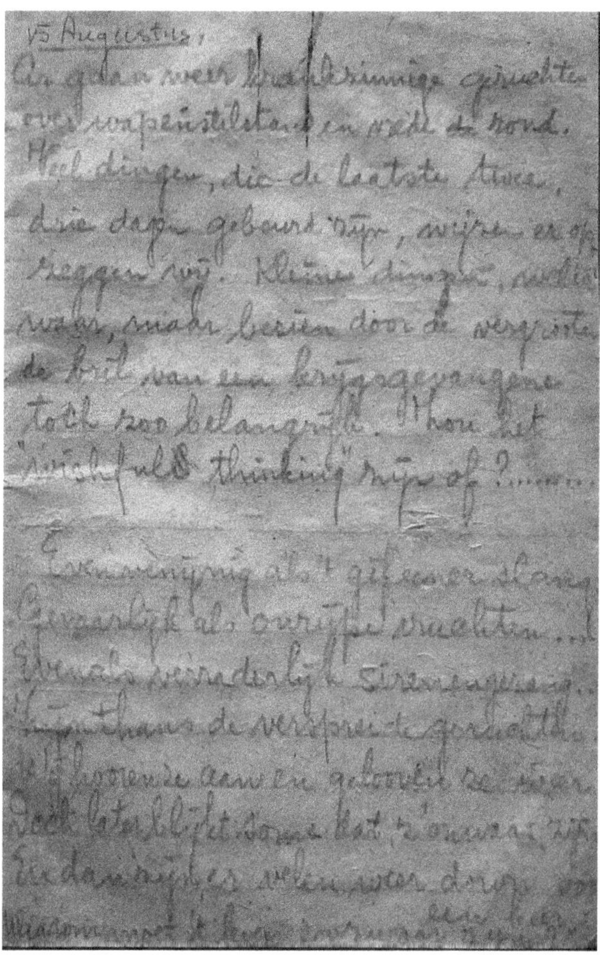

Diary 15 August 1945

"Fat Man". Public domain

"

There are certain thoughts

that you,

no matter what,

always keep to yourself

Courtesy of:
Author: Haruki Murakami
Book: *Colorless*
Publisher: Penguin Random House LLC (US)

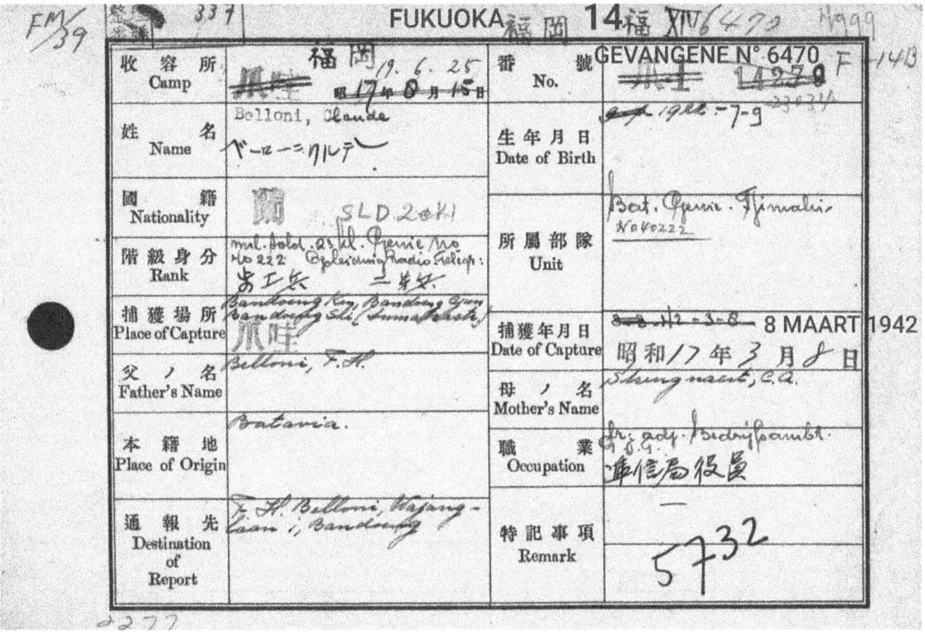

Partial name list of the prisoners of war, Fukuoka 14B, Nagasaki, page 1

Partial name list of the prisoners of war, Fukuoka 14B, Nagasaki, page 2

The sun of freedom. Public domain

# PART III
# THE SUN OF FREEDOM IN CLAUDE'S EYES
# 3. FREE! 1945

A cow,

a goat and

sweet faces

"

I fear all we have done

is to awaken

a sleeping giant and

fill him with a terrible resolve.

*Isoroku Yamamoto*

# 3.1 The capitulation of Japan, 15 August 1945

I believe there'll come a time when all the horrors of being a POW under the Japanese will fade into just a really bad memory.

*B*ut for those who made it out alive, that moment of survival will stick with them forever. Yet, their hunger didn't end there. Now, they were starving for something different – they craved the truth, updates on what was happening in the world, and solid facts to grasp onto.

Claude's diary August 1945.

Insane rumours about ceasefire and peace are going around again. Many things happened in the last two or three days point to this. Small things, admittedly, but seen through the magnifying glasses of a prisoner of war, seem so important. But could it be wishful thinking?

Vicious rumours spread like the venom of a snake, dangerous unripe fruit, or as captivating as a siren's song. We hear them and believe them. But later they turn out to be untrue. And then we feel deflated. Why does life have to be so hard?

On 12 August, Emperor Hirohito made a move by ordering Japan to surrender without any conditions. This was a historic moment because, for the first time ever, his voice was broadcast live on the radio, on the 15th of August. He announced the surrender declaration to the Japanese people himself. Then, on 2 September, that unconditional surrender was officially signed. Just like that, the Second World War came to an end. Over in Europe, Germany had already thrown in the towel back in early May.

Looking through the list of POWs from Fukuoka 14B, there's a note that Claude was checked into the camp hospital right around when Japan surrendered. Why he was there, I can't say. He never talked about it.

Partial name list Prisoners Of War, Fukuoka 14b: Claude in hospital

## Free! Peace!

Claude's fervent wish for peace and freedom keeps running through his head. He knew he'd be happy if that wish ever became reality. But for that to happen Japan had to surrender first.


Claude's diary 19 August 1945.


On 19 August we were called together. The camp commander stood on an empty barrel and he informed us in Japanese that there was peace. Nothing was said about surrender. We realised that we were free. God, oh God, it is true.

Peace at last!

We were stunned, there was no talking, no laughing, only sobbing and crying. Men hugged each other. The rumours had finally come true. What we had longed for had become a reality after so many years. The war was over. We were finally free! Peace, a wonderful word bestowed by God. The day had finally come.

Today, our friends from Fukuoka 2 sent meals to our camp to celebrate our liberation. What a feast we had. We celebrated our freedom with wild joy and at the same time there was great concern about our families. Had they survived their internment? The first news arrived only a few months later.

The next day, 20 August, we got up. Not with the fearful feeling of expectation of bombing with those parachutes, not with the expectation of being forced to work in the factory. Twelve long hours of daily slavery, servitude and humiliation had ended.

Now as free men we look forward to feel like human beings again. To put on clean clothes, sleep in a good bed, eat something other than rice and soup, soup and rice, rice and soup, three times a day.

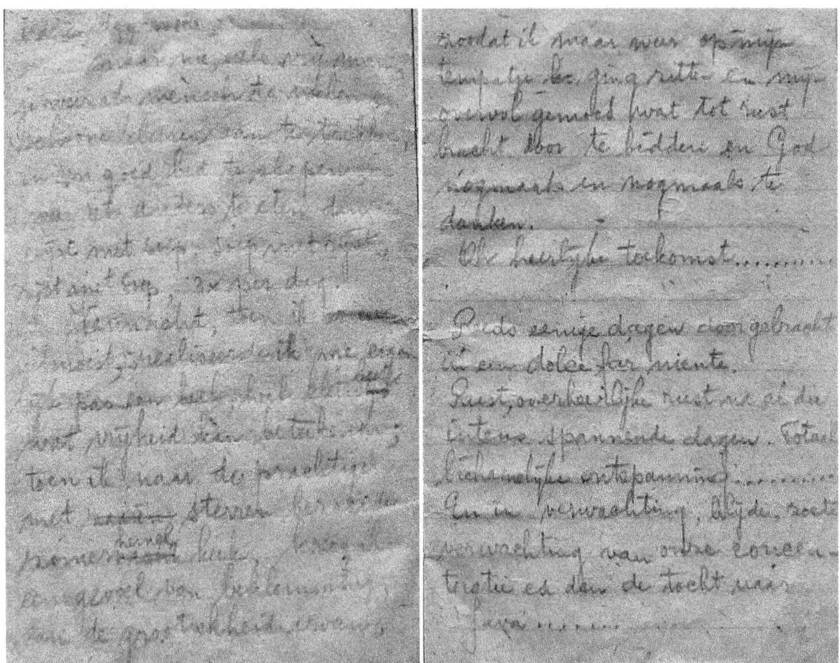

Diary 23 August 1945. Dolce far niente

Last night, when I had to go out, I realised only a very, very small part of what freedom could mean. When I looked at the beautiful starry Summer sky, I got a feeling of oppression from the greatness of it, so I sat down on my 'tempat', sleeping place, again and calmed my mind by praying and thanking God over and over.

Oh could a wonderful future await us all?

I had already spent a few days in a 'dolce far niente', pleasant relaxation, rest, delicious rest after many intense days. Total physical relaxation with anticipation of a happy journey back to Java.

For the time being, we were not allowed to leave the camp because of radio active radiation which we unfortunately had been exposed to.

Overmorgen de 25e wordt een Am. vliegtuig verwacht, die één of ander pakket zal uitgooien. de 26e worden de Yanks hier verwacht. Wat een gericht zal dat zijn..

26 Aug. -

Mijn lieve ouders zijn vandaag 31 jaar getrouwd. Innig gefeliciteerd, hoor! Wat een tijd al: 31 jaar. Evenmin, na 3 jaren van elkaar gescheiden te zijn, het weer tezamen te mogen vieren in vrijheid. Helaas kan ik nog niet bij Ul beiden zijn, maar wees er verzekerd van, dat deze, al niet thans deze dag toch gevierd zal worden.

Diary, 24 August 1945. Hooray!

Hooray, camp Fukuoka 2 has come up with Red Cross stuff for the 'poor bombed' of ex-camp 14B again. Delicious food. What a treat. The day after tomorrow, 25 August, an American plane is expected to drop some food packages.

On 26 August, the Yanks are expected. What a sight that will be. This day is also the 31st Wedding anniversary of my parents. Congratulations to them! After three years of separation would we be able to celebrate this together in freedom? Unfortunately, I cannot be with you both yet, but rest assured that nevertheless this day will be celebrated, admittedly in Japan, thousands of kilometres away from you, but as a free man. May God grant that you may celebrate this day many, many times together with all of us in the family circle. Good health, 'lieve Mam en Pap', dear Mum and Dad.

In the evening, after a beautiful walk to the sea, we came back to our barracks. One of our boys had smuggled a 1.5 litre bottle of saké. Bartered trade was going on secretly with the population. Food traded for cigarettes. So I was able to drink to both your health after all. A good omen, perhaps?

On 29 August we went down through Nagasaki, or rather what was left of Nagasaki. We were asked to find urns in the debris of the Urakami Cathedral. We carefully placed some ashes in empty urns we collected from a Buddhist temple and identified the ashes in writing. We transported the urns in cloths to the temple where we left them for the time being. There were 113 urns in total which the Americans transported later back to America.

On 30 August a request was made to the camp-commander for more rice, better soup, meat and fish. Of course there were huge objections, but this morning we were able to buy a large cow for two pairs of American shoes and a pen. How is it possible that American shoes could be worth that much? A cow in exchange for shoes? Japan is certainly a country of contradictions. From today we took over the Japanese watch. I have to get up at 7.00 hrs. tomorrow morning. 12 hours of guard duty awaits me.

Today, 31 August, is 'Koninginnedag', Queen's Day. After six years of having to commemorate her birthday abroad, our Queen finally celebrated her 65th birthday in her home country. Our joy was increased by the fact that at about 12.00 hrs. American planes dropped 15 parachutes, each with double drums filled with food. What a feast. Such a pleasure to eat European food again. What a joy, what a joy, what a wealth, what a wealth.

The so-called Japanese management and Japanese guards are drifting off and we get their guns and ammunition. I had never ever thought of being on guard with a Jap gun.

On 3 September we had visitors. Three Swiss and a Swede from the Red Cross arrived. The first American journalists showed up for a visit on 9 September. It was only then that we heard from the Americans that we had to deal with an atomic bomb attack. During those last days I walked with a rifle over my shoulder like other camp residents.

Before the war I had read 'A Farewell to Arms' by Hemingway. I longed for that too, a farewell to arms. It took a long time before we, the Dutch Indisch, could go home.

Claude continues, 8 September 1945.

We have a wicked sociable group, full of commercial spirit. Last night the fun reached its climax. Mars came in with Steph Broese, my 'slapie', bunk mate. He had a whole live 'kambing', goat around his neck. And I can assure you he was received with loud cheers. Steph's birthday is today. And he had a good birthday, I say that because we made 'saté' kambing, goat meat on a bamboo stick, and 'gulé', kambing, goat meat dish. To complete the day, two B-29s dropped parachutes with more supplies again. We now have so much tinned food that we first have to clear our 'tampat tidor', sleeping place before we can lie down.

Claude's diary continues, 12 September 1945.

Today we are expected to embark onto the hospital ship in the harbour. We are being disinfected, then dressed only in pyjamas we will be taken to the aircraft carrier. At last we are leaving this country. It is hard to comprehend what a great feeling this was for us, former prisoners of war.

13 September 1945.

We were disinfected, the Americans gave us new clothes. I saw the first sweet faces in years, of the nurses of the hospital ship. I helped them as an interpreter and helped with filling in forms et cetera. What a pleasure it was to hear a civilised female voice again after hearing only the voices of those ugly little bastards here in Japan.

We were taken to Okinawa on the small aircraft carrier the U.S.S. Chenango and from there to Manila by plane. We spent the next few days in a 'dolce far niente' again. No more anxious feelings. Divine food and cinema in the evening. Holy cow, it's just hard to take it all in. On 16 September, we were supposed to arrive in Okinawa, but we had just sailed past this city, our destination, because there was a cyclone in the area. The next day there was another heavy storm, which rocked the ship terribly. On 18 September, we steamed into Okinawa harbour and were accommodated in tents.

On 21 September, around 4.00 hrs., we left for Manila in a B-29 aeroplane. I am now flying above the clouds, I am in the clouds ... , filled with joy and a little closer to home. The sun has just risen. Oh God! How wonderful it is to be free! If anything gives you the feeling of freedom, it's the plane, that bird, up there so high in the sky. Oh wonderful freedom! Around 8.30 hrs. we arrived in Manila. From the plane we were loaded onto a truck and driven to the 29th Replacement Camp and later to the 5th Replacement Camp. We were given fresh food in a Red Cross canteen. We were vaccinated. How similar the Philippines are to Java. Banana trees, mango trees, everything is so similar to Java. I wish they would send us back to Java soon, because I had heard that the island is still in such a mess and I want to be there.

From Claude's diary, 23 October 1945.

I was delighted to get two long letters from home which affected me emotionally so I went to our sweet little church in our camp to cry quietly. There I became calm again.

We are told that we will leave for Java on 2 November. Whether we get to our homes is of course another question. We were completely overwhelmed by this unexpected information. Together with several soldiers, I was trained again. New KNIL units were formed. We had to restore the Dutch authority in the Dutch East Indies. What is in store for us now?

Joy over the capitulation and peace was soon gone. The end of military service, the laying down of arms, was a great desire for Claude and the other prisoners of war, but reality turned out differently. Before he knew it, Claude was wearing a KNIL uniform again and he was back in the service of the KNIL.

Claude in Manila, 5th Replacement Camp. He already gained some weight due to the abundance of food in the last month.

Claude didn't end up going back to Java, where he had hoped to pick up the pieces of his life. Instead, he was rerouted to Balikpapan on Borneo. There, KNIL units, including Claude, were flown in. Australia was playing it cautious, not wanting to stir up trouble with the nationalists in Java. So, the reassembled KNIL units got moved again, this time from Balikpapan to South Celebes aboard a British Navy ship, landing Claude in the middle of efforts to reestablish Dutch control in Makassar.

Makassar, a key port city vital for trade, sits in a bay with waters deep enough for big sea vessels to dock easily. It was a bustling place, especially with the Chinese dominating the trade scene there.

But for the Indo-European community, this move spelled another stretch of growing unease, filled with fear, violence, and disorder.

Before he fully realised what was happening, Claude was back in uniform for the KNIL, tasked with bringing order to the turbulent Celebes. His mission included disarming the revolutionaries of the newly proclaimed Republic of Indonesia by President Sukarno. Many of Claude's comrades weren't up for this new task; the toll of their recent ordeals had left them too weak physically to face another challenge.

Claude's diary 27 October 1945.

Around our camp, while we were in Fukuoka 14B, machine gun posts were set up everywhere. As soon as the Americans landed, the Japs would shoot us all. This was what the Japs kept telling us. The Japanese could not afford that, when the time came, they would also have to maintain a kind of second front within their own territory. Nevertheless, I sincerely hope that the atomic bomb will never be used again against people. Unfortunately, that decision is not mine to make.

After Japan threw in the towel, all those places they'd taken over during the war started breaking free. President Truman, the man who said 'yes' to the bomb, never looked back. He figured not using it would've cost a lot more American lives. "How could I face anyone," he argued, "knowing I had something that could end the war and didn't use it?"

Fast forward a bit, and you've got loads of people, for years, getting sick because of the bomb's fallout in Hiroshima and Nagasaki. They're called *'Hibakusha'* in Japan, the bomb survivors.

Now, you might think Claude got hit by that radiation too. But whenever he talked about being in Nagasaki when the bomb dropped, he was clear: he dodged that bullet. He came out of it all right, lived a good life, got married, had a couple of daughters, and even saw his grandkids grow up.

The U.S.S. *Missouri*, stationed in Tokyo Bay at the time, served as the venue for the official surrender ceremony on 2 September, 1945. General MacArthur signed the unconditional surrender document on behalf of the Allied forces.

In a turn of events that differed significantly from the fate of many Japanese military leaders — who faced long prison sentences — Emperor Hirohito was spared from having to stand trial for his wartime actions. It seems he had General MacArthur to thank for this leniency. MacArthur himself was of the opinion that Hirohito should remain as Emperor.

David Bergamini, who experienced life in a Japanese camp in the Philippines as a young boy, delves deeper into the topic of the atomic bombs in his book *'Japan's Imperial Conspiracy'*. He reveals that the bomb dropped on Nagasaki three days after Hiroshima was a different type. Interestingly, Nagasaki wasn't the primary target; it was actually a backup. The original plan was to target Kokura, a historic city on the northern coast of Kyushu, with the second atomic bomb. However, due to poor weather conditions making visibility over Kokura bad, the bomber was redirected to Nagasaki, the secondary target.

The bomb aimed for Nagasaki had a specific spot in mind, right past the train station, set to wipe out the bay and the old parts of town tucked into the Urakami valley. But that day, just like in Hiroshima, clouds covered the sky. They found a gap in the clouds, though, and that's where they dropped "Fat Man." Thing is, it didn't hit where it was supposed to. It ended up somewhere else in Nagasaki, which kind of dialled down the disaster from what they had planned. By some stroke of luck, this mix-up meant the men at Fukuoka 14B POW camp got a break and weren't in the direct line of fire.

When that bomb went off, it pretty much erased everything within a couple of miles from Nagasaki's heart. The blast was so fierce it ripped through people nearby, mangling bodies and bursting lungs.

Now, there's this place in Nagasaki, right between where the bomb hit and the museum they set up to remember it. They've got this monument there, put up by the Monument Nagasaki Foundation. It's to remember the 545 POWs from Fukuoka 14B. They unveiled this marble monument on 4 May, 2021, with all the proper ceremonies you'd expect in Japan.

On the monument, there's a crane, which everyone knows stands for peace. And there's a clock stuck at 11:02 a.m. — the exact moment Nagasaki's world turned upside down. Right in front of it, they've laid out shapes to show where the barracks of Fukuoka 14B used to be, kind of bringing a piece of that past into the present.

Memorial statue of Fukuoka 14B, Nagasaki, 2021. © Foundation Monument Nagasaki

Newspaper article Leeuwarder Courant, 7 August 1979

## A Reunion

After the Dutch East Indies were freed, Boy made his way from Japan to Makassar in South Celebes. He started searching for his family with some help from the Red Cross. His folks had sent word they'd moved to Makassar by the end of 1945. His dad, Fred, landed a gig with the Celebes Government as the Head of Housing. Margot, Nettie's daughter, showed up in Makassar early 1946, after having her son, and snagged a job as a teacher. Dési, on the other hand, stayed back in Bandung, got hitched in February 1946, and by 1947, she and her new husband headed off to the Netherlands.

Claude didn't take long to track down his parents. Seeing them again was everything he'd hoped for, but the happiness was tinged with sadness.

René, with his cockpit crew

He was hit with the heartbreaking news that his brother, René, had been killed back on 3 March, 1942. René, who was a 24-year-old second lieutenant pilot observer, didn't make it back from a mission out of Kalidjati.

On 1 March, 1942, the Japanese had caught everyone off guard at Kalidjati, north of Bandung, by attacking and seizing the airbase there. The crew at the nearby Andir military base had no clue about the take-over and thought it was still safe. René and his crew were sent to scout Kalidjati airfield on 3 March, with orders to land and pick up some baggage if they could. After they landed at Kalidjati, nothing more was heard from René and his crew members.

In Leidschendam, the Netherlands, my father shared with me a story from years after the war.

René, KV no. 159518, KNIL

He was at this gathering in Hotel Des Indes in The Hague when he bumped into a medium. Dad wasn't planning to talk to him, but something pulled him over. During the session, my father brought up René, wanting to know more. The medium asked if he had a photo of his brother. Sure enough, Dad always carried René's picture in his uniform in his wallet. The clairvoyant took the photo, ran his hand over it a few times, and after a while handed it back. He mentioned feeling a profound sadness and said, "I don't feel his head." That struck a chord with my dad, leaving him horrified and drowning in grief. He left right then and there, never finding out if what the medium said held any truth. The real details of René's death remained a mystery. Rumours had it that René might have been executed, but nothing was ever confirmed. He was just 24 years old. René Belloni was awarded the Bronze Lion for bravery posthumously. There's also a cross bearing his name at the Dutch Field of Honour Ancol in Jakarta, at section I, row 40, location number 41.

Flowers in honour of René Belloni at the cross of honour in Ancol, Jakarta, 15 August 2023

Every year around 15 August, the War Graves Foundation in the Netherlands offers the opportunity to have flowers placed at the memorial crosses on the Fields of Honour in the Netherlands and Indonesia. In 2023, I made use of this again to honour uncle René.

Bamboo runcing, Merdeka! Public domain

# 3.2 Uprising in Nirvana

## Mid 1945 -1949

For Claude, it felt like the storm never really passed. The dream of returning to his pre-war life in the East Indies, his paradise, seemed more and more like a distant memory. Even after Japan's surrender, he was itching to be demobilised, to put the war behind him.

*B*ack in the Netherlands, the focus was on rebuilding and recovering from the devastation of World War II. But over in the Dutch East Indies, the power dynamics had shifted dramatically after the Japanese left. The Indonesians took charge.

This shift led to an important moment on 17 August, 1945, just two days after Japan surrendered. The Indonesian Nationalist Party, seizing the instant, declared independence, establishing the '*Republik Indonesia.*' Sukarno, an engineer turned political leader, was named President, with Hatta serving as Prime Minister. Both had been imprisoned and exiled for their nationalist views but now stood at the forefront of their country's push for sovereignty. They made the independence announcement right from Sukarno's home in Pegangsaän, East Batavia, not too far from where Claude had been held. Broadcasted over Radio Jakarta, Sukarno's voice marked the beginning of a new era for Indonesia.

Sukarno, born Kusno Sosrodihardjo (1901-1970), emerged as Indonesia's first President. In Indonesia, he was affectionately known as '*Bung*' Karno, with Hatta being '*Bung*' Hatta — '*Bung*' being an honorific title meaning something akin to 'Father of the Nation,' in line with an old Javanese tradition.

The push for independence wasn't just a political manoeuvre; it was fuelled by the pressure from militant youth groups, creating a tense and often dangerous atmosphere. The Indo-European community, eager to return to their former lives, found their hopes dashed as they faced a new reality. Instead of liberation, they entered a period of uncertainty and fear, a time marked by the word '*Bersiap*' — meaning to be ready or alert. Shouts of '*Merdeka*' — freedom, independence — filled the air as Indonesian flags waved, signifying a dramatic change for everyone involved.

Right after the war, the Netherlands found itself in a tough spot, unable to immediately reestablish control over the Dutch East Indies. I've learned that Great Britain agreed to step in temporarily, but it took about six weeks for British forces to actually land there. During that time, there was basically a power vacuum, with no one officially in charge. Since the Dutch Colonial government was still in exile in England and there weren't any troops ready to take control from the Japanese army, the responsibility weirdly fell back to the Japanese soldiers who were still around. Meanwhile, many Europeans remained stuck in what used to be Japanese internment camps.

Seeing the Japanese take on this role of authority was surreal, to say the least. It wasn't long before the Dutch Indisch community realised that the Indonesians, who they once viewed as comrades in suffering, were now on the opposite side. The shift was stark, with some Indonesians turning hostile, often targeting civilians.

In a strange turn of events, the Japanese soldiers were now tasked with protecting the internees from these attacks. Their demeanour had changed dramatically; they no longer barked orders but instead bowed and nodded politely, much like the internees had been doing not so long ago.

Meanwhile, Indonesian nationalists were quickly gaining control over vast areas of Java and Sumatra. With the Indonesian freedom struggle heating up, it was too dangerous for the internees to leave the camps. Various places like churches, monasteries, hotels, old internment camps, prisons, and even tea and coffee plantations were repurposed to keep people safe. Protection was provided by the Japanese and, in some areas, Indonesian police forces.

Under the directives of Allied General Louis Mountbatten, the Japanese were tasked with keeping the peace. Suddenly, things in the camps started looking up: food supplies increased, and items like oil, sugar, meat, and fruit began making their way in. The camp staff's attitude shifted towards being more friendly, and the strict monitoring of movements in and out of the camps was relaxed.

But this improvement was short-lived. Before long, the conditions reverted back to something similar to the Japanese regime. Comforts like beds were scarce, food rations were minimal, just a small portion per serving, and medication was hardly available. The internees found themselves battling hunger and the same diseases that had plagued them under Japanese rule. Mountbatten initially ordered Europeans to remain within the camps for their safety, advising against venturing out into the streets. This restriction, however, didn't extend to the Dutch-Indo community living outside the camp boundaries.


## British troops on Java

When British troops landed in Batavia towards the end of September 1945, the situation got even more intense. The British forces, including English, Scots, Indian Sikhs, and Gurkhas from Nepal, were all about protecting European civilians and helping those who had been in Japanese camps. They even helped evacuate Japanese people, but they had strict orders not to engage with the pemudas.

The *pemudas*, young radicals, were dead set on making sure the Dutch couldn't regain any sort of control. They were ready to do whatever it took to run their country on their own terms, fighting tooth and nail against the Dutch colonial powers. The place that was once the Dutch East Indies was quickly turning into a land where the Dutch were no longer welcome.

During the war, the Japanese had trained local militias to fight against the Allies, and now, these groups were eager to use their training. Armed with machetes, rifles, and bamboo spears known as *'runcings'*, these villagers, schooled by the Japanese, were ready for battle. Meanwhile, Japanese soldiers who'd gone into hiding across the islands began to support the leaders of the new Republic of Indonesia, fuelling the flames of the Indonesian Revolution. Japan had promised Indonesia independence after the war, and now they were helping make that promise a reality, encouraging Indonesians to fight for their freedom.

This support from Japan empowered Indonesian nationalists and freedom fighters to establish their own strongholds. With the training received during the war and a growing number of fighters joining their cause, the movement for independence gained momentum. The call for freedom grew louder and the fight for it increasingly fierce, as the struggle for Indonesian independence entered a new and more violent phase.

The revolutionary actions during this time were essentially a bold declaration: the days of colonial rule were over. The revolutionaries, fuelled by a fierce determination to end foreign domination, resorted to extreme measures. Incidents of stone-throwing, verbal abuse, rape, and even murder against Dutch citizens became alarmingly common. Indonesian youths, emboldened and perhaps influenced by the brutal tactics previously employed by the Japanese, engaged in widespread violence and intimidation.

Massacres became horrifyingly routine. The streets saw armed Indonesian youths detaining Europeans, conducting searches, and at times, taking them captive. Driven by desperation and fear, some Europeans sought refuge in nearby internment camps, hoping to escape the wrath of these fanatical groups. Meanwhile, Dutch-Indo residents found themselves pursued into forests, only to become prey to other Indonesian factions.

Men, and later women, who were not in the so-called "protection camps," were forcibly removed from their homes, which were then looted, destroyed, or set ablaze by the pemudas. To locate their targets, the Indonesian revolutionaries utilised the Japanese *'Tonari-gumi'* system —

a neighbourhood association and civil defence mechanism established by the Japanese. This system enabled them to pinpoint addresses and locations of unprotected internees with chilling efficiency.

This fervent quest for independence ignited a passionate zeal among the Indonesian kampong youth. A potent mix of nationalism and desire for freedom led to a deep-seated resentment towards anything associated with the Dutch, marking a period of intense strife and upheaval as Indonesia fought to redefine its identity and future.

"

A life full of pain is

like a life full of sorrow

when nobody sees it.


But do not give up,

because life is a gift.


So look for that one bit of sunshine,

that sun will give you hope and courage

to go on living.


Overcoming that pain

will not be easy.


But with enough

sun in the eyes, hope and courage

it will surely be all right again.



*Author: Unknown*

## War of Independence

Many Indo-Europeans were either still in the former Japanese camps or had only recently been released. Their physical appearance — skin colour, eye colour, and the language they spoke — made them easy targets for the pemudas. On 1 October, 1945, pemuda leaders ordered their followers to view all Dutch people as enemies, marking a significant escalation in hostility. Around this time, despite Allied commands to the contrary, the Japanese began arming the pemudas on a large scale.

Sukarno, foreseeing the danger, warned of a racial war where the safety of the Dutch could not be ensured. From October to December 1945, Indonesia saw a surge in violent raids across the country.

For those who were free on Java, life became even harder after Sukarno decided to cut their food supply on 4 October. This move signalled to the pemudas that their actions had Sukarno's tacit approval.

By the end of October 1945, the British attempted to quell the rising tension by airdropping pamphlets over Surabaya, urging Indonesian troops to lay down their arms. This only fuelled the anger of pemuda leaders. On 10 November, British forces, backed by heavy artillery, entered Surabaya, sparking the Battle of Surabaya. This bloody conflict saw pemudas ready to die for their cause, leading to fierce street battles with the British forces that resulted in numerous casualties on both sides. The violence that swept through Surabaya, especially the horrors reported at the *Simpang* Society, *Bubutan* prison, and *Werfstraat* prison, was beyond words.

By the end of November, the British had taken control of Surabaya, but peace and order were still far off. It wasn't until early March 1946 that additional troops arrived in Surabaya to assist in stabilising the situation.

In Bandung, the situation took a turn for the worse. There were simply too many Indo-Europeans in the city for them all to be rounded up and placed in protected camps. As a result, they were left vulnerable, essentially treated as outlaws, while the frenzy among the pemudas and others in Bandung escalated. Vehicles were seized, communication and water supplies were sabotaged, and looting became rampant. The atmosphere was charged with fear as numerous Dutch, Ambonese, Chinese, Mena-donese, and even supportive Indonesians were abducted. Given the high number of individuals who went missing, it's likely many were tortured or killed. In one of the numerous outbreaks of violence in Bandung, the southern part of the city was engulfed in flames in March 1946, an event remembered as the Bandung Sea of Fire.

The situation in Makassar mirrored the commotion in Bandung. The city became a dangerous place, with the disruption of public life instilling growing fear among its residents. Some pemudas in Makassar had undergone military training by the Japanese on Celebes, and they used this training to oppose the Dutch authority. Despite increased patrols by the British army, they were unable to provide adequate protection for the Indo-Europeans against the threats they faced.

Claude wrote in his diary, December 1945.

There was virtually no news in Makassar. Chaos reigned in the city. At one point we were attacked by the 'permista', Indonesian forces. Everyone was shooting at everyone. I thought to myself, I don't want to die. But if I am not careful, they will shoot me. An all-out war ensued and lasted for some time. Many people were killed. I was in a pavilion in the middle of the city and could see everything. Republican Indonesian soldiers were in our yard. Suddenly some Ambonese came around the corner. When the Ambonese were attacked they became really angry and made short work of their opponents. There was a short truce. I crawled through the drains to my parents who lived 300 metres away to see if anything had happened to them. Corpses lay around me everywhere.

On 30 December, 1945, despite British objections, 800 Dutch marines hit the shores of Java at Tanjung Priok, Batavia's port. Not long after, the first Dutch ground troops arrived. The KNIL, bolstered by the newly formed First Division '7 December', was tasked with bringing order and peace back to the Dutch East Indies. This division, made up of over 18,000 soldiers from the Netherlands, faced the monumental task of reclaiming control from the freedom fighters, despite being poorly prepared. Somehow, they managed to retake territories and ensure the safety of internees, who were then moved to major cities in trains with windows blacked out to avoid detection. However, negotiations between the Netherlands and Indonesia broke down, causing tensions to spike and violence to erupt once more.

By July 1946, the Allies green-lit the Netherlands to take back Celebes. Around this time, the last of the evacuated Japanese troops were leaving, and by 30 November of that year, the last British forces departed the Dutch East Indies, leaving a trail of casualties behind. Makassar's people, including those who had sided with the Dutch, endured significant hardships. Claude, although not directly involved in the combat, felt the weight of these troubling times. He recalled the atmosphere in Makassar as particularly stifling.

Claude and his fellow KNIL soldiers did what they could, always on high alert, yet struggling to match the sheer numbers of the revolutionaries.

Between March and April 1947, Great Britain acknowledged the Indonesian Republic as a de facto government, with other nations soon following suit. The Netherlands, however, only recognised Indonesia about two years later. The Dutch government aimed to establish order and enforce the law through military operations, termed 'police actions', refusing to acknowledge The Dutch East Indies as an independent state, instead viewing it as a colony.

The first major military operation by the Dutch, known as 'Operation Product', kicked off in mid-1947. Then came 'Operation *Kraai*' (Operation Crow) towards the end of 1948 or early 1949. Despite an armistice being signed, the Indonesian independence fighters, feeling unbound by the treaty, violated it multiple times. This led to a cycle of guerrilla warfare and countermeasures, causing casualties on both sides. The conflict continued even after a ceasefire was announced in the latter half of 1949, coinciding with the sovereignty transfer talks from the Dutch East Indies to Indonesia.

Under significant international pressure, the Netherlands finally handed over sovereignty of its colony in the Dutch East Indies to the Republic of Indonesia on 27 December, 1949. This historic event took place at the '*Paleis op de Dam*' (Palace on the Dam) in Amsterdam, witnessed by Queen Juliana of the Netherlands and Mohammad Hatta of Indonesia. A corresponding ceremony was held in Batavia, at the Governor-General's palace. The documents of transfer were penned in English, Dutch, and Indonesian, marking the official end of Dutch colonial rule in the region.

Additionally, a deed was signed to establish the Dutch-Indonesian Union, a partnership between the Kingdom of the Netherlands and the newly-formed United States of Indonesia, led by Queen Juliana. This union aimed to foster mutual interests between the two nations.

After four long, brutal years, Indonesia's fight for independence culminated in its recognition as a sovereign state. This momentous occasion signalled the start of decolonisation in Asia. The Netherlands retained control of New Guinea, leaving it as the last piece of the Dutch colonial empire in the region yet to be resolved.

Sukarno made his way to Batavia a day after the sovereignty transfer to set up his new residence in the palace. Even with the colonial era officially ending, the violence that erupted four years prior didn't cease immediately. After getting rid of the federal states, Sukarno declared Indonesia a unitary state with the 'Republik Indonesia' in 1949, introducing a temporary constitution. Indonesia was charting its own course now. But even into the 1950s, local gangs continued their assaults, particularly targeting Europeans and Chinese among others. For many, the Bersiap period and the War of Independence, stretching from 1945 to the end of 1949, was as devastating, if not more so, than the Japanese occupation, marked by extreme cruelty and hardship.

The Netherlands views the defeat by Japan and the violent end of its colonial rule in the Dutch East Indies as dark chapters in its history. The brutal Bersiap period has left a lasting mark on countless Indonesian and Dutch families, haunted by experiences of violation, attack, and deep emotional scars.

My mother's family was among those scarred by the violence of the Indonesian War. They carried the weight of their traumatic memories quietly, rarely speaking of what they endured. My father, having faced the horrors of Japanese aggression, bore his own psychological and emotional wounds. Like so many Indo-Europeans who lived through nearly a decade of conflict in the Dutch East Indies, my family's experiences made them lifelong victims of those turbulent times. Their silence on these matters often spoke louder than words could ever convey.

"

And once the storm is over,

You don't remember how you got through it,

How you managed to survive.

You're not even sure

If the storm is really over.

One thing is certain.

When you come out of the storm,

You will not be the same person

Who came in.

That's what the storm is about.

Courtesy of:
Author: Haruki Murakami
Book: *Kafka on the Shore*
Publisher: Penguin Random House LLC (US)

## Finally, no more weapons

After enduring more than five gruelling years amidst two wars, facing unimaginable hardships, suffering as a prisoner of war, labouring in men's camps, surviving being torpedoed, and witnessing the devastation of the atomic bomb attack, my father, Claude, was finally allowed to put down his weapons. On 2 February, 1948, he received his 'Leave' pass from the KNIL, marking the end of his rigorous service. From 2 August, 1941, to 2 February, 1948, Claude and his fellow KNIL soldiers had been on constant alert, day and night. It was a long, exhausting period filled with challenges and dangers. But at last, my father was honourably discharged from the KNIL service and reserve duty, closing a significant chapter of his life marked by duty and sacrifice.

# KONINKLIJK NEDERLANDS-INDISCH LEGER
# KONINKLIJKE LANDMACHT

### HOOFDKWARTIER VAN DE ADJUDANT GENERAAL IN NEDERLANDS-INDIË.

Nr.

04094.

Dienst : Aflossing en Demobilisatie

BATAVIA, de ....2-2-.... 1948 1)

### BESCHIKKING/VERLOFPAS.

I.  Wordt met ingang van ...... Subsistenten Kader   2 Februari 1948 afgevoerd uit de sterkte van het ........ Subsistenten Kader ...... 2)

te ...te Makassar de Mlt.sld. BELLONI C. Stbnr. 40222 ...... 3)

geboren ... 9 Juli 1922 te Batavia ...... 4)

laatstelijk ingedeeld bij ... Subsistenten Kader te Makassar ...... 5)

(schrijven van de Legercommandant dd. 21 April 1947 Nr. 6/AD. en van H.K.-A.G. dd. 10 November 1947, Nr. 575/AD. Spoed, alsmede van 25 Nov. '47, Nr. 650/AD. Spoed).

II.  Betrokkene wordt met ingang van ...... 2 Februari ...... 1948
groot-verlof verleend voor zolang hij ...... de Ministerie v.Voorlichtingen N.I.T. te Makassar. ...... werkzaam is. 6)

Zodra de werkzaamstelling komt te eindigen, heeft betrokkene zich ten spoedigste voor opkomst in werkelijke dienst te melden bij de Plaatselijk (Militair) Commandant.

Indien betrokkene naar een andere werkgever wenst over te gaan, dient aan de Adjudant Generaal om overschrijving van deze verlofpas te worden verzocht. Een zodanige overschrijving heeft alleen plaats met goedvinding van de oude werkgever.

*Het groot-verlof sluit niet in dat betrokkene Nederlands-Indië mag verlaten.*

" Vermoent betrokkene aanspraak te kunnen doen gelden op
" evacuatie Nederland volgens de daaromtrent voor niet-
" militairen getroffen regeling, dan heeft hij zich
" binnen twee maanden na de datum van demobilisatie ter
" registratie daarvan te wenden te Batavia tot het Kan-
" toor voor Reiswezen (Rijswijk 11) en overigens tot de
" burgerlijke evacuatie-kantoren el.q. de Hoofden van
" Plaatselijk Bestuur."

Leave pass , Claude Belloni, 2 February 1948

Local houses in Flores, 1948

## Back in Flores

Back in 1948, at the age of 26, Claude was still in Celebes but decided to move on to a new chapter in his life. He took a job in Makassar as an Information Officer/Public Relations Officer at the Ministry of Information, focusing on promoting the then-state of East Indies. In his role, he was tasked with being a liaison to the former President Sukawati of East Indies, accompanying him on various business trips throughout the state.

A work assignment brought Claude to Flores, a place that held a mix of memories for him. He thought of his good friend Rudy, with whom he had endured so much to survive, and of the many comrades who had succumbed to dysentery and were cremated there. Memories of hardship, Korean guards, and sleeping on the jungle floor flooded his mind. Yet, upon returning, Claude saw Flores from a completely different perspective — it was stunningly beautiful. He was especially captivated by the three-coloured crater lakes of the Kelimutu volcano, each a different colour: red, blue, and yellowish-green, with their hues changing daily. Local lore suggested these lakes were the spiritual resting places of ancestors. Claude hoped to one day return with his family — his wife, my sister Louise, and me — to share the beauty of these lakes, serving as our guide. Sadly, he passed away before he could fulfil this wish.

Claude sometimes reminisced about his time as a public relations officer, considering it one of the best jobs he ever had. Besides his official duties, he indulged his passion for writing and sports by working as a reporter for the '*Makassaarse Courant*' and serving as the sports editor for '*Sportief,*' a weekly magazine published in Batavia, showcasing his diverse talents and interests even after the war.

Anita Belloni, about 1960

# 3.3 An introduction to Anita and her family

## A little in love

So, how did Claude end up impressing a lady who was all about sports, especially after they got off on the wrong foot? Well, it all boiled down to Claude being a smooth talker, in his own quiet way.

*T*hey bumped into each other in Makassar, right on a tennis court, of all places. Both of them were big on tennis, really into the game. This time around, Claude found himself playing referee during a women's doubles match where Anita was playing. They kicked the match off in the late afternoon, with Claude chilling behind his shades.

Things got a bit heated in the second set. Anita decided not to hit a ball flying her way, convinced it was going out. Then the squabble kicked off – Anita was adamant the ball was out, but umpire Claude wasn't having it. Anita tried showing him exactly where the ball landed, totally sure it was out. She wasn't the type to keep her thoughts to herself, either. She pointed out to Claude that there was no way he could see the court lines properly with his sunglasses on, especially since the sun had already dipped down and wasn't blinding anyone anymore. Her partner kept trying to cool things down, but Anita kept at it, telling Claude he'd better get himself a new pair of glasses if he planned to keep umpiring from his lofty chair.

In the end, Claude didn't budge, and Anita had to suck it up and accept the call that didn't go her way. They even had a bit of a back-and-forth about it after the match. But, somehow, by the time the afternoon was wrapping up, they'd moved past their spat.

It was a bit of a rocky start for Claude and Anita, but that awkward tennis court showdown? It turned out to be the unlikely beginning of something special between them.

Turns out, Anita was pretty smitten with Claude's way of winning people over; he had a knack for charm, and they hit it off as friends. It wasn't long before they started seeing each other, always with a chaperone tagging along, just like the custom was back then. Sometimes it was Anita's older sister, other times a friend of her mum's. Back in those days, getting cozy, like kissing or even holding hands, was a big no-no. Maybe they'd sneak in a cheek peck when saying goodbye, but that was as daring as it got.

Despite the awkwardness early on, their tennis games kept on without a hitch. They teamed up for mixed doubles, learning all there is to know about each other's game — weaknesses, strengths, the whole nine yards. They had this way of balancing each other out on the court, which actually led them to snag a bunch of trophies together.

Eventually, their friendship evolved into something deeper, turning into a love story that was way smoother than their bumpy start. After a while, Claude went the traditional route and asked Anita's mum, Loes Kempff, if he could propose to her daughter. The proof that her mum gave the thumbs up is in a photo of them, surrounded by flowers, celebrating their engagement in Makassar on 12 June, 1948.

Engagement Anita Kempff & Claude Belloni, 12 June 1948

* An abbreviated family tree of the Kempff family is in the appendix.

## Dramatic times for Anita's family

Life in Surabaya for Anita's family, the Kempffs, was pretty straight-forward before the war hit. They ran a small dairy, nothing fancy, just enough to get by and keep the family of eleven afloat. Anita's dad, Piet, her mum, Loes, and their oldest kids pitched in. Mornings were early, filled with the sounds of clinking bottles and the smell of fresh milk. It was hard work, but they were a tight-knit crew, and they made it work.

Then, 1942 rolled around, and everything changed. The Japanese invaded Surabaya. Anita, only twelve at the time, saw her world turn upside down. Their house, once filled with the mundane noise of daily life, now echoed with the terrifying sounds of bombs and gunfire. One day, a bomb blew up so close that shrapnel flew right through their living room. Miraculously, no one got hurt, but the fear stayed with them.

The occupation forced the Kempffs into a situation they'd never imagined. They ended up in the Darmo camp, all crammed together, except for Piet, who was sent elsewhere. The first few months were bearable; they had enough to eat, and while the fear of what might happen next was always there, they managed to keep it together. Loes, Anita's mum, was a rock. Even when they pulled her in for questioning — who knows why — she kept her cool and protected her kids.

When they finally got out, they thought they could go back to their old life. But their home wasn't theirs anymore; the Japanese had taken it. They had to move, becoming "outer campers" in a city that no longer felt like their own. Loes had to figure out how to feed nine kids when food was scarce, relying on Red Cross vouchers and whatever else she could scrounge up.

Through all of this, Anita stayed quiet about her experiences, leaving it to her younger sister, Puck, to fill in the blanks years later. The family's resilience during those years was something else. Loes, especially, did whatever it took to keep her children safe and fed. And when Piet finally came back in 1943, it was like a small piece of their old life returned to them. They were together again, facing the challenges as a family, holding onto hope that they'd make it through the rest of the occupation.

After the Japanese occupation, just when the Kempff family thought they might catch a break, things took a turn for the worse. This next chapter in their lives, known as the Bersiap period, was a whole new level of nightmare. The air was thick with tension, and the streets of Surabaya echoed with the harsh call of "*Belanda* dogs" from the loudspeakers, a derogatory term aimed at the Dutch and Indo-Europeans people like the Kempffs. The message was clear: "You have to go to the camps where you will be better protected." But protection felt like a hollow promise, and the Kempff family decided to stay put, outside the camps, hoping to avoid becoming targets.

By late September 1945, their situation grew even more dire. Surabaya was a city on the brink, with pemuda fighters, young Indonesian nationalists, taking to the streets. These weren't just scuffles; they were full-blown battles, with the pemudas now armed with Japanese rifles and mortars. The Kempff's neighbourhood turned into a war zone overnight. The family's home, once a place of safety, was now in the line of fire, quite literally. Bullets and mortars didn't discriminate; the Kempffs found themselves dodging danger at every turn.

Food, which had been a challenge, became an even greater one. Sukarno's Belanda boycott cut them off from any source of sustenance. It didn't matter if friendly Indonesians wanted to help; accepting food was off-limits. The Kempffs were trapped in a vicious cycle of hunger and fear, with every day bringing a new struggle to stay alive and unharmed.

The nights were the hardest. The continuous sound of gunfire and the distant booms of mortars were a constant reminder that peace was far from reach. For the Kempff family, these moments weren't just about survival; they were about clinging to the hope that they'd see the end of this violence, that they'd once again find some semblance of the life they'd lost. Amidst the havoc, their bond as a family was both a lifeline and a source of relentless anxiety, knowing each day could be their last together.

## Tears in Surabaya

Surabaya in October 1945 was a powder keg about to blow. With the British trying to muscle in, the Japanese barely out the door, and the Dutch itching to get back in control, the city was tense. For the young Indonesians, it was now or never to push for independence. They grabbed whatever weapons they could from the Japanese and dug in, ready to fight for their city, their future.

The Kempffs were right in the middle of this mess. Piet, trying to keep his head down and his family safe, found himself in a nightmare scenario. His little girl got sick, the kind of sick where you know you've got to do something fast. So, Piet did what any dad would — hopped on his bike and pedalled like mad to the nearest pharmacy, hoping to get back with medicine in time to make a difference.

But the streets weren't just streets anymore. They were battlegrounds, with the pemudas, those young fighters, everywhere. Fired up and armed, they were stopping everyone, suspicious of any move they didn't understand. Piet ran into a group of these guys. He tried to explain, probably, but things were so heated, so fearful, that nobody was really listening anymore.

And just like that, Piet was gone. No dramatic exit, no goodbye, just a dad out to save his daughter and never seen again. Back at home, Loes and the kids waited, hoped, and then slowly, the hope turned to despair. They had to face the fact that Piet wouldn't be coming back. The family was shattered, Loes now the sole pillar holding up the remains of their world.

Surabaya wasn't kind to the Dutch-Indisch during those days. Between the Japanese taking what they wanted and the fight for independence turning everything upside down, the Kempffs, like so many others, ended up with nothing. No home that felt safe, no belongings to speak of, just the clothes on their backs and a bunch of empty stomachs to fill.

It was rough, real rough. But Loes, she was made of tough stuff. With Piet gone and the city in turmoil, she kept her family together, making do with what little they had, navigating through each day's new challenges.

It was about survival, about keeping her kids alive through it all, with the hope that someday, somehow, things would get better.

My aunt Puck shared more about the hardships. Her story brings us right into the heart of the family's struggle during a particularly harrowing time in 1946.

"It was now our family's turn to suffer again. In mid 1946 Opa Kempff was no longer with us by then. Our door was banged on. My elder sister Eleanora opened the door carefully. The noisemakers were three young pemudas who stood there threateningly in front of the door with their sharp bamboo runcings. Mother Loes fell to her knees and begged the rioters to leave her family alone. She asked them not to harm her family. There was quite some consternation. Eleanora was lying on the floor. She had fainted, probably from fear. The pemudas did not answer the pleas of mother Loes. We, the five oldest children, apart from Eleanora, had to go with the Indonesians. We were not allowed to grab any of our belongings. They took us away immediately. Before we knew it, we were separated from the rest of the family. Suddenly, we were in a truck that took us to the Wonokromo camp, where we experienced many moments of fear. There was heavy fighting in the area. Grenades hit our camp regularly. Each time this happened, the camp residents were startled. We slept on mats. Grenades were also regularly thrown at night. When the time came, the five of us and other camp mates would stand scared stiff beside our mats. More and more people came into the camp. At one time we only had about 35 cm to sleep on our mats. We only received a handful of rice with a few scraps of vegetables once a day. At some point, we all had to evacuate at night to the Wonokromo railway station, a distance of about two kilometres. When we arrived there, there was no train to be seen, so we had to walk back with bullets and grenades flying around us. The next day we were ordered to walk the same road again to see if a train was coming, but this time it was raining. We had no idea what the purpose of this evacuation was. In this camp, we learned everything a camp child should know. Defending oneself, being responsible, taking care of one's things, being on one's guard, going out for food, bargaining, taking care of the elderly, burying people.

The climate and the work meant that our clothes soon became rags, besides being too small. If tea towels were available we used them to clothe ourselves. Our sister Anita had guts and she was good at *'gedekken'*, bartering. She did this on a deck built of bamboo mats and barbed wire. Anita bartered with people outside the camp and with Nepalese Gurka's who had little money. She would secretly trade some things for some clothes for her siblings. Or she would trade something for food. All sorts of things passed over the 'counter'.

From this camp, we were temporarily transferred to Sidoardjo. I do not know why. From Sidoardjo we had to go to the Wonokromo station. From there we left by train for Wonoya. The windows of the train were boarded up. Once in Wonoya, we were interned in a rope factory for a few months. The food and hygiene here was pathetic. Medication was not available. It was bad here.

At the beginning of 1947, we were in the overcrowded Sumobito internment camp. The camp consisted of 14 servants' houses, each with 4 or 5 rooms. The zinc roofs made the houses as hot as ovens. Hygiene and food were also sorely lacking here. The quality of water was bad here and often there was no water at all. The older children, including Anita, your mother and her older sister, took care of the many old people in this camp. There was malaria and dysentery. Anita's body was covered with tropical sores, which could not be treated because of the lack of medication. The dead were buried in burlap bags. Often the children did not get permission to bury the dead so the dead bodies were buried too late, which made the whole area reek of decaying bodies. The internees, including Anita and her sister, dug graves for the deceased.

After almost a year, the five of us were taken on an overcrowded train again with boarded up windows via Solo to Batavia. I think it was the Tjideng camp, where we were crammed with others into a space of three by four square metres. We were not permitted to receive any letters nor to have contact with Oma, our sisters or brother. It was not permitted to receive any post from outside the camp and it was not allowed to send any post from the camp to the outside. Finally, we were handed over to the Red Cross.

Through secret channels, we found out that our mother and the rest of the family were now staying in Makassar. Oma's boarder had persuaded her to move to Makassar, where he had arranged accommodation for the family. The Red Cross had already signed us up to go to Surabaya. Fortunately, thanks to the support of the Red Cross and the help of our good family friend Ronald, we managed to change our destination and go to Makassar. Almost a month later, the five of us were reunited with mother Loes and our sisters and brother."

As young girls and boys, they had bravely endured the internment camps. Each member of the Kempff family had, in his or her own way, managed to endure the misery in what used to be a paradise before the Japanese occupation. The Bersiap period and the war of independence had changed all this.

Each family member carried his or her experiences within him or her. None of them revealed much about the past years of turmoil, fighting, uncertainty or fear. Nor did they express the hope of seeing their father again, hope that the violence would stop or the hope of seeing the rest of their family. These periods of intimidation, humiliation and pain were experienced by every Kempff family member and by many other families who were scarred for life.

Could the Javanese legend from a thirteenth century book have a grain of truth after all, which states, 'After years of foreign domination, a yellow-skinned people would come who would not rule for too long. And then the delightful liberation would arrive.'

## Fearful thoughts

Claude wrote in September 1947.

Along with many Dutch Indisch people, our dream had been shattered. Both materially and morally we had to start all over again. We tried to move on with our lives. Everyone had to deal with a certain amount of hardship in life. What terrible things can a person do to his fellow men? Our boundaries of resilience were continually shifted. Counting our blessings did not help. You began asking yourself, what are we doing in this rotten world? What is the meaning of life? We had physically survived these wars but spiritually we were broken. Again and again, those fears came and negative thoughts dominated our thinking. Fears got the upper hand more and more and miserable images of those experiences filled our minds. We could not escape the mental trauma. This trauma caused many people terrible mental anguish for the rest of their lives, which was very noticeable. It remained an ongoing struggle.

Enclosure "A"

<u>EX-PRISONERS OF WAR</u>

<u>MILITARY</u>

Nationality: DUTCH

Service : ARMY

| NAME (Last) (First) (Initial) | Rank or Rate | Serial Number | Physical Condition |
|---|---|---|---|
| 1. BAX, Antontheddorus | Soldier | 173517 | Good |
| 2. BECHTUGIAN, G. C. | Brigidier | 88915 | Good |
| 3. BELLGEW, Bernard, L. V. | Private | 12109 | Fair |
| 4. BELLONI, Claude | Private | 40222 | Good |
| 5. BOGHARDT, J. | Private | 106123 | Good |
| 6. BOMHOUVER, Z. F. | P.F.C. | 87400 | Good |
| 7. BOLLEMYER, Hendrik G. | Soldier | 13012 | Good |
| 8. BOS, Harm | Private | 41823 | Fair |
| 9. BOURGHE, Edward K. | Soldier | 127823 | Good |
| 10. BOUMEESTER, Frederik H. | Soldier | 94 | Fair |

Partial overview of former-KNIL-Prisoners Of War

"

You can hide your memories

But

You cannot erase the history that produced them

With thanks to:
Author: Haruki Murakami
Book: *Colorless*
Publisher: Penguin Random House LLC (US)

Wedding of Anita Kempff and Claude Belloni, 9 November 1948

# 3.4 Choices to make

After all the havoc of the past few years, Claude really hoped for a break, a chance to take things easy for once. But life had other plans, and he found himself at another crossroads, needing to make some tough calls.

*O*n 9 November, 1948, Claude and Anita Kempff tied the knot in Makassar. It was a family affair with Claude's parents, his sister Margot, mother Loes, Anita's brothers and sisters, and some of their friends celebrating the couple's big day. The tradition of showering the newlyweds with flowers was alive and well, and Anita and Claude were no exception.

But then came 27 December, 1949, when the Dutch handed over control to the Republic of Indonesia. This huge change meant that Dutch Indos like Claude, along with the families of Moluccan KNIL soldiers (since the Moluccas were now part of Indonesia), had to decide where their loyalty lay.

The Dutch were leaning on the Indo community pretty hard, pushing them to choose Indonesian citizenship, to become '*Warga Negara Indonesia*' (W.N.I.). They hoped most Dutch Indos would stay. If you picked Indonesian citizenship, you could stay put. But if you wanted to keep your Dutch nationality, you had to pack up and leave. Suddenly, there wasn't really a place for Dutch Indos in Indonesia anymore. At first, a lot of them wanted to stay — it was their home, after all. But when the Republic of Indonesia didn't keep some key promises from the 'Round Table' agreement that were supposed to protect the Dutch Indos, staying became a lot less appealing.

The brutal memories of the Japanese occupation from 1942 to 1945, the violent Bersiap period right after the war, and then the fight for independence from 1945 to 1950 were more than enough reason for many to want out. The fear of another Bersiap, of being targeted and mistreated again, was real. Dutch Indos were getting harassed in the streets, spat on, and booed. Public schools shut them out, and speaking Dutch was off-limits. To put it simply, Dutch Indos felt like outsiders in their own country, and for many, leaving Indonesia seemed like the only option left.

For the Indisch community, it was time to make a big decision, one that felt like breaking up with a long-time love — the Dutch East Indies. All the dreams they had for a better life there were shattered. The Dutch Indos who wanted to hold onto their Dutch citizenship had a hard deadline: leave Indonesia within two years.

The message from the newly independent Indonesia was clear: "Go back to where you come from." The rules for leaving were strict. You could only bring one suitcase. Some managed to pack a trunk with a few clothes and some small personal items, but that was it. Everything else had to be left behind. To get out, the Dutch government required proof of Dutch nationality. Just having served in the armed forces wasn't enough proof, but most Indo-Europeans managed to confirm their Dutch roots.

This uprooting turned their lives upside down. Countless Dutch Indos and Moluccans had to say goodbye to the land that felt like their motherland and start over. It was a heart-wrenching move. Even though many had never even been to Holland, knowing it only from geography classes or stories, they set their sights on it. By 1950, every passenger ship out of Batavia, freighters included, was packed.

Back in Holland, the number of migrants coming in overwhelmed the government, specifically the Drees Cabinet. It turned out there were way more people arriving to stay than they'd anticipated. Settling in the Netherlands was tough for the Dutch Indos. Even getting loans for boat tickets was a struggle. And when they finally arrived, the welcome was anything but warm. The stories I've heard from several Dutch Indo families all echo the same sentiment: The reception in the Netherlands was cold, with little sympathy or understanding for what the Dutch Indos had been through.

The Dutch had a way of seeing things that didn't always make sense to everyone. They believed that a lot of Dutch soldiers ended up fighting in the East Indies mainly because of the Dutch Indos, who were caught in the middle of conflicts with rebellious Indonesian youths. Back in Indonesia, the Dutch Indos faced discrimination, and when they arrived in Holland, they found they didn't quite fit in there either. Most Dutch citizens didn't know much about their own colony, the Dutch East Indies. Some were even surprised to hear the Dutch Indos speaking Dutch so well, albeit with an Indisch accent.

When the Dutch Indos finally made it to what was supposed to be their homeland, they had pretty much nothing — no money, no belongings. They were placed in temporary housing spread all across the Netherlands. The Moluccans, who were part of this group, got an especially rough deal. They were isolated and put into camps or barracks with no heating and only cold water, many around Hoogeveen in Drenthe, in the north. At first, there wasn't even a whisper about giving Dutch citizenship to the Moluccan community. That only came much later.

The Dutch people didn't really see the Dutch Indos as their equals. They weren't interested in their stories or their history. The Dutch Indos were often judged by their accents and the colour of their skin. Meanwhile, the Dutch were dealing with their own post-war struggles — the aftermath of World War II, the damage and hunger they'd faced. Some even said their own "Winter of Hunger" was tougher than anything the Dutch Indos might have experienced back in the Indies. Plus, the Netherlands was in the middle of rebuilding itself, with industries wrecked, homes destroyed, and jobs scarce. To many, the Dutch Indos seemed like uppity colonials who would've been better off staying away. There was hardly any recognition of the hardships the Indisch people had gone through.

To add insult to injury, the Dutch government didn't even acknowledge the Dutch Indos as war victims. It was as if they'd forgotten that these same people had contributed significantly to the Dutch economy, with revenues from the Dutch East Indies playing a major role in the country's wealth, even helping to build Dutch railways. The contributions and sacrifices of the Indisch people were largely overlooked.

There were some harsh words spoken in the Dutch parliament, with some saying the Dutch Indos got what was coming to them for supposedly exploiting the local Indonesians back in the Dutch East Indies.

By spring 1950, the Dutch government was scrambling to find housing for families arriving from the now-former colony. They asked owners of empty hotels and boarding houses to help out, setting up a contract accommodation plan. But this effort by the Drees government just wasn't enough. They ended up using barracks and camps to deal with the housing shortage for the Indisch people. Those who got jobs had to fork over part of their wages for their stay, and those without work saw their lodgings as a debt that needed to be paid back once they found employment. On top of that, any pensions or savings over three thousand guilders got taxed. The government also made everyone buy second-hand warm clothes and furniture, adding to the financial strain and making the whole situation feel even more degrading.

Given all this, it's no wonder some Indo-Europeans decided to leave Indonesia or Holland altogether, aiming for the U.S. to chase the American Dream, or heading to Canada, Australia, Brazil, the Netherlands Antilles, and elsewhere. This was the start of a widespread Dutch Indo diaspora.

New Guinea was left as the last Dutch hold in Southeast Asia and was considered a new potential home or stopping point for Dutch ships. International deals from the Round Table Conference in 1949 meant the KNIL officially disbanded on July 1, 1950. That same day, the *'Van Heutsz'* Regiment was established back in the Netherlands, keeping the KNIL spirit alive. Some KNIL folks were let go or joined the Indonesian army, while others, including Moluccans and retirees, were sent to the Netherlands. For those KNIL soldiers left in Indonesia, it was a tough pill to swallow. The army had been their life, and instead of being demobilised in some honourable way, they felt like they were just cast aside.

On 25 July, 1950, Claude got some well-deserved recognition from the KNIL for his commitment and honourable service to his country during the war from 1940 to 1945. He was also honoured for his role in restoring order and peace after Japan surrendered. As a nod to his efforts, he was given the right to wear the KNIL insignia. On top of that, the Minister of Overseas Territories awarded him the Badge of Honour for Order and Peace with clasps for the years 1945 through 1948.

There's this book, *The Japanese Experience in Indonesia: Selected Memoirs of 1942-1945*, penned by Imamura Hitoshi among others, with Anthony Reid and Oki Akira providing the introduction. Imamura, who played a significant role during WWII, didn't face the death penalty at the war tribunals. Instead, he was sentenced to a decade behind bars for the war crimes his forces committed. Imamura had a pretty extensive career, both in diplomacy and the military, with postings in Germany, Britain, Italy, China, and the British East Indies. He climbed the ranks to become the top dog, the commander of the Sixteenth Japanese Army, tasked with taking over the Dutch East Indies. By 1943, Imamura Hitoshi

DE MINISTER VAN OVERZEESE GEBIEDSDELEN

Gelet op het Koninklijk besluit van 2 December 1947 Nr. 4 (Nederlandse Staatscourant 12 Januari 1948 Nr. 7);

kent toe het

ERETEKEN VOOR ORDE EN VREDE

MET GESPEN "1945-1946-1947 en 1948"

aan

C. BELLONI

's-Gravenhage, de 24e December 1949

De Minister voornoemd,

Decoration for Order and Peace with Clasps '1945-1946-1947 and 1948'

Medals Claude, 1948

was promoted to general, cementing his place in military history.

Since August 17, 1945, Indonesia has marked its Independence Day, being the first nation to declare its freedom post-World War II. As the 1950s rolled in, a lot of people in the Dutch East Indies who had chosen Indonesian citizenship started second-guessing their decision. Life got tough for them. The relationship between the Netherlands and Indonesia went south, especially after Indonesia decided to call it quits on the Dutch-Indonesian Union in 1956. They were fed up, partly because of the Dutch still hanging around in Indonesia and the ongoing tussle over New Guinea, which the Dutch weren't ready to let go of.

Come 5 December, 1957, President Sukarno made a bold move by nationalising Dutch companies in Indonesia. The folks running those companies had no choice but to hand them over to the Indonesian army. This wasn't just about businesses; Dutch banks and agricultural ventures got taken over too. The Dutch still in Indonesia were suddenly seen as a threat to national security. Dutch education got the axe, they were banned from taxis, and a lot of them found their phone lines cut.

This situation forced many Indo-Europeans to leave Indonesia for good, further straining the ties between the Netherlands and Indonesia. For those who had picked Indonesian citizenship back in 1949, it meant having to leave their homeland behind. The political mess, the economic instability — none of it made staying in Indonesia an appealing option anymore. So, they headed to the Netherlands, where they eventually got their Dutch citizenship back. But settling down and finding peace wasn't easy. The anti-Dutch sentiment in Indonesia, dubbed '*Zwarte Sinterklaas*' or 'Black Saint Nicholas,' left a dark stain on the festive season and even led to the banning of the Saint Nicholas children's party in Indonesia.

So, what about Claude and Anita, who were still in Makassar in 1950? What was next for them? What choices did they face, and what decisions would they make for their future?

Map of Dutch New Guinea. With thanks © heirs Mr. W.A.L. van Doorenmaalen

One of Hollandia's beautiful vistas

# Part IV
# A new future of freedom
# 4. Pioneering in New Guinea

## With a microphone in the inland

Manokwari, along the *Geelvinkbaai*, Yellow parrot bay

# THE FORGOTTEN EARTH

## 4.1 TERRA INCOGNITA

After everything Claude had been through, especially as a prisoner of war, staying in the tropics but having to leave his homeland, his only option was Dutch New Guinea. It was considered the most remote part of the world back then.

*T*his is what Boy said about it.

> Your mum and I didn't think it was an option to live in the Republic of Indonesia. As we both preferred to stay in the tropics, we chose New Guinea together, despite the fact that we knew we would face a tough and primitive time, as there was so little on the island. It became our new home in the unspoilt paradise of the bush. Together we stood strong, both not averse to roll up our sleeves. We thought we would make it, just the two of us. You see, despite everything, we managed to build a future of freedom.

So, in 1950, Boy and Anita, decided to start fresh in New Guinea, still under Dutch rule at the time. This move meant leaving their life in Makassar behind, saying goodbye to many possessions, and heading off to what was pretty much unknown territory with just a few suitcases. They had to leave their cherished East Indies behind for good.

By 27 December, 1951, every Dutch citizen in Indonesia had to make a tough call: stick with Dutch nationality or switch to Indonesian (*warga negara*). This put a lot of people, especially the Indo-Europeans who had grown up in this country, in a tight spot. The decision was more than just about which passport to hold; it was about choosing where to live — stay in Indonesia, head to the Netherlands, or move somewhere else entirely.

Beach at Nangari, Biak, Noemfoor district

Back in 1950, not much was known about Dutch New Guinea. The land in the western part was mostly infertile, crisscrossed with wild, impassable rivers in the north and covered in dense jungle in the interior. The whole western area was tough to get through.

New Guinea, a tropical island twelve times the size of the Netherlands and located north of Australia in the Pacific Ocean, is a place of stunning natural beauty. It's part of the Melanesian archipelago and falls under the continent of Oceania. The island is split between Dutch New Guinea and Papua New Guinea (PNG). New Guinea's landscape is unlike anywhere else, with one of the largest rainforests in the world. Above the snow line are high peaks and alpine meadows, while the lower areas feature dense tropical jungles and savannahs dotted with eucalyptus trees. Closer to the coast, there are mangrove swamps and sago palms in the peat bogs, all surrounded by beautiful coral reefs.

In the lowlands of Dutch New Guinea, cities like Hollandia (now Jayapura) in the north, Manokwari in the northeast of the Bird's Head Peninsula, Sorong in the west of the Bird's Head, and Merauke in the south, are pretty warm. The average temperature hovers around 30 degrees Celsius, but at least there's some relief from natural sea breezes.

Hollandia, in particular, has a pretty sweet spot, nestled at the foothills of the Cyclops Mountains which give it some shelter, and with Humboldt Bay protecting it from the rough Pacific waves. Plus, the bay is deep enough to be a good port for big ships.


## Nueva Guinea

The name "Nueva Guinea" came about when Portuguese explorer De Menenez noticed the coastline looked a lot like Guinea in Africa. It wasn't until 1606, when a Dutch ship called *'Het Duyfke'* (The Dove) cruised along the southern coast, that the Dutch found out about the island. And it took until 1616 for Dutch explorers Schouten and Lemaire to map the northern coast, even naming an island there after Schouten.

The Dutch East India Company (VOC) wasn't too keen on the island at first, especially since Spain had control over it. But after a few fights, the Dutch took over. They didn't do much with it, though, just built a couple of forts. Dutch influence slowly started to spread, first through trade and then through Christian missions.

The island also became a place for exiling political troublemakers. Between 1928 and 1942, two camps were set up along the Upper Digul River, deep in the jungle and surrounded by not-so-friendly Papuan tribes. This was where persons labeled as communists or nationalists, basically anyone seen as a threat to the status quo, were sent. It was meant to be a re-education spot, to cut them off from any outside influences. Notably, Mohammed Hatta, who'd later become Indonesia's vice president, and Sutan Sjahrir, the first prime minister of Indonesia, were held here. Until World War II kicked off, West New Guinea was pretty much off the radar economically and largely unexplored.

## Japanese and the Allied forces

Throughout World War II, the Japanese forces didn't manage to take complete control over New Guinea. Specifically, Merauke — a town in the southeast of the western part of New Guinea, surrounded by the ocean on one side and swamps and jungle on the other — remained out of Japanese hands.

However, Hollandia, located on Humboldt Bay, became a significant place during the war. By April 1942, it had fallen under Japanese occupation, and all Europeans in the area were captured and taken to Ambon to be interned. The Japanese set up two infantry regiments, a marine regiment in Hollandia and built three airfields near Lake Sentani. The town turned into a crucial support and supply hub for the Japanese, storing large quantities of food, clothing, and medicine.

By early 1944, there were indications that Japan intended to relocate its troops from East New Guinea to Hollandia. In response, the Americans established a military base on Biak, a coral island with white sandy beaches and palm trees to the north, and near Hollandia on Mount Ifar, where they quickly set up the headquarters for their Pacific operations. Under General Douglas MacArthur's command, the Americans carried out a surprise operation code-named 'Reckless' in April 1944, targeting Hollandia. The Japanese were caught off guard by the landing and fled into the jungle en masse.

Hollandia, with its strategic Humboldt Bay, was chosen as a key location for coordinating actions against the Japanese in the Pacific. Yet, the town lacked any real infrastructure. MacArthur ordered the rapid construction of an airfield, a harbour, roads, and several buildings. This feat was remarkable, given the challenging jungle terrain the American forces had to navigate. Ultimately, Hollandia was developed to accommodate over 100,000 American soldiers, serving as a pivotal base in the Pacific theatre.

## New Guinea in those days

Back then, the Dutch government saw the western part of New Guinea as a blank slate, a place with hardly anything, where both the land and its people were seen as projects to be developed from scratch. After the Dutch East Indies was handed over to Indonesia in December 1949, the Dutch doubled down on their presence in New Guinea, aiming to boost their international status. They were caught in a tough situation, though. On one side, they saw themselves as bringing progress and freedom to New Guinea and its Papuan inhabitants. But at the same time, they also wanted to use the island to beef up their influence in Southeast Asia.

Comparing New Guinea to the Dutch East Indies was like night and day. The Dutch East Indies was a well-established colony, while New Guinea was virtually untouched, a forgotten chunk of land across the murky Arafura Sea, its coasts lined with mangroves.

Just past the mangroves were endless swamps, home to head-hunting Papuan tribes who'd been living there for millennia, almost like they'd stepped right out of the stone age. These tribes were isolated, reachable only by navigating the often impossible maze of rivers and streams.

Not many outsiders braved this harsh, unyielding environment. The soggy ground and water could easily swallow you whole, and the damp climate was a nightmare for anyone's health. The area was teeming with a dizzying variety of insects, snakes, and crocodiles, thriving among the dense forests and towering mountain ranges that made human life all but impossible. Despite these challenges, New Guinea remained a stunningly pristine island, untouched and full of natural beauty.

In the early 1950s, the Dutch saw themselves as New Guinea's long-term guardians, but by the mid-1950s, they started pushing for the territory's self-determination. Dutch officials ventured into the interior to establish a solid Dutch presence, symbolising Dutch authority. Often, "administration" meant calming down tribes that were at odds with each other. These young civil servants had to be clever and adaptable, especially in applying the law in situations unfamiliar back home, like cannibalism. They leaned on 'adat', or local customs, to form the legal basis, recognising that Dutch laws couldn't cover everything.

Aside from setting up a legal system, the Dutch also kick-started medical care and education. Missionaries, who were the first Westerners to take an interest in New Guinea's inhabitants, laid the groundwork for these efforts. Dutch became the language of instruction in schools, with both primary and secondary education being established.

## Papua New Guinea

On the other side, Papua New Guinea (PNG), the eastern part of the island, is a land of mountain ranges, tropical rainforests, and coastal plains. The Papuans, mainly living in the highlands, rely on agriculture. With a mostly tropical rainforest climate, the country also experiences earthquakes and tsunamis due to its location along a tectonic fault line. Interestingly, PNG is one of the equatorial countries where it snows regularly on mountain peaks like Mount Wilhelm. The region is rich in minerals, oil, and gas.

Culturally, Papua New Guinea is incredibly diverse, home to around a thousand different ethnic groups, each with its unique traditions and costumes. Music is a big part of their culture, with George Telek and O-Shen being notable musicians from the area. Sports play a significant role too, with many Papua New Guineans excelling in Australian football and rugby, playing in leagues abroad.

Since 1884, Papua New Guinea (PNG) was split into two main parts: the Northern area, which was a German colony known as German New Guinea or Kaiser-Wilhelmsland (named after Kaiser Wilhelm II, the last German Emperor), and the Southern part, which became a part of Australia in 1904. German businesses had their eyes on the Pacific Ocean's western part, setting up strategic points across various islands. In 1882, the German New Guinea Company was created to, among other goals, acquire colonial territories in this region, conduct research, and manage plantations.

The company brought in many Chinese workers for its operations in German New Guinea. These workers were employed in various capacities, including working on coconut and tobacco plantations, shipbuilding, running shops, and other jobs. After World War II, many of these Chinese workers moved to Western New Guinea, other parts of Asia, and Australia.

From 1884 to 1899, Germany annexed several islands and island groups to the north and east of German New Guinea. By 1899, it became clear that the colony wasn't very profitable or safe for private companies, so control was handed over to the German Empire. Signs of German influence remain in places like Finschhafen (named after Otto Finsch), as well as the Bismarck Sea, Bismarck Archipelago, and Bismarck Mountains, all named after Otto von Bismarck.

When World War I broke out in August 1914, the Japanese Imperial Navy took over the northern parts, including the Carolinas, German Mariana Islands, and Marshall Islands, while Australia took control of the rest of German New Guinea. Following the Treaty of Versailles in 1919, Japan and Australia, under the League of Nations mandates, officially took over the territories they had occupied. Australia was given a League of Nations mandate in 1920 to govern German New Guinea.

## Kokoda trail

In 1942, during the thick of World War II, the Japanese set up their headquarters for the eastern part of New Guinea in Buna, shifting away from Darwin in Australia's Northern Territory. The Allies, on the other hand, stationed their command centre down south in Port Moresby, PNG's capital. Buna and Port Moresby were divided by a rugged mountain range, with the Kokoda Trail serving as the only path through the mountains connecting the two.

Japanese forces made their way through the dense jungle towards Port Moresby, managing to get dangerously close to the city. However, their advance was halted in the mountains by Australian troops at the Kokoda Trail. Here, the Australians mounted a successful defence of Port Moresby, partly thanks to a massive effort that included carving out a staircase of about 4,000 steps from the rock, creating the only viable passage from the north to the south of the eastern part of the island.

The Kokoda Trail is known as one of the most challenging and gruelling paths a soldier could face. The battle to fend off the Japanese invasion along this trail was a pivotal moment for Australia in World War II. The Australians managed to hold the Japanese back at Kokoda and eventually drove them back to the northern beaches of Sanananda by 1943, marking a significant victory.

To this day, many Australians participate in an organised trek known as 'The Kokoda Track' every year, a pilgrimage that allows them to experience and learn about the hardships and heroics of this critical battle. Much of the trail remains as it was in 1942, offering a vivid glimpse into what Australian soldiers endured.

The Japanese had anticipated an American assault on the coastal town of Wewak, leading them to station part of their forces there. Early in 1944, Japan aimed to relocate its troops from East New Guinea to Hollandia, but American forces successfully thwarted this manoeuvre.

Since 1975, PNG has been an independent country, officially recognised as the Independent State of Papua New Guinea, with Port Moresby serving as its capital.

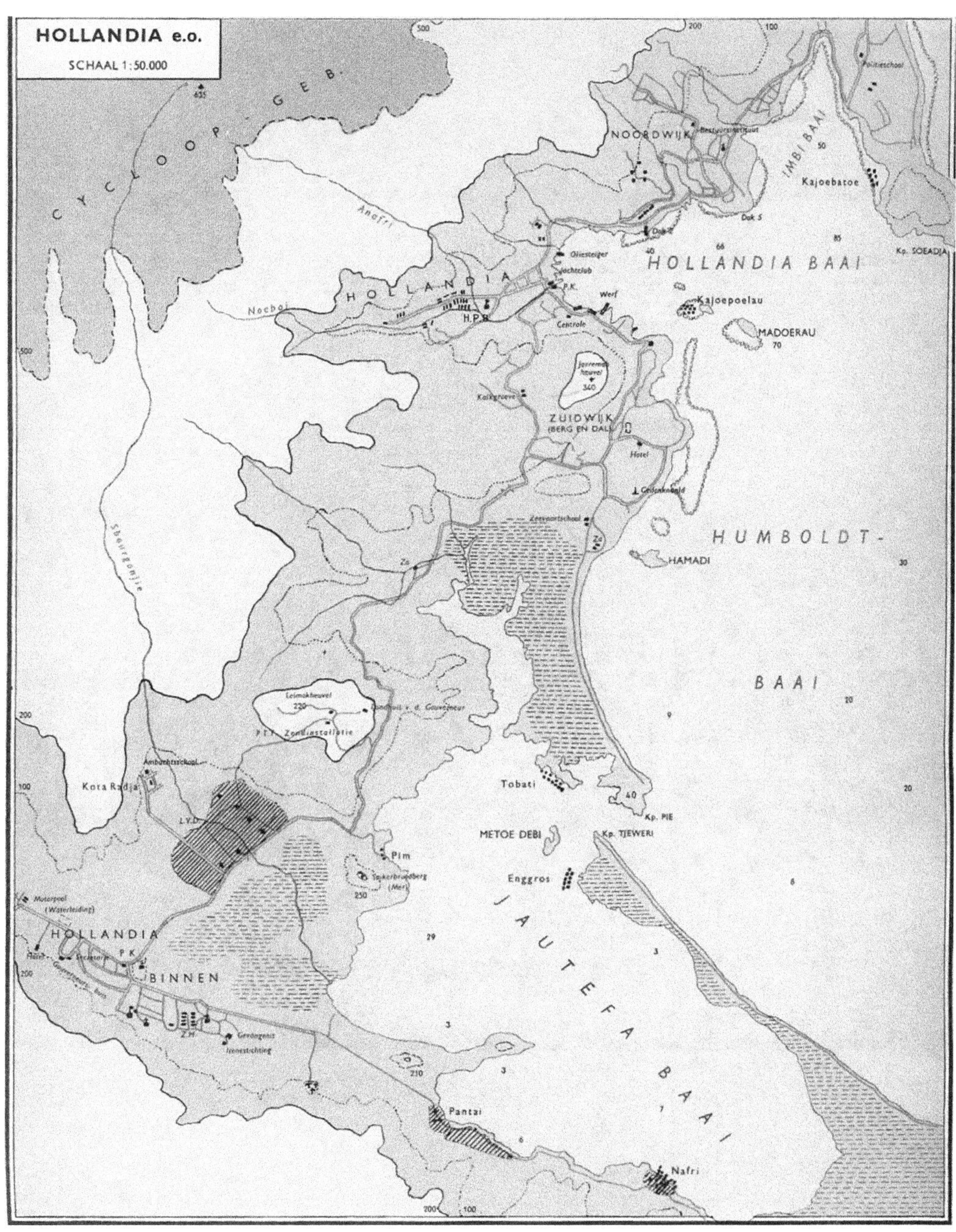


Environment map of Hollandia. School atlas of New Guinea, drs. H. Eggink, W. Versluys NV, Amsterdam, 1956

Aerial photograph, Hollandia

# 4.2 Hollandia and surroundings

Hollandia, the old capital, was where the Belloni family decided to give life another shot. After all the turmoil they'd been through, the real question was, could they get used to living somewhere so untouched and simple?

*B*ack in April 1942, things took a turn when Japan took over Hollandia. It was just a small place, but suddenly all the Dutch people living there had to pack up and leave for Ambon in the Moluccas. The Japanese had big plans for Hollandia, wanting to turn it into a storage spot for all the important stuff like medicine, food, and clothes. But by 1944, everything changed again. The Allies hit hard, lots of Japanese soldiers didn't make it, and the ones who did ended up running for the hills, leaving everything behind in a mess. After that, the Americans stepped in. They started fixing up the place, setting up bases in the damaged ports of Finschhafen and Hollandia, calling them Base F and Base G. They even built eight docks in Humboldt Bay, getting ready for more action against Japan.

### 'A beginning of the beginning in Hollandia'

Nico van Vliet, a colleague of Boy, wrote an article in the magazine *'Kroniek'*, Chronicle, in 1955 about what preceded at Hollandia's fiftieth anniversary.

On 28 September, 1909, when a Dutch steamship, the *'Van den Bosch,'* made its way into Humboldt Bay, right near the Numbay River. They were there to set up shop for future exploring. So, they sent a small boat with four guys to find the perfect place. They ended up picking a location on the beach by the Numbay River, where the sago palms grew and the land was hugged by gorges. They called their new camp *Kloof,* which means Gorge Camp.

By 7 March, 1910, they were raising the Dutch flag in Hollandia, officially starting a new settlement and a spot to run things from. This move was kind of an answer to a place the Germans had set up in what's now part of Papua New Guinea. They unloaded all their supplies and building stuff, and after three days, the *'Van den Bosch'* took off, leaving behind a group that included four officers, eighty soldiers and their families, and a bunch of porters and workers. Their big job was to figure out the border between the German and Dutch territories in New Guinea. For Captain Sachse and his team, that meant a lot of walking around in places no white man had ever been.

And right away, things got tough. The swampy ground was full of mosquitoes, any path they cleared in the jungle would just grow right back, and diseases like malaria and beriberi hit them hard and fast. One of their trips along the *Keerom* River, Turnaround River, turned deadly when they ran out of rice after losing a bunch of their supplies.

Not long after they set up camp, a biologist came to join the crew but quickly ran into trouble. He got hit with a nasty bout of Malaria Tropica, caught Indisch Thrush, ended up with a liver abscess, and even forgot who he was for a while, which meant he had to be rushed out of there fast. Despite all the hurdles and the endless jungle that seemed to close in on their little spot of civilisation, the people kept their spirits up. When they weren't busy, they found ways to make their corner of the world feel more like home, even putting together a swimming pool in the river and making their own furniture out of whatever wood they could find. By February, feeling like they finally had some roots down, they decided it was time their settlement had a proper name. So, on 7 March, 1910, they stood up and said, "In the name of the Queen," and just like that, Hollandia was born, with high hopes that its flag would keep on flying.

As time went on, Hollandia started to pull in more people. Chinese merchants showed up, looking to do business, and gold prospectors came through, dreaming of striking it rich. They even sent out big expeditions to take a closer look at all the plants and animals nobody had messed with yet. Before long, both Japanese and American folks found reasons to come by. The American military did some impressive stuff there, even though they were pretty much making do with what they had — dealing with lousy mail service, eating out of cans, and trying to keep cool and sane in the brutal heat and isolation.

Someone once described the place like this: "One terrible island after another, the mouldy smell of the jungle, the rain, scorpions, malaria, mosquitoes, and lice are always on your back."

The Humboldt Bay operation was part of something bigger called 'Operation Reckless'. It was right in those same waters where Captain Sachse had dropped off Dutch soldiers back in the day that the American Sixth Army showed up. Their job was to free people like Vic de Bruyn, also known as the Jungle Pimpernel, acting governor Jan van Eechoud, sergeant Mauritz Kokkelink (KNIL), captain J. Willemsz Geeroms (KNIL), and a few others. These guys were part of a guerrilla group hiding out in the jungles of the *Vogelkop* (Bird's Head Peninsula), giving the Japanese a hard time. Even though those days are way behind us, you can still see the traces of the Americans' stay — houses made from poles and rusty zinc sitting on concrete floors, a whole world away from what the Dutch were used to.

Nico van Vliet


## As it was in the early fifties


Boy and Anita were under no illusions — picking up their lives and moving to Hollandia was going to be tough. But they were up for it. Back before they left the Dutch East Indies, Boy had gotten a job from Governor S.L.J. van Waardenburg: set up a radio station in Hollandia. It sounded like a lot of work, sure, but it was also a chance to really make a difference in this new place.

On 16 September, 1950, Boy headed out to Hollandia by himself, leaving Anita back in Makassar. It was a heavy goodbye, knowing they were leaving their old life behind for good. Anita was six months pregnant, working at a perfume shop, and had to wait a bit longer to follow Boy. She was going to come over once Boy had found them a place to stay. When Boy finally sent a telegram saying she should come, flying over by herself wasn't really an option because of the baby on the way. Luckily, they managed to get permission for her fifteen-year-old sister, Puck, to go with her. It was a big relief for Anita, and for Puck, it was a chance to get away from the growing troubles back in the East Indies, where there was a real risk of young folks being taken by the radical pemudas.

Landing in Hollandia with hardly anything to their name, Boy and Anita were starting from scratch with barely anything to go on. They were the embodiment of that adventurous spirit the Dutch government kept talking about, saying it was exactly what New Guinea needed. Their new life was kicking off with Boy heading out on tough trips to the southern parts of New Guinea, laying the groundwork for their future in what was still pretty much a wild frontier town, standing right on the edge of enormous changes.

When the Dutch East Indies stopped sending supplies to New Guinea after sovereignty was transferred, things got tough. Everything needed had to come all the way from the Netherlands, over 14,000 kilometres away. The situation got so bad that the area almost hit famine levels. The bit of food locals and Chinese merchants had wasn't nearly enough for everyone. It got to the point where leftover American military canned food was what kept many people going.

Luckily, the Americans didn't just leave canned food behind; they also built some pretty useful stuff like paved roads and bridges around Hollandia. These roads linked important places like Kota Baru, Sentani, Ifar, and Tanah Merah, making it a bit easier to get food and whatever else was needed around. Growth was slow, really relying on the few resources they had, along with a lot of hard work, hope, and excitement from everyone. It really was just the start of something new.

When Boy was looking for a place for his family to stay, he found a place in Sentani, not far from the airstrip, in an old American quonset hut. These were simple, semi-circle shaped huts made of metal, originally for storing US Navy gear. But the new Belloni home wasn't empty; it came with mice and rats that had made themselves comfy in the walls and were always swiping stuff, even socks.

Anita, who was pregnant and not exactly thrilled about the rodents, had Boy on constant rat-catching duty. She'd sit on a chair, watching him go at it, half-joking that their kid might end up looking like one of those critters. Despite her worry, they managed to keep things light. She even had a special nickname for Boy, "*jong*," an endearment of *jongen*, boy.

Living in Sentani, Anita started keeping chickens in the yard and growing veggies, trading with neighbours. It was their way of making do, creating a sense of community, and starting anew. They were building a life from scratch, filled with simple joys and the teamwork needed to tackle the challenges of their new home.

## Boy and his energy

Boy got his spark from so many things around him. His job, his family, his friends, the local Papuans, and just the outright stunning nature of Hollandia – it all fuelled him. There was something about the place that could make you stop and stare, even on a bad day or when you were up against it. Like this one time, he was driving, right? Out of nowhere, this massive rainstorm hits, and this little creek he needed to cross suddenly looked more like a raging river. He was stuck, no phone, no way to call out, just him and the storm for what felt like forever.

At work, Boy did a bit of everything at the Radio Broadcasting Company New Guinea. He wasn't just spinning records or reading the news; he was putting together shows, out there getting stories, really making things happen. But the best part? It was the people he met, especially the Papuans. Their stories, their lives, it got to him. He wasn't just about telling their stories; he wanted to do right by them, help out any way he could.

Then there were the dinners at Boy's place. He and Anita loved having people over, especially reporters from all corners of the globe. And Anita, she was something else in the kitchen. She could whip up a feast out of nothing, making every meal an event. Their guests couldn't get enough, always sending notes afterward about how amazing everything was, all thanks to Anita.

But when it all comes down to it, it was Boy's family that kept him ticking. His love for them, his dedication – that's what his life was really about. They were his rock, the ones he leaned on when things got tough, the ones who made all the crazy, beautiful, and hard stuff worth it.

When Indonesia became its own country in 1949, the Dutch realised they had a new role: to help New Guinea develop. They came up with the Department of Economic and Technical Affairs, or D.E.T.A., just for this. It was their way of giving young guys from the Dutch Indies a shot at doing something meaningful. These "DETA-boys" were fresh out of school, coming from all sorts of backgrounds — military, business, government. They'd seen some things, having lived through the Japanese occupation and the wild, dangerous times of the Bersiap period back home. Sticking with their Dutch roots, they left the new Republic of Indonesia behind, hoping DETA would be their chance at a new beginning, maybe get back a bit of what they'd lost.

To get into DETA, you were supposed to be 18, fit, and Dutch. But rules were flexible; sometimes kids as young as 15 or 16 got in. The mission was about more than just putting up buildings in Hollandia. It was about giving these guys a purpose, letting them be part of building something from the ground up.

Signing up meant you got a ticket from the Indies to New Guinea and a few essentials to get you started: a camp bed, a blanket, a mosquito net, and a basic set of dishes. That was about it. They knew life wouldn't be easy, but they were ready for the challenge.

Claude enjoying the vista in Hollandia

The pay was nothing to write home about — just 1.50 guilders a day. But they had a place to stay, food to eat, and some kind of medical attention, even if "attention" is putting it generously. Conditions were tough: the food was basic, and medical help was pretty much just malaria pills and band-aids. A good chunk of their pay went towards trying to find something decent to eat.

They lived in Kloof Camp, crammed into military-style barracks made of corrugated iron and set up on stilts by the river. These barracks were like half-circles, just big enough to fit their beds with hardly any space left over. It was cramped, not exactly comfortable, but it made them a tight-knit bunch.

This group was like a mini-version of the Dutch Indies, with all kinds of faces, skin tones, hair, and eyes. They were a mix of everything, a true reflection of the diverse world they'd left behind. Together, they faced the tough times, sticking it out with hope in their hearts, playing their part in shaping New Guinea's future.

Listening in on their conversations, you'd catch a unique blend of Dutch Indisch, Malay, and *petjoh* — a colourful mix of Dutch, Malay, and Javanese.

It wasn't an easy life; they pretty much got the same treatment as contract labourers, roughing it out in huts that were barely holding up. But it wasn't long before their spirit and resilience shone through. Unwilling to settle for less, they started building their own homes using whatever they could find around them. There was this hope, you see, a bright spark in their eyes about one day reuniting with their families. That hope, along with a youthful eagerness to learn and grow, kept them pushing forward, even when picking up new skills felt like climbing a mountain.

For kicks, they'd take a dip in the makeshift 'swimming pool' behind Kloof camp — a spot they had crafted by damming the Numbay River. If the mood struck, they'd go wild boar hunting or fishing. Saturdays were for movie nights, a little slice of escape, and Sundays offered a change of scenery with trips to Base G, the beach, or a chance to splash around in the sea.

Anita's younger brother, Hans, had also made the trek to Hollandia and found himself working with DETA. It was from him that I got the lowdown on what being a DETA boy was really like. Hans was upfront about it — none of them shied away from hard graft or the tough life that came with the job. But there were perks, like getting their car and motorbike licenses, a rare opportunity back then. Hans even bagged his truck license, learning to handle those ex-American military beasts on wheels. His journey didn't stop there; he climbed his way up to a position with the Hollandia Port Authority. It goes to show, hard work paid off. And for many, the dream job was landing a gig with the government — Hans made that dream a reality, sticking with it until he left for the Netherlands in 1960.

As time marched on, the remnants of American construction faded into memory. The coastal towns buzzed with new activity, laying down water pipes, setting up electricity and telephone lines. Before long, the landscape transformed with bridges, houses, schools, churches, shops, offices, warehouses, jetties, and airports. It was a time of building, of growing — a time when dreams started to take shape in concrete and steel.

In the early days on the island, you could say the place was more wild than wired — decent roads were a fantasy, and public transport was virtually nonexistent. The main way to get around? Flying.

*"The Kroonduif,"* or Crown dove, was the pride of the skies — a sturdy 'Beaver' plane run by the Netherlands New Guinea Aviation Company, NNGLM, an offshoot of KLM, Royal Dutch Airlines. This plane wasn't just about its sleek design; it was a lifeline, carting passengers, post, clothes, and food across the island. Named after a stunning pigeon known for its regal crown of feathers, the Kroonduif was a symbol of connection in a place where paths were often skies.

But the hard graft wasn't just about getting from A to B. It was a time of laying down the groundwork — literally and figuratively. Schools, churches, and the first stone houses began to rise from the ground in 1952. The island buzzed with efforts to educate, to plan economically and agriculturally. Boredom was unheard of; there was too much to do, too many dreams to build.

The spirit of those who came to work on the island was something else. It wasn't all about the money; it was about the mission. With a mix of optimism and a good sense of humour, everyone dug in. Hard work wasn't just accepted; it was embraced. So much so that a five and a half day workweek became the norm — a testament to their dedication and drive. The Dutch government even gave a nod to the women, marvelling at how seamlessly they adapted to the ever-shifting sands of island life.

The ultimate prize? Preparing the Papuans for independence. Back in Holland, people had this idea of tropical living as some kind of extended holiday, especially for the women. But for the Indo-European women in New Guinea, luxury was a world away. Governor Jan van Baal put it best, saying there were people so wrapped up in their mission that their work and personal lives blurred into one.

That was the story for my parents too. They threw themselves into their roles, facing every new challenge head-on. Anita built a safe, loving nest for the family, caring for baby Louise with all she had. And Boy? He managed the purse strings and poured his heart into his job at R.O.N.G., *"Radio Broadcast New Guinea"*. For him, like many others, the line between work and home just didn't exist. Their lives were their work, and their work, their lives — a complete circle, driven by dedication to a cause far beyond themselves.

Kroonduif 'Beaver'. Near Manokwari, Geelvinkbaai

Vista of Hollandia

## Boy as radio broadcaster

'You are listening to the Dutch radio broadcast in New Guinea in Hollandia.'

## From amateur transmitter to radio station

Boy landed himself a once-in-a-lifetime gig: getting a radio station off the ground in Hollandia. This job with R.O.N.G., *"Radio Omroep Nieuw-Guinea"*, wasn't just any position — it was a role within a government agency, starting from the ground up. Imagine kicking things off as a community radio, working under the most basic conditions, and then watching it transform into a full-blown professional outfit.

For most, the setup would be a nightmare — basic, to say the least. But Boy thrived on this kind of challenge. It was his chance to dive headfirst into a sea of creativity, to be the master of his own ship, navigating through uncharted waters with nothing but his wits and a hefty dose of improvisation.

He'd always light up talking about the early days, building the broadcasting company from the ground up with two mates of his, Lapré and Rubens, both RAF veterans from Biak. These guys had a bit of experience running a makeshift station for the military people on Biak Island, playing tunes and sharing news. They were using whatever they could scrounge up — turntables, records, the whole shebang from an old military setup called 'Radio Garut' in West Java.

Their project, YDZ, first hit the airwaves on 24 March, 1950, as 'Radio Biak'. It was modest — just an hour of music twice a week — but it was theirs, and it was a start.

Then, the operation moved to Hollandia, transformed into R.O.N.G., and officially went live on 30 September, 1950. Their 'studio'? If you could call it that. It was basically an old shed near the Sentani airstrip, at the base of the Cyclops Mountains. The place was a mess, filled with empty oil drums that had to be cleared out before they could even think about broadcasting.

But Boy and his team didn't see obstacles; they saw opportunities. Clearing out that shed, setting up the old American transmitter left behind by the war, they were making do with what they had, turning a rundown shack into the heart of their new radio world. It was more than just a job for Boy; it was a mission, a chance to connect, to create, and to carve out a little slice of history in the wilds of New Guinea.

Radio broadcasters in New Guinea. In front of the 'new' R.O.N.G. building in Hollandia. Left to right: Rubens, Lapré, Belloni

Boy continues his story.

The passion with which we worked as broadcasters knew no bounds. From the first radio broadcast, we played some records and so on. "You know your stuff, so begin, they told me." A few times a day we could use the telex to signal to the Netherlands for an hour. A young lady at the post office then typed the copy. We processed radio news through the press agencies, like the ANP, "Algemeen Nederlands Persbureau" (General Netherlands Press office) news reports that came in by telex. Communication with the ANP, the largest news agency in the Netherlands, was only by telex.

Together with Dick van Os, programme director, we turned it into a real radio station, though it was in New Guinea style. A studio in the old petrol shed with a roof of brown rusted iron corrugated sheets. Not a big studio with a nice interior and modern equipment. No, just a modest studio with 75 seats which we had built ourselves with a soft board. There was no sound-absorbing material, so we cut up military blankets to make acoustic strips that hung down from the ceiling. It took us eight days to complete it. Anyone, who wandered onto the 20 metre band in the evenings on his receiver, could hear a Dutch voice on the air, announcing: "You are listening to the Dutch radio broadcast in New Guinea at Hollandia". R.O.N.G. had made its entrance, although the first beginnings were very brief. That old American radio transmitter from the bush had only 350 Watt capacity and had to cover an area that was almost twelve times the size of the Netherlands. We had a few vinyl records and two old turntables. Everything had to come from the Netherlands and that made it expensive. In New Guinea, such things were unobtainable. No wonder a man once joked, "You have forgotten a 'W' before R.O.N.G." By which he meant that the reception of the broadcasting station was poor. Yet for us, it was an enjoyable time.

Later on, I was not only a broadcaster but also a programme leader, in which I was in charge of the daily management of the radio, as well as being an administrator and an accountant, responsible for the financial management of the broadcasters. In the beginning, we pilfered news from the airwaves. Later, it all became a bit more official. These times remained the exquisite years of my life.


Landing in Hollandia, Boy found himself right where he belonged. Back in Makassar, he had a taste of the work as an Information Officer/ Public Relations Officer, and it seemed like luck was on his side once again. Pioneering wasn't just something Boy did; it was part of who he was. Journalism came naturally to him, as did connecting with all sorts of people, as long as he had the room to breathe and create.

But it wasn't all smooth sailing. Boy had his battles, especially when it came to boosting the quality and variety of the radio programs. He tackled this head-on, mixing national and regional news with deeper dives into significant topics, all while keeping the tunes flowing. News from back home in the Netherlands also made the cut, making sure everyone stayed in the loop. In a place like New Guinea, where the Dutch community was spread thin across the island and entertainment options were slim, R.O.N.G. became a lifeline, a way to break the monotony of isolation.

As New Guinea's population started to swell, so did R.O.N.G.'s popularity, not just among the Dutch but also with the local population on the western side of the island. By the end of 1952, things were really taking off. The Office for Information and Radio Broadcasting New Guinea was established, and the station moved to a new location in Hollandia Haven. They weren't messing around — a brand new studio was built, and they upgraded to a 3-Kilowatt transmitter, leaving the old 350-Watt one in the dust. Suddenly, R.O.N.G. was at the forefront, a state-of-the-art operation with a massive music library and top-tier equipment, a stark contrast to the traditional ways of life still prevalent among some of the Papuan communities.

Claude interviewing former Minister for Overseas Territories, Prof. Dr. Mr. W.J.A. Kernkamp
in front of the R.O.N.G. building

In this evolving world of media, Boy found his calling as a second journalist. Together with his colleague, they dove deep into the heart of New Guinea, covering stories, keeping tabs on global events, and exploring every topic under the sun. Their commitment to thorough research and storytelling enriched the station's offerings. His collaboration with the information office meant he kept churning out documentaries and interviews, painting a picture of New Guinea for listeners near and far. This wasn't just a job for Boy; it was where he was meant to be, doing what he did best — informing, connecting, and exploring.

Boy was doing something right. His work with R.O.N.G. wasn't just for the people in New Guinea; newspapers and magazines back in the Netherlands ate up whatever he sent over. It was a win-win. He was sharing pieces of New Guinea with the world, and they couldn't get enough.

As the second journalist, Boy has to hang out with the colleagues working on films and documentaries for the office. This switch-up came from the top. Governor Jan van Baal thought it made more sense to do the voice-overs for New Guinea documentaries right there in New Guinea, instead of sending stuff back and forth to the Netherlands. So, after a bit of time off in 1956, Boy packed his bags for a three-month internship at Multifilm N.V. in Haarlem. It was all about getting the inside scoop on making films that told stories about where he was living.

Coming back to New Guinea, Boy jumped into a new role almost straight away. He became the go-to guide for a group of Dutch parliament members visiting New Guinea. Basically, it was his job to show them the real New Guinea, beyond the postcards and stories. He was the go-to guy, explaining what life on the island was all about.

Boy was on a roll with writing, guiding, and even hitting the radio waves. By 1958, he was everywhere — working as an ANP correspondent with his foreign correspondent-ships of Reuters and he was an employee of *Stringer*, a division of the American weekly *Time and Life* magazines and he got his stories out through the British magazine *Daily Express* and of the American radio and television station NBC, *The National Broadcasting Company* in New York. He was also behind the New Guinea Chronicles spreading the word about New Guinea through the 'Royal Society East & West' and the 'National New Guinea Committee', both based in the Netherlands.

All this hard work paid off. Boy ended up leading the Information Bureau of the Government in Hollandia. The job was more than just work; it was what made him happy, giving him the freedom to tell New Guinea's stories his way, especially knowing that his stories were making waves back home.

While Boy was making his mark, his family was growing too. In 1951, he and Anita welcomed their daughter Louise in the military hospital in Ifar. She was the apple of their eye, and they made sure everyone back home knew about her, sending photos and letters all the time. Those pictures of Louise, especially the ones showing off her full head of hair, were a hit with the family in The Hague and Makassar.

Anita, Claude, Louise, Hollandia, 1951

Boy was out there making waves with his radio and journalism work, while Anita was holding down the fort at home, looking for someone to help look after their bundle of energy, Louise. They found Esther, a *"babu"* (nanny), who had her hands full. Louise was a little firecracker, always on the move. There's this one time she zipped down a slope on her scooter, way too fast, ending up with a bleeding lip and a scraped knee. Poor Esther barely had a chance to catch her breath, let alone keep up with Louise's adventures.

Anita wasn't just managing home life; she carved out her own space in Hollandia's workforce as a secretary. And Puck, she found her spot working at 'Pharma', Mr. Samuels Brusse's drugstore. The commute was no joke — a 45-minute drive in the pitch dark, on a road missing any kind of safety features, like crash barriers or lights.

It was a busy life, and then, six years after Louise made her entrance, I came along. My earliest memories? They're bits and pieces, really. I remember spending hours in my playpen, our house and garden, and Spanky, our dog, who was always around. The beach is in there too, and these fuzzy moments of my parents chatting and laughing on the terrace, or the sound of Papuans singing and whistling. It's hard to tell if these memories are truly mine or if they've been stitched together from the stories that have been told and retold at home, not to mention the films and slides my dad loved to show.

What anchors these memories to something real, though, are Dad's journals.

Boy's journals aren't just a collection of news and events; they're deeply personal. They tell the story of his adventures, the tours and expeditions he went on, and most importantly, they show his love for New Guinea, how he saw and cherished the island's beauty and its challenges. They're like a time capsule, filled with his observations and experiences, capturing all the details of our life in New Guinea.

In 1951, a significant move happened for the family. They shifted to Hollandia Binnen, also known as Inner Hollandia or Kota Baru. This place was a little world of its own, housing not just homes but also the famous *Toko Ong Ak*, a place where you could indulge in some ice cream. The

Radio broadcaster in New Guinea, Claude behind his desk at the Secretary in Hollandia Harbour, October 1960

community was complete with schools, a hairdresser, offices, churches, clubhouse, even a police station, hospital, and prison. Kota Baru, nestled about forty kilometres inland from Hollandia Harbour, offered a slice of civilisation amidst the wild.

Their new place was by the northeast side of Lake Sentani, in a more traditional setup known as a *"gabba gabba"* house. These houses had a charm to them, with roofs made of crescent-shaped sago palm leaves, though some sported zinc roofs. The walls, too, were crafted from sago palm leaves, while concrete floors gave the structure a solid foundation. But living here came with its own set of challenges. The sago palm leaves were a magnet for insects and mosquitoes. Come dusk, their home would be under siege by mosquitoes, finding their way through the tiniest of gaps. The only defence against these nightly invaders was a mosquito net draped over the beds.

Despite the challenges, their home was humble — a straightforward three-room house with an outside toilet. It was a stark, yet authentic experience of life in New Guinea, far removed from the conveniences of the modern world but rich with the essence of the place they were learning to call home.

Aunt Puck shared with me some of the everyday challenges they faced living in New Guinea.

One thing that stuck out was how, when the rain was heavy, the tap water would stop running. If you had clothes to wash during those times, you had no choice but to head to a nearby creek, or *"kali"*, and do your washing there.

By the end of 1951, as the deadline approached for the Dutch to exit Indonesia, our family welcomed some new arrivals. Oma Loes, along with her youngest son, Ferry, and her two youngest daughters, came to stay with us in our gabba gabba house in Hollandia Binnen.

Vista of Hollandia. On the left Humboldt Bay, right Jautefa Bay. The Humboldt Bay is named after the German explorer Alexander Von Humboldt, who, by the way, never visited the area

Hollandia, Kota Baru

Sure, it was a tight squeeze, but we made it work. Oma Loes and the kids bunked down in one room on bunk beds, while Puck claimed a corner of the living room, cordoned off by a curtain for some privacy. Boy, Anita, and Louise had the other bedroom to themselves.

A couple of years later, in 1953, our family moved to a more solid setup — a stone house known as an Essestijn house, right on *Pantaiweg* (Pantai Road) in Hollandia Binnen. Oma Loes and Anita's siblings stayed back in the old place, keeping the gabba gabba house warm.

Then, in 1958, we moved again, this time to Boslaan in Dok V. This place had a view to kill for — you could look out from the garden and see the bay and the Cyclops mountains in the distance. This house was also built from stone and came with some modern comforts like a bathroom, an indoor toilet, electricity, and running water. Still, we had to boil the water before drinking it. But, a kerosene stove in the kitchen? That was a game-changer for my mum.

Our garden was a little slice of paradise. We had a kaffir lime tree, a cherry tree, and a banana ("*pisang*") tree, not to mention the herbs and pineapples we grew. We even kept a few chickens around. Louise, she was our little adventurer, always up the cherry tree, munching on cherries like they were going out of style.

In September 1954, my mum's family faced a heartbreaking loss. Her youngest brother, Ferry, was only fourteen when he caught Malaria Tropica. Despite the family's hopes and prayers, he couldn't beat the illness. On the 7th of September, 1954, Ferry passed away and was laid to rest in the general cemetery in Hollandia Binnen. His grave is a lasting reminder of the family's loss, still there to this day.

Vista Hollandia Harbour

Around the same time, the political climate surrounding New Guinea was heating up. President Sukarno of Indonesia was making moves, bringing New Guinea's status to the forefront at the United Nations. Indonesia argued that New Guinea was rightfully part of its territory, citing geographic and historical ties. The Netherlands, on the other hand, pointed out that the Papuans were culturally and ethnically distinct from Indonesians, being Melanesians. The Dutch government believed that the Papuans should have the right to determine their own future when they were ready. This debate over New Guinea's fate became a recurring topic at the United Nations, but no definitive decision was reached for a long time.

The uncertainty and political tensions made many Dutch Indisch people anxious about their future in New Guinea, including my Oma Loes. She felt that moving to the Netherlands would offer her family more stability and safety. So, in mid-1957, she made the difficult decision to leave New Guinea with her three youngest daughters. They arrived in Amsterdam on 22 September, ready to start over in what was now their new home country. Initially, they stayed in a 'contract pension' in Amersfoort, a temporary housing arrangement for repatriates. Eventually, Oma Loes found a small apartment in Nijkerk, not too far from Amersfoort, where she settled with her two youngest daughters. Meanwhile, her son Hans and my mum, Anita, chose to stay behind in New Guinea, facing the uncertainties of the times head-on.

## Relaxation and fun

In New Guinea, life wasn't all work and no play. My family and their friends made sure to carve out time for relaxation and fun. Boy, especially after a busy week, would take us out on Saturday afternoons or Sundays for some much-needed family time. It was a reminder that life wasn't just about work; it was also about making memories together.

Boy described Lake Sentani.

The impressive Lake Sentani is an enclosed bay of the Humboldt Bay and is known for its beauty. At the same time, it is also a mysterious lake, where beautifully coloured Veil fish moved gracefully through the water. There were also gold-coloured fish, amongst the deep green water plants where freshwater crocodiles lived. In the deep water, large fish such as Swordfish swam around as well.

Lake Sentani was one of those places where we found our slice of peace. Imagine a vast freshwater lake, over 100 square kilometres in size, sitting 75 meters above sea level. The lake is dotted with more than 20 islands and surrounded by about 25 kampongs and villages. It's encircled by rolling hills covered in tall reed grass, "alang-alang", which can shoot up to two metres. The lake, fed by clear freshwater rivers, is a haven of lush tropical greenery, with peaceful creeks and sandy shores. But it's not always quiet — large green grasshoppers can break the silence with their piercing calls. You'd often see white herons perched on tree trunks and dragonflies fluttering over the water, their blue gossamer wings glinting in the sunlight. The lake's beauty is breathtaking, with the vibrant reds and oranges of 'flame of the forest' flowers reflecting in its still waters, under the golden rays of the sun. Yet, this serene scene can quickly change as treacherous winds whip the lake into a frenzy of swirling waters and high waves.

The road to Lake Sentani, built by the Americans during the Second World War, snakes through this picturesque landscape. It stretches from the lake to Hollandia and on to Sentani Airport, beside the Cyclops mountains and lined with coconut trees. This road, known as the 'black snake' for its winding path through the mountainous terrain, offered stunning views of Jautefa Bay, weaving through the hills. Driving along it was a bit of an adventure, with the steep inclines, sharp descents, and hairpin turns, but the breathtaking views of the water and hills made every trip worth it.

Right along Lake Sentani, you'd spot these bamboo houses perched on stilts right in the water, their roofs covered with atap. Back then, canoes were a common sight, gliding through the lake's tranquil waters.

Boy was pretty versatile when it came to lake activities. Sometimes he'd be behind the wheel of the water-ski motorboat, or he'd take on the role of a spotter for the water-skier, making sure communication with the driver was spot on. And then there were days when he'd strap on the water skis himself, taking to the lake with ease.

Like the 'exotic Lago Maggiore', Lake Sentani

Evening mood, Lake Sentani

The lake wasn't just about the thrill of water sports; it was a place of stunning beauty that drew visitors in. People could spend hours just soaking in the magnificent sunsets, watching the colours dance and change across the sky. The lake was alive with activity — sailing races, water skiing, or kids playing along the sandy shores, creating a picture-perfect scene.

Snacks and meals were part of the lakeside experience. We'd dig into the goodies we'd brought along or grab a plate of nasi goreng, fried rice, at Bellevue. Then there was Huize Meerzicht, a popular place to be for water sports lovers, where you could get all sorts of tasty treats. It felt like our own 'exotic Lago Maggiore' right there in New Guinea.

Papuas in Proa, Lake Sentani

Relaxation and joy on the banks of Lake Sentani

Around the lake, you'd often find women swimming or skilfully guiding fish into traps, while men tended to the vegetable gardens. The older Papuans might be seen lounging by the lake, enjoying the view, and chewing betel nut, lost in the tranquility of the moment.

Our Sundays sometimes took us to the Sentani market to pick up fresh veggies or fish or to visit friends living in those stilt houses above the water, some nestled on quaint little islands. The Papuans we met were always welcoming, their smiles wide, though they shied away from discussing old traditions, pretending not to catch our curious questions. Legends whispered of spirits dwelling in quiet corners of Lake Sentani, places considered taboo, where even the fishermen and women would steer clear. There was a tale about a man who dared to venture into one such forbidden spot, only to be found dead in the lake the next day.

Lake Sentani. Boy, Anita, Puck and friend Harry

## Beach, sea, shovel, bucket and tyres
## The beautiful beaches near Hollandia

Boy loved the beach at Base G. If you took the road from Hollandia-Haven, past the landmark known as *Kaju Batu*, the wooden rock, you'd find yourself in a peaceful valley with a small kampong. Our family, along with others, made it a ritual to spend Saturday afternoons on the stunning white sandy beach there. The water was so clear and shallow, never deeper than a meter, letting you see your feet clearly against the white sand. Louise and the other kids would be laughing and floating on inner tubes from cars, while I preferred to stay cool in the shade, busy with my bucket and shovel, crafting sand castles and feeling the hot sand beneath me. Baalbek beach was another favourite, famous for its beautiful rock formations that framed the shore.

Sundays were for exploring with family and friends, often heading to the Marine bath near the Ifar military encampment, about an hour's drive from our home in Hollandia. We'd pack the car with food my mum and aunties made and spend the whole day there, enjoying the waterfalls and big rocks. Sliding off those boulders into the chilly water was a thrill we never tired of, and we often had the place to ourselves.

We also looked forward to the events the Government threw, like New Year's Eve, Queen's Day, and St. Nicolas Day. Those gatherings were a break from the everyday, a chance to unwind and have some fun. Dancing was a big part of my parents lives too, thanks to the many bands around New Guinea in the fifties and sixties. From The Royal Hawaiian Minstrels in Manokwari to The Rocking Teens in Hollandia, music was everywhere. And there was this Papuan band with *Putih*, the albino lead guitarist who sang Dutch songs, adding a unique twist to the scene.

Getting a radio at home changed everything. It became the heartbeat of our house, always tuned to the music station. Friends and family would come over, and they'd all end up dancing to the radio tunes, creating our own little parties. And those organised dress-up parties and fashion shows were something else. Louise, Mum, and I had our moments of fame, strutting down the catwalk in our best outfits, basking in the applause and laughter.

One way traffic, Lake Sentani

Rural peace, Lake Sentani

Anita and Boy. The gypsy couple in the jungle. Ready to party

Baalbek, Hollandia, a beach with nice rock formation. Boy and Louise on foreground

# Queen's Birthday in the jungle

A radio talk show. Boy behind the microphone during Queen's Day in the jungle.

On 30 April, 1952, Queen's Day out in the New Guinea jungle was something else — a real highlight for everyone, Papuans and Dutch alike. It was a day nobody wanted to miss, a chance to come together, share some laughs, and enjoy the camaraderie. Our family always made sure to be part of the "Oranje" (orange) festivities. Boy was the one bringing it all to life on the radio, sharing everything he saw, heard, and felt right from the heart of the action.

The excitement wasn't just confined to Hollandia. Over the Cyclops Mountains, some 2,300 meters right behind the town, the kampong was buzzing. Women were prepping for the day, loading up their woven carrier nets — those braided bags they wore around their heads — with sweet potatoes and sago lumps, ready for a feast. The men were getting into the spirit too, etching designs onto their long bow arrows and dabbing red dye for patterns on their faces, thinking ahead about the crafts and trinkets they could trade. They laid out black cassowary feathers, getting the drum skins tight for the music that was an essential part of the day's joy.

Kids were right there with the adults, rolling up reed mats and gathering bamboo flutes of all sizes, from the tiniest to ones over a meter long. The whole community was in motion, gearing up for 30 April, knowing there was a hefty journey to Hollandia ahead. That trek was no joke — six days through the mountains, crossing high watersheds, navigating narrow, slippery paths with their goods and gifts in tow. But the pull of Queen's Day made the tough journey worth it.

The sound of flute orchestras filled the air, setting the scene for Queen's Day, a celebration that swept through every corner of New Guinea. From the bustling streets of Hollandia to the remote villages in Sarmi, Manokwari, Sorong, Merauke, and Tanah Merah, the excitement was palpable. These last few days leading up to the 30th of April saw everyone pitching in with a smile, ready to honour Queen Juliana's birthday in style. For the Papuans, this day was the highlight of the year, a festivity embraced with open hearts, supported by government funds to ensure it was the grandest day of all. The dedication of those from inland areas, willing to trek for days to join in, speaks volumes of the day's significance. And if you made it to the celebration without a place to stay, no worries — there was always a spot with relatives or an open field under the stars to rest your head.

The games played on Queen's Day were a spectacle of fun. One of the most eagerly awaited challenges was the greased bamboo pole competition. Imagine an eight-meter-long pole, slick with green soap, towering above the crowd with prizes like bright shirts, shorts, handkerchiefs, and cans of corned beef dangling temptingly from the top. The goal was to climb to the top and claim a prize, but with the pole slathered in soap, it was easier said than done.

The scene was always one of chaotic fun. The competition was fierce and filled with laughter. Peter, making it halfway up, finds himself bogged down by John and Nicholas, who cling to his legs, dragging him back to the ground, much to the amusement of onlookers. Others try to form human towers to gain an advantage, but the pole, under the strain of the eager climbers, starts to sway. Just when it seems like it might topple. The crowd held its breath until Markus made a valiant attempt, and the pole began to topple, sending everyone into an uproar of laughter and cheers. It was instants like these — filled with laughter, struggle, and the thrill of competition — that made Queen's Day unforgettable.

Over on the other side of the field, some of the Papuans are trying their luck riding bikes through an obstacle course of barrels. It's not as easy as it looks. The barrels are spaced in a way that you have to be pretty good to zigzag through without wiping out. A few manage to do it, making it look smooth, but for most, it's a bunch of stops and starts, and a couple of near misses that get a laugh from the onlookers.

Nearby, a boxing match is going on. It's informal, with a European guy who's been training the local youths acting as the referee. The boxers are young, eager, and full of energy. They are not holding back, throwing punches like they mean it — right hooks, uppercuts, you name it, glistening with sweat in the hot sun. It's clear they're enjoying the challenge, feeding off the crowd's cheers.

A bit further out, there's something completely different happening. The people from the Nimboran Plain are doing the cassowary dance. It's a big deal, very showy. They have these 'cassowaries,' guys dressed up with big feather bundles, darting around while others, pretending to be hunters, chase them. It's all pretend, of course, with no real arrows flying, but it's done so well you get caught up in it. The dancers are all in, decked out in bright yellow and moving to the beat of the drums, really giving it their all.

Dancers drumming on their Tifas. Queen's Day, Hollandia

Cassowary dance. Making fire. Dancers of the  Nimboran Plain. Queen's Day, Hollandia

Preparing walking over hot coals. Queen's Day, Hollandia

Anyone who thought they'd catch some extra sleep on 30 April was in for a rude awakening. In New Guinea, dawn breaks around five in the morning, but even before the sky starts to lighten, the air is filled with music. Flute orchestras and small bands start their march through the streets, making sure no one misses the start of the day. Their tunes float through the air, lively and persistent, turning the idea of sleeping in into a distant dream.

Flute orchestra. Queen's Day, Hollandia

Bands march around playing songs like 'Piet Hein, His Name is Small', 'Dutch Flag You Are My Glory', 'In the Name of Orange, Open the Gate', and 'Where the White Top of the Dunes'. They play with a lot of heart and a bit of make-it-up-as-you-go. If you decide to step outside to watch, you might find yourself caught between two groups playing different tunes at the same time —' Piet Hein' in one ear, the 'Geuzenlied' in the other. It's such a jumble of music that you might think about heading back inside. But sticking around is the thing to do. The players are hoping for a little something for their efforts, maybe some food or a few coins.

The houses where the big shots of the city live get the most attention. High-ranking officials like the resident, the top boss of the local government, and even the Aspiring Controllers get a personal concert. Around eleven, the Joka choir, a big deal in New Guinea, sings patriotic songs outside the Governor's place, entertaining him and his guests. Then, Papuan young men sing 'Alle menschen werden Brüder' from Beethoven's ninth symphony, a song about all people becoming brothers.

Queen's Day is a big deal here, a time for everyone, Papuan and Dutch alike, to enjoy music, singing, and eating together. It's the best day of the year, where everyone comes together, forgetting their differences for a while.

## Outdoor activities

### Tennis

Tennis was the sport of choice for both Boy and Anita. They weren't just casual players; they were passionate about the game. They hit the courts regularly, not only playing for the love of the sport but also competing in tournaments across New Guinea. They played everywhere, from the Dutch territories to the eastern parts of Papua New Guinea. Their home boasted a collection of trophies and prizes, all neatly displayed in glass cabinets, a validation to their skill and dedication on the tennis court.

Boy and Anita with their tennis friends

## Hunting

Hunting was another thing, especially for Boy, once work was done for the day. He'd grab his gun and head out with friends, hoping to bring back something extra for the dinner table. Anita, however, had one rule for when he returned from these hunting trips: he had to strip down outside the house. The reason was simple; the hunt left him and his clothes smelling pretty bad, and she'd get straight to washing everything outdoors.

Boy had his hunting stories. Bringing home something extra was always a win. He once mentioned that a *"tjèlèng"* (wild boar), could fetch a hundred guilders from a Chinese restaurant in Hollandia. There was even a time he and minister Jense accidentally ran over a boar. "It's not every day you run into a hundred guilders," the minister had joked. Despite the accident, that boar still earned them a hundred guilders.

Whenever Boy managed to bring home a piece of boar, a large *couscous*, a possum, or a rabbit, Anita's first instinct was to share. She believed in giving part of their bounty to others. What they kept was turned into dishes like *"dengdeng"*, dried meat. They'd slice the meat thin, cure it with salt and saltpetre to draw out the moisture, then after eight days, they'd wash the strips and dry them in the sun. It was much later, back in Hollandia, that their options for food, including meat from PNG and Australia, started to expand.

A group of hunters after a pig hunt. Friend Ecky in front left and Boy behind him with sunglasses

## Fishing

Fishing was another activity Boy enjoyed, heading out with friends not just for the sport, but for the catch. Unlike back in Holland, where catch-and-release was common, here the goal was always to bring something home. They rarely used fishing rods, preferring nylon lines or spears instead. Boy was quite successful, often returning with enough fish to share with family or friends.

Cleaning the fish was Boy's job, as Anita wasn't fond of doing it. Once cleaned, Anita took over, turning the fresh catch into delicious meals. She had a special talent for making *ikan bali*, a spicy fish dish that was always a hit. The freshness of the fish, combined with her culinary skills, made for an unbeatable meal. Plus, the fish in New Guinea were significantly larger than anything they'd caught in the Netherlands, making each catch even more rewarding.

Boy, the proud angler

## The 50th Anniversary of Hollandia!

Hollandia hit a big milestone — the 50th anniversary of its founding — on 7 March 1960. The town was originally established by a Royal Dutch Navy detachment back on 7 March 1910. Fifty years on, the celebration was nothing short of spectacular. High-profile guests included the Governor, the Resident of Hollandia, Navy and Marine commanders, and the head of local administration, among many others.

Our family was there to see it all. The ceremony kicked off bright and early at 7:15 a.m. A (longboat) *barkas*, made its way to the shore, carrying veterans dressed as KNIL soldiers, the same uniforms they would have worn back in 1910, reenacting Captain Sachse's historic landing. Once the boat was docked, two men, swords drawn, took their positions as the rest of the troops, fully kitted out in old KNIL gear, marched up to the flagpole at the monument under the lead of Captain Sachse.

The main event was the hoisting of the flag, followed by the unveiling of a white monument marked with *'Hollandia 1910-1960'* in black letters. A large platform, adorned with colourful flowers shipped in from the Netherlands, stood in front of it. The whole monument project was funded by Hollandia's citizens. In his speech, the Resident emphasised the importance of working together towards a common goal to build a thriving community. He wrapped up by revealing a new street sign, *Captain Sachseweg'*, in honour of Hollandia's founder. The Governor even declared 7 March an official holiday.

The celebrations, organised by the *'Oranjecomité'*, included everything from bicycle and proa races to sailing. The day was rounded off with a parade of decorated cars and the opening of the *'Pasar Malam'*, a local market, marking a day of remembrance and community spirit.

Monument 50th anniversary, Hollandia

Papuan demonstration, Hollandia 1962

Hollandia Harbour

# 4.3 The curtain falls

Life in the tropics for Boy and Anita suddenly came to an abrupt end. They once again had to make an important decision.

*I*n August 1962, everything changed. They, along with other Dutch friends, had just six weeks to pack up their lives of twelve years into a few suitcases because of some political deal made far away. They managed to find new homes for Spanky, their dog, and the chickens, and sold off what furniture they could. It was a tough pill to swallow.

They loved New Guinea. It wasn't just about the place; it was the life they built there. Boy and Anita would often talk about the simple things that made it special. The endless green bush around their home, the friendly faces of the Papuans, the vast, blue Pacific Ocean, beaches with coral peeking through clear water, the soft white sand, palm trees that danced in the wind, and the clear, fresh water in lakes and rivers. It was the sounds at night, the feel of the air, the sense of being a small part of something huge and beautiful. They felt free there, in a way they couldn't explain, surrounded by nature's beauty that seemed to have no end.

But then, the situation with Indonesia turned everything upside down. West Papua's takeover wasn't just a news headline; it was a real, scary turn of events that hit too close to home. The Dutch and Papuans alike had been trying to make things work, really putting their hearts into building a community together. But now, it felt like all that effort was for nothing.

As 1962 began, the threat of Indonesian forces moving in hung heavy. Some people packed up and left, driven by the fear of what might happen. Others couldn't bring themselves to go, their love for the island rooting them to the spot despite the danger. Boy and Anita were torn, like everyone else. Leaving was hard, but the thought of staying, of watching their beloved island change under force, was even harder.

Leaving New Guinea wasn't just about moving; it was like saying good-bye to a part of themselves. My parents often reflected on how the Dutch, once integral to the island's life, now felt like outsiders. They had poured their hearts into the place, believing they were making a difference. They worked alongside the Papuans, helping to put New Guinea on the map, offering education, medical care, and improving the local infrastructure. They built schools, hospitals, and houses, hoping to give the Papuans a better future.

But as the political tide turned, all those efforts seemed to vanish overnight. "It's like we've been played," my parents would say, feeling a familiar sting of displacement they'd known too many times before. This wasn't just another move. It was a forced farewell to a home they had loved, a community they had become a part of, and dreams they had nurtured. Including the hardships of Japanese captivity, the Bersiap period, the War of Independence, and the transfer of sovereignty in 1949, this felt like yet another upheaval in a long history of dislocation for them.

Was this the end, or the start of something new? That question lingered as we packed up, leaving behind more than just belongings — a part of our hearts stayed there, too. Along with thousands of others, we were uprooted, leaving the island that had become more than just a home.

Louise and I felt the weight of that goodbye. New Guinea, with all its familiar faces and places, was now a memory. In mid-June 1962, Mum, Louise and I together with others set off for Sydney, and on 20 June, we boarded the M.S. *Willem Ruys* for the Netherlands, carrying not just our belongings but our Indo heritage, our upbringing, and a tapestry of memories from our time on the island.

Despite the chaos, there was a moment when hope for the Papuan peoples had shone brightly. On 5 April, 1961, the New Guinea Council was established, a step towards self-determination with leaders like Mr. J.H.F. Sollewijn Gelpke, Mr. Nicolaas Jouwe, and Marcus Kaisiëpo at the helm. It was a time of cooperation and progress, with independence seeming within reach. The sovereignty transfer ceremony on 1 December, 1961, in Hollandia was a landmark moment, symbolising a new chapter for the Papuans, even though full independence was still out of grasp.

M.S. *Willem Ruys*

Boy got to see something really special that day. For the first time, the people of the Dutch colony raised their own flag, a symbol of their struggle and hopes. Nicolaas Jouwe explained the red on the flag stood for their fight to be independent. The star? That was the Morning Star from the island stories, promising good things and a hero's journey. The flag's colours, blue and white, were all about home, representing the places they came from in Western New Guinea. They called it the Morning Star flag, and watching it fly, you couldn't help but feel a bit of that promised hope.

The song they sang was old, the words by Reverend Isaak Samuel Kijne from back in 1925, set to a tune by Marius Brandts Buys. It was a love letter to Papua, their home, promising undying love. Watching them sing, you could see it wasn't just a song to them. It hit deep, stirring something so strong that many choked up, lost for words. Boy felt it too, seeing the pride in their eyes, the way they were moved by their own anthem.

After the council got elected in '61, seeing that flag next to the Dutch one was a big deal. But the joy was short-lived. They couldn't have guessed then how quickly things would change, that Indonesia would take over so soon. All the dreams of stepping out on their own seemed to crumble overnight. The celebration turned bittersweet, and not long after, the air got thick with worry about skirmishes and soldiers sneaking in.

Meanwhile, politics played out far away from New Guinea. Talks between Minister Luns and President Kennedy, even Prince Bernhard got involved, trying to sort out the mess without forgetting the people right in the middle of it. Prince Bernhard had this secret plan, tucked away in some archive for years, all about finding peace and making sure the Papuans got a fair shot at deciding their own future.

In early 1962, Indonesia wasn't just talking tough; they started sneaking military folks into New Guinea by boat. It wasn't long before they upped their game, dropping paratroopers into the mix. This all kicked off with a clash at Vlakke Hoek, the starting gun for Indonesia's 'Operation Trikora' — a full-on plan to grab Western New Guinea by force. And then, there were these Indonesian torpedo boats lurking around at night, trying to drop off more infiltrators. The Dutch Navy caught one and set it on fire. Indonesia, with its new stash of weapons from Russia, was suddenly a bigger threat than before.

The Netherlands sent over soldiers to try and keep a lid on things, but by May 1962, Indonesia was making it clear they were ready to escalate, signalling a big invasion could be on the horizon. It got to the point where the Dutch government couldn't promise to keep everyone safe anymore.

That's when a lot of Dutch people started to think about getting out. Plane and boat tickets out of there started selling fast, especially when the whispers of war started sounding a lot more like shouts.

Boy, who was running the government's Information Bureau, was right in the thick of it, getting the lowdown on all the high-level talks about New Guinea, including what was being said between the Dutch government and the United Nations. He couldn't help but wonder what all this Indonesian push was going to mean for the people and the place he'd come to call home.

Even with all the meetings and talks, no one could hammer out a deal for the longest time. That left Boy, Anita, and everyone else in this limbo of hope and worry. They'd been told back in the '50s that New Guinea was going to stay Dutch for the long haul. Now, it looked like that was just a pipe dream. With Indonesia turning up the heat and the Netherlands looking like it might lose its last foothold in the tropics, Boy and Anita started thinking it might be time to pack up for the Netherlands, just to be safe.

I never really got around to asking my parents why they chose the Netherlands of all places. It probably had a lot to do with family. Both sides already had roots there, making it feel like a natural spot to start over. Having relatives around meant they wouldn't be starting from scratch; there'd be some familiar faces to help them get settled.

Then, on 31 July, 1962, the news dropped that would change everything. A deal had been struck about New Guinea, and just like that, it was handed over to Indonesia. For Boy and Anita, it felt like the final piece of their world, the Dutch East Indies they knew, was slipping away.

The 15th of August, 1962, marked the day it all became official. The 'Treaty of New York', also known as the 'Plan Bunker', was signed off by the Netherlands, Indonesia, and the United Nations, outlining the future of Western New Guinea without any input from the people who called it home. The Papuans, who were promised a say in their future, were left out in the cold, their voices drowned out by political manoeuvring. Their protests and banners, questioning the price of their homeland, went ignored. The treaty flipped their world upside down, not just for the Papuans but for the Dutch Indos like Boy and his family too. The details of the agreement, which spread quickly, only added to the sense of loss, despite many having already made plans to leave, sensing the end was near.

With the ink dry on the agreement, a ceasefire kicked in right away, and a UN team rolled in to make sure everyone played by the rules. The Dutch military pulled back, while the navy and air force kept watch over the area. Meanwhile, the Indonesian infiltrators, all 1500 of them, had to lay low, now under the watchful eye of the UNTEA, the United Nations Temporary Executive Authority. By 1 October, 1962, Dutch New Guinea was no more, handed off to a UN interim administration. Rolz-Bennett from Guatemala took the reins, tasked with keeping the peace alongside the General Police and a small UN security force, mostly made up of Pakistanis, with a little help from American and Canadian air support. Commanded by Said Uddin Khan, they were the new law in town, marking a final end of an unforgettable period for Boy, Anita, and everyone else caught up in the shifting sands of history.

During the initial transition period up to 1 May, 1963, there was a clear rule: no Dutch or Indonesian could be in charge of the top eighteen jobs in the administration. By the time 1 October rolled around, most of the Dutch civil servants, Boy included, had already made up their minds to leave New Guinea. To fill the gap, thirty-two international staff were brought in, and eleven Dutch officials stayed on with UNTEA to help keep things running smoothly.

But May 1963 was the real turning point. New Guinea was about to become Irian Barat, or West Irian, officially under Indonesian control. Right after the switch, the New Guinea Council was shut down, marking the end of an era.

For my parents, this felt eerily familiar. It was like a replay of their departure from Makassar in 1950, another tough goodbye, another forced move. Once again, they found themselves packing up a life they'd built with love and hard work, not for a return trip, but for a one-way journey. Leaving behind their cozy stone house in Dok V, a place they'd made their own with its three rooms, indoor plumbing, and the doors they'd leave open to catch the breeze and the views — closing those doors felt like closing off a piece of their hearts.

The thought of saying goodbye to their Papuan friends, to the life they'd known in the lush jungles of New Guinea, sent a chill through them. It was a harsh reminder of how much they were leaving behind, not just a home but a whole world of memories and connections that had become as much a part of them as their own skin.

For Boy, the time had come to leave New Guinea, a departure that weighed heavily on him. The thought of not seeing another sunrise or sunset there was a bitter pill to swallow. As Torey, a Papuan, put it, the chapter of Dutch history in West Papua had closed.

According to the New York Agreement, Boy, one of the eighteen high-ranking officials named, was required to step down from his role as the head of the Government Information Bureau. His position was handed over to Ali Khalil, an Egyptian representative, who would hold the post until 1 May, 1963.

The departure wasn't a solitary affair. Boy, alongside friends like Ecky

Dankmeyer, Han ten Cate, and about a hundred others who were evacuating, joined the last Dutch Governor-General, Dr. Pieter Johannes Platteel, in his final moments on the island. During his goodbye, Dr. Platteel urged the people to support the incoming United Nations administration, which promised to look after the safety of New Guinea's inhabitants.

On 28 September, 1962, a significant send-off took place for Pieter Platteel. He was escorted by José Rolz-Bennett, the top UN official, Brigadier-General Said Uddin Khan, and several Papuans. A guard of honour, including members from the Royal Land Forces, Air Force, Navy, Papuan Police, and the Papuan Volunteer Corps, stood by as Platteel made his last inspection of the 'Pakistani UNTEA Honour Guard', a part of the UN's security force. The inner thoughts and feelings of the Governor during these moments remained private, but it was clear he, like everyone else affected by the transition, was deeply sad and disappointed. This was not just a personal farewell but marked the end of an era for the Dutch kingdom in the region.

The Platteel party left from Sentani strip, heading first to the coral island of Biak. From there, they'd start a long journey back to the Netherlands on 1 October, flying KLM via a route that stitched together Tokyo, Hong Kong, Bangkok, Beirut, Athens, and Vienna, before finally landing in Amsterdam on 25 October, 1962. It was a one-way trip, a final farewell to the life they had known.

Boy had his flat blue KLM suitcase with him, a parting gift from the airline. As he boarded the plane, he was leaving behind more than just a location. He was saying goodbye to a paradise, to friends, and to a life filled with memories. On the plane, hidden behind dark sunglasses, Boy couldn't hide his emotions. With tears in his eyes and a lump in his throat, he was among many who felt the weight of this departure. I can only guess, but speaking must have been hard for him, choked up with emotion as he was at the thought of leaving his home behind.

Home wasn't just a place for Boy; it was the bay where he lived, the docks where he worked, the bush, the water, the air, and the people — both Dutch and Papuan — who shared in this journey. The pain of leaving was intense, a mix of sorrow and loss tearing at him. As he sat there, memories of his colonial years in the Dutch East Indies and New Guinea played back like a movie, marking an end of a long period.

In his heart, Boy was probably sending a silent message to the friends he left behind, a promise of remembrance and a wish for their safety: "So sorry you are on your own again. Until we meet again, take care of yourselves, dear Papuan friends."

On 1 October, 1962, the skies over Hollandia opened up, pouring down rain like it hadn't in ages. That day, under the heavy rain, the flags of the United Nations and the Netherlands flapped side by side — a sight never seen before. It marked a big change: for the first time, the UN was taking over a whole area, stepping in to govern.

The handover happened early in the morning, at 8 a.m., on the Imby field. There was this instant during the ceremony, broadcasted on the radio, that really hit everyone hard. The announcer, his voice shaky, made it clear this was a big deal. He said, in Dutch first, then in Malay, that everyone was about to hear the Papuan folk song for the very last time on this broadcast. "Papuans, keep this song in your hearts," he said. It felt like a punch to the gut, knowing it was the end of something big.

After that, things felt different, like everyone was left hanging. Sukarno of Indonesia had made promises to be fair to the people of mixed European-Asian descent, but given his track record, people were skeptical. And sure enough, his eyes turned to New Guinea, aiming to scoop up the last bits of what used to be Dutch territory in the East Indies.

Leaders from Papua, fellows like Nicolaas Jouwe, Zacharias Sawor, and Marcus Kaisiëpo, ended up stuck far from home, feeling totally ditched. It wasn't just the Netherlands that let them down — it felt like the whole world did, including the big players like the United States and the UN. This just cleared the path for Sukarno to go after New Guinea without much in his way.

As soon as 1963 rolled around, and Indonesia officially took over, renaming it West-Irian, everything changed for the Papuans. They were told their anthem and the Morning Star flag, symbols of their identity and freedom, were off-limits. Singing that song or flying their flag was like asking for trouble, the kind that could land you in prison for years.

It was a rough time, with folks trying to hold onto who they were while everything around them was trying to snuff that out.

Sukarno had his eyes on the prize — New Guinea's untouched riches. The Netherlands had never tapped into the vast deposits of copper, gold, and cobalt lying beneath the island's surface. So, in 1962, Indonesian paratroopers descended into the jungle, moving towards the barracks left by the Dutch army, which had been working towards setting New Guinea on a path to independence.

The highlands of Papua were known since 1936 to be a treasure trove of high-grade ores. Yet, it wasn't until the mid-60s, under the guidance of an American mining company, that the region started to be mined for copper, gold, silver, and nickel. West Papua quickly gained a reputation for having the biggest gold and copper mines on the planet, not to mention other bountiful resources like oil, gas, and sought-after tropical hardwoods like ironwood and ebony. Despite this wealth, the Papuans, especially those in urban areas, saw little improvement in their living conditions.

In 1969, Indonesia organised a referendum among the Papuan population — the Act of Free Choice — as part of the sovereignty transfer agreement, giving Papuans a say in whether they wanted to join Indonesia. But this vote didn't exactly meet the international standards for fairness. It was conducted using the Javanese Moshawara System, with 1,025 delegates handpicked by Indonesia, which hardly represented the entire population. The chosen few, tribal elders, and village chiefs, voted for integration, but the wider Papuan dream of independence didn't fade.

By 1965, the first seeds of resistance were sown in Manokwari with the founding of the *Organisasi Papua Merdeka* (OPM), or Free Papua Movement, under the leadership of Permenas Awom, a sergeant from the Papuan Volunteer Corps. The Morning Star flag was adopted as the symbol of their fight for freedom.

Fast forward to March 2024, the OPM is still very much active, continuing its struggle for the independence of the Republic of West Papua. They're not just fighting on the ground; they're making their case on the international stage, pushing for the rights and self-determination of the indigenous Papuan Melanesians at the United Nations in New York.

Joy of life in New Guinea

# Part V
# Crisscross through New Guinea
## 5. Expeditions to almost impassable paths

Magic and

the rich culture of the Papuans

Father and son. Kapaukoe, Wisselmeren

# 5.1 The unique people of New Guinea

Boy's time with the Papuans was packed with moments that you'd have to see to believe. He found himself in situations that could make you laugh one minute and have you on the edge of your seat the next.

*T*o him, the Papuan peoples were fascinating, not just because of how they lived but because of their flair for making something out of nothing, their traditions, and their way of seeing the world.

Calling everyone from New Guinea "Papuan" is a bit like saying everyone from Europe is the same. It doesn't quite fit because there's so much variety among them — different languages, customs, and ways of life.

While they're all called Papuan, their languages split into two main groups: Melanesian and Papuan, with over 100 languages and 800 dialects scattered across the island. The word "Papua" itself has a couple of stories behind its origin. Some say it comes from the Malay *"poewa-poewa,"* referring to their frizzled hair. Others think it's from *"Papa-Ua,"* a term from the Sultan of Tidore meaning "not united" or "not involved", which kind of fits when you think about how spread out and varied everyone is there.

The island's rough terrain — mountains, rainforests, marshlands, and tricky rivers — played a big part in keeping its people apart. Coastal Papuans, of average height, and the shorter mountain dwellers, sometimes called "dwarf Papuans," lived very different lives, hardly ever crossing paths. These mountain people, possibly the island's oldest residents, don't often grow taller than 1.55 metres. Village life was typically small-scale, with populations rarely exceeding a few hundred. The various tribes kept to themselves, mistrusting and sometimes warring with their neighbours over ancient sorcery beliefs.

Although being neighbours, they had so little contact with each other. Villages were small, often no bigger than a hundred people, and seeing a crowd bigger than three hundred was rare. Trust wasn't easy to come by, and fights between tribes weren't unusual, often sparked by old rivalries or accusations of sorcery. Yet, despite these differences, everyone pretty much agreed on one thing: not much care for someone telling them what to do. In Papuan society, it didn't really matter who you were; everyone was seen as equal.

Despite these divisions, Papuan society was notably egalitarian, showing little deference to authority figures. Their diets reflected their environments: mountain communities relied on sweet potatoes and cassava, while coastal groups fished and harvested sago from wild palms. Processing sago was a labour of love, taking about two weeks to beat and rinse the starch from the palm for a supply that could feed a family for months. Sago larvae, a protein-rich delicacy, were enjoyed raw or roasted. Along the coast, coconut palms were indispensable, providing food, drink, and materials for building.

Sago, food of the nation of New Guinea

My shell necklace from the Wisselmeren

Papuans live close to nature and create their clothes and jewellery from natural materials.

Papuans have this amazing way of living right alongside nature, and it shows in pretty much everything they do, especially in what they wear and the stuff they use daily. You could see it in their clothing and jewellery, all crafted from the bounty the land offers.

For the men, wearing a '*koteka*' is the norm. It's like this tube made from a dried-out gourd that they wear around their privates. It's practical and works for them. The ladies stick to skirts made from whatever's handy, like grass or leaves, or sometimes they use tree bark. It's all about using what the environment gives you.

In the bigger places, like Hollandia, you'll see Papuans dressing a bit more like what you'd expect in a city, wearing shirts and pants, which is totally different from the traditional wear. Mums carrying their babies around in these handmade nets called '*nokkeng*' is something else. They're made from fibres of orchids or pineapples and even have a bit of tree bark thrown in for extra support so the little ones have more room and won't get all tangled up. These nets aren't just tossed together; they're carefully crocheted, using hooks made from bird bones.

Hunting's a big deal for getting food, and they're all about making their tools. Canoes are carved straight out of tree trunks using stone axes, which is no small feat. And pigs, well, they're pretty valuable, sometimes even more than money or other things. They use these cowrie shells as money too, which is pretty cool.

There are still places where people hadn't seen much of the outside world until not too long ago. Like, the whole concept of a band-aid was alien to them. And some groups, like the Asmat, they don't bother with clothes at all.

Their rules about what's right and wrong, their adat, are way different from what the Dutch brought over. There was this big mess over in the *Wisselmeren,* (Change lakes) with the Obano Rebellion because their way of dealing with serious accusations was to sort it out with arrows. The Dutch had to step in to calm things down.

Aerial photograph Wisselmeren

Wisselmeren

Lady with her handmade basket, Waropen, Geelvinkbaai

Papuan lady. Basket maker

Woodwork with stone axe, Baliem Valley

The Papuans are very creative when it comes to decorating their bodies or utensils.

Sturdy man. Baliem Valley

And then there's the way they live, like the Korowai tribes in the Baliem Valley,  making these incredible tree houses way up high or how every tribe has its own take on art, be it carvings, jewellery, or how they build things. It's all about making do with what's around them — bones, bamboo, you name it. They've got this whole system figured out that works with their way of life and keeps them close to their roots.

Asmat men's house, Baliem Valley

Asmat, Baliem Valley

Two young ladies having fun

Playing with spears

Pigs, the richest possession in New Guinea

# 5.2 PAYING WITH PIGS FOR A WOMAN

On his trips, Boy saw firsthand some unique traditions among the Papuans, especially in how men and women interacted. They kept to separate quarters — men in their communal houses and women and children in theirs, meeting only in the forest, away from their living spaces.

*L*ife for the Papuans was a mix of hunting, fishing, and a deep love for music, dance, and singing. They came alive during their celebrations, all decked out in elaborate gear — feathers, painted faces, or bodies smeared with mud — coming together to celebrate. They'd drum on the *tifas* and dance till the first light of dawn broke through the darkness.

Tribal loyalty was everything. Being part of a tribe meant you were looked after — food, a place to live, safety — all covered. In return, your loyalty to the tribe was unwavering. You'd support your tribe members, especially those in charge, no questions asked. Wealth wasn't about how much cash you had but about what you contributed to the tribe. The chiefs were respected figures, thought to be wise and even magical.

Agriculture and pigs were their bread and butter. When it came to marriage, pigs were literally the currency. The Baliem Valley had this system where a man's wealth was measured by the number of wives and pigs he had. Getting married meant a man's family had to trade, often around five pigs, for a bride. Sometimes, it wasn't just pigs but also shell money, food, or other goods changing hands. Even big parties and celebrations had pigs at the centre of it all.

Men shared living spaces in what's known as men's houses, built on stilts a good way off the ground, while women and children stayed up in treehouses, safe from any threats. These communal men's homes weren't just simple structures; they were built to last, raised on a forest of poles, a testament to the communal and structured way of Papuan life.

## Magical thinking

Boy really got the hang of how the Papuans think and live. They're big on spirits and honouring their ancestors, which is a huge part of their culture. Boy saw them doing rituals to try and make stuff happen or change things, using spells and special items to call on powers beyond what we see. To him, it felt like there's a whole side of Papuan life that's just beyond most people's understanding.

Even with Christianity making its way in, the Papuans didn't just drop their old ways. They kept their traditions alive, which Boy really respected. He saw them pushing for a better future, getting involved in schools and hospitals, but also noticed some folks preferred to stay out of the spotlight, sticking to the quiet life.

To Boy, it was clear they weren't out to cause trouble. They had a solid sense of community and respect for each other, which made him feel safe around them.

When it comes to religion, the Papuans are all about spirits — the good ones and the not-so-good ones. They believe these spirits are all around, keeping an eye on things. That's why they have all these ceremonies and rituals, to keep the spirits on their good side. But it's not all smooth sailing; they're pretty cautious about spirits, especially the ones they think might be up to no good. They have rituals to deal with those too, even using needles on themselves to keep the spirits at bay. And when it gets dark, that's when they're really on edge because who knows what's lurking out there.

Rain was always messing things up for the Papuans, especially when it came to their hunting gear. The extra moisture would slacken their bows, leaving the arrows too limp to be of any use. But for the Papuans, life wasn't just about the practical stuff; their beliefs in spirits and honouring ancestors were woven into pretty much everything they did. They saw the world around them — the sky, the moon, the sun, the stars, and the sea — as realms filled with meaning.

They've got this strong tradition of passing down stories, which helped keep their culture and beliefs alive. From when they were just kids, they were brought up to respect their ancestors.

Boy got to be part of something really special in the Asmat region – the *Bisj* festival. It's a ceremony all about the spirits they believe in, and Boy said those three nights he spent there were something he'd never forget. They'd bring in these big tree trunks to the chief, and from these, they'd carve out Bisj poles. These weren't just any poles; they were carved to represent ancestors, sort of like they were standing on each other's shoulders.

The whole thing went on for several nights, and it was during this time that they believed the spirits would come back to the villages they used to live in. The Papuans would dance to music played on their homemade instruments, and there was this promise made to the spirits — that they'd seek revenge on their enemies. At the festival's end, they didn't just leave the Bisj poles lying around. They placed them out among the sago palms in the forest. The idea was that the spirit of the deceased, now in the pole, would pass on to anyone who ate from those palms, making sure there was always plenty of food for the Asmat people.

Tifa with snake skin. On the right Bisj pole with ancestors standing on each other's shoulders

Bisj pole with tsjémen, made of tree roots, on which enemy skulls hung

Mourning Marind woman, with braided sago strands

Asmat Papuan, Baliem Valley

# 5.3 TOUR ON THE ISLAND

Boy was right at home in Dutch New Guinea. He thrived on the adventure, roaming into places where it felt like time hadn't moved, meeting all sorts of Papuan tribes, headhunters included.

## Southwest New Guinea. The Asmat region

*H*anging out with the Asmat was a huge deal for Boy. They're a group with a real talent for creativity, something that caught Boy's attention right away. But the Asmat have a bit of a rep for being headhunters, which is part of what makes their corner of Southwest New Guinea so mysterious.

Their culture's rich, filled with amazing carvings and a spiritual life that's pretty intense. They believed in keeping things balanced by head-hunting and even practiced cannibalism. They lived off the land, getting their food from the forest and the sea, like sago, jungle animals, and fish. To stay safe from floods and any unfriendly neighbours, they built their homes way up in the trees.

Art's a big thing for them. Next to Bisj poles they made shields, and even the backs of their canoes are works of art, shaped like fish, birds, or people, and coloured with natural dyes. Their war shields and the skulls from their raids were decked out in scary patterns, kind of like a warning sign to anyone who might want to mess with them. They also made these figures called *korwais*, which were sort of like statues that housed the souls of the dead, who they'd then ask for advice.

Music was another way they kept in touch with their ancestors. The

Asmat made their drums out of a whole piece of wood and used them to feel closer to their ancestors. They put beeswax on the snakeskin part of the drum to make sure it sounded right. These drums had special designs or pictures on them that meant a lot spiritually.

When someone died because of fighting or what they thought was witchcraft, the Asmat saw it as something that shouldn't happen. Families would often look to settle scores after such deaths. Bisj poles were a big deal for remembering the dead and for their ceremonies. They made these poles from nutmeg tree trunks, and they were pretty tall, around five meters. They put pictures of ancestors and people who had recently died on these poles. The top of each pole had a part sticking out, called *tsjémen*, where they'd hang the skulls of their enemies. This was a way of showing their strength and remembering their conflicts.

The people who were good at making these Bisj poles used old-school tools like animal teeth, shells, and stones to do their work. This wasn't just about making something look good; it was their way of keeping in touch with the past and honouring those who had passed away.

Back in the day, the idea of dying from natural causes didn't really sit well with many Papuans, especially the Asmat. They had this belief that they came from the trees themselves, carved from wood, which made the forest feel like an extension of their community. Because of this deep connection, headhunting, especially down south, wasn't just some random act of violence — it had its place in their society.

When someone in the family passed away, the women had their own way of showing grief. They'd wear these mourning outfits made from braided sago strands around their necks. The heavier the outfit, the more important the person who died was to them. Mourning meant putting life on pause — no parties, fishing, or even eating. It's no surprise then that women were pretty keen on getting through this period quickly. But the mourning only really ended when the men brought back skulls from their raids. Skulls were also key in arranging marriages; the more skulls a man had, the more appealing he was. So, it kinda made sense that women were supportive of headhunting.

The Asmat believed that if things were going south in their village, it must be because enemies had cursed them. They'd sleep on the skulls of those enemies, thinking it gave them powerful protection. This belief made headhunting more than just revenge; it was a way to strengthen the whole community.

Around 1951, it was estimated that about a thousand heads were taken each year in South New Guinea, not even counting other killings. The local government thought even that number might be low. When someone died, the blame usually fell on sorcerers from rival tribes, believed to be trying to weaken them. Taking an enemy's head was seen as a way to grab some extra life force for themselves and their people.

Victories and successful hunts were big deals, marked by ceremonies where men would dress up, decorating themselves with chalk, natural dyes, and headdresses made from the feathers of parrots or Birds of Paradise. These birds, with their stunning feathers, were seen as creatures of paradise, earning them the title 'birds of the gods'. Hard to catch, living high in the trees, they were symbols of unity for the Papuans, playing a big role in their celebrations and passed-down traditions.

Bird of Paradise. Bird of the Gods

## The Casuarine coast, Southwest New Guinea. With the most primitive of the primitives

Boy said: "It is a revelation every time you come to these kampongs to see the most primitive of the primitives."

They greeted each other, "Omen, omen." "Hugh!"

## An outpatient clinic in the wilderness

In October 1957, Boy was asked to accompany the second medical expedition to the then almost unknown, area, which was part of the Asmat. In his journal, he shared some wonderful reflections and wrote about his long and impressive journey, which began in Merauke. Here he experienced how the Papuans on the Casuarina Coast reacted to white men.

## An extract from Boy's journal, 'Reflections on a medical patrol' Expedition 29 October/November 1957

A few people realised that in this century there were still areas where time seemed to have stood still. One of these areas is the Casuarina Coast in the Southwest of Dutch New Guinea, unknown to many as most of the villages and rivers, which flowed here, did not appear on any map. Dutch pioneers, like Doctor Visser were drawn to this part of the country. As a leader of this team Dr. Visser wanted to protect the population in the area from this disease, Framboesia. The anti-Framboesia campaign was considered necessary before a Government settlement could be established there.

Framboesia was an infectious tropical disease, which mainly affected the skin, covering it with ulcers. It also affected the bones which at a

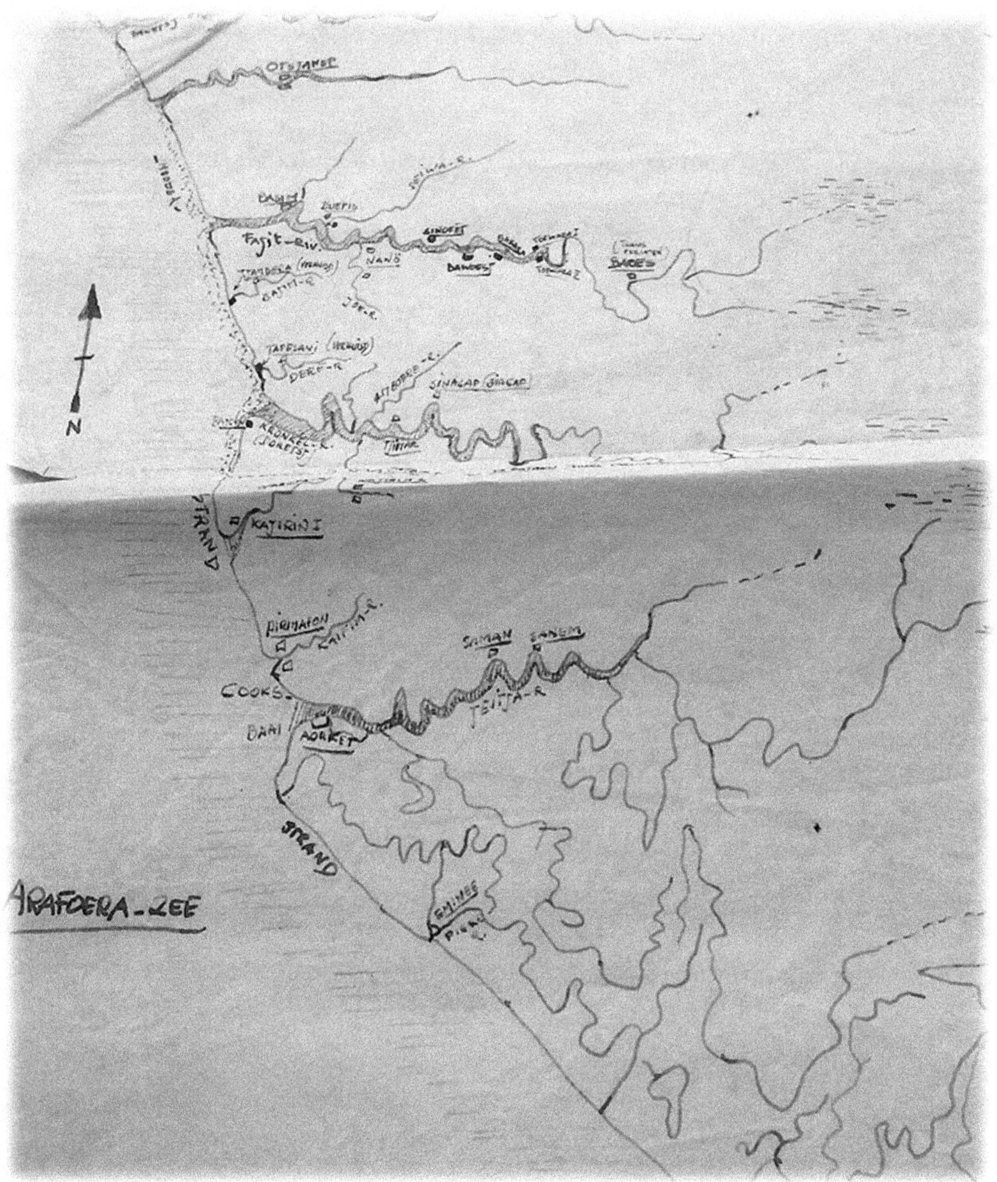

Map of the Casuarina Coast, drawn by Boy

Boy in conversation with doctor Visser and the Chief constable

later stage became deformed. Hundreds of flies sat on those sores and caused terrible suffering. Children were mainly affected by Framboesia. The name was derived from the raspberry-like growths on the skin, which was related to the bacteria of Syphilis.

This medical team travelled with two patrol vessels, a larger one called 'Tasman', named after Abel Tasman, the Dutch seafarer and explorer, and a smaller one called 'Eendracht', Unity. The expeditions in April and October/November 1957 aimed to vaccinate the population against Framboesia on the Casuarina Coast. The vast majority of the inhabitants had never seen such larger sailing vessels before, and the team wondered how the inhabitants would react to vessels larger than proas and to white men. These questions remained open for now.

The expeditions were under the auspices of UNICEF and WHO, the World Health Organisation. The entire population of the jungle on the Casuarina Coast, was to be inoculated with a penicillin injection PAM, to cure them of Framboesia. It was important to reach as many people as possible to either cure them or prevent them from getting the disease. Because the disease could easily spread among the entire population even if there was just one infected person.

The medical team travelled to all the villages on the Casuarina Coast. Most of this area had not been mapped. Only a few white men, mainly missionaries had been here before, because this was headhunter country. Many tribes had been converted to Catholicism and practised a mixture of Catholicism and their traditional customs. Funnily enough these headhunters often wore rosaries around their necks.

Doctor Willem Visser gives PAM injections, Casuarina coast

Thanks to Catholic Fathers Verschueren and Meuwese, this region was developed. Both of them belonged to 'The Sacred Heart Missionary' on the South coast of New Guinea. By working for many years among the Papuans, they had acquired knowledge of their cultures and dialects. On one of their trips, the Fathers discovered a new river, which was recognised on 6 September 1948, the day that Dutch Queen Juliana was inaugurated. From then on the Dutch Government called this river Queen Juliana River.

The Casuarina Coast was a strip of about one hundred kilometres which included its hinterland and was known as one of the most wild and unknown areas of Dutch New Guinea, because of the headhunter and cannibal tribes. These tribes lived in fear of evil spirits and their neighbours. In this area, nobody could be sure of not being killed or being victims of barbaric tribal acts.

After a few days, we arrived at Queen Juliana River, the beginning of the Casuarina Coast. They had named this coast after the Casuarinas, a type of pine tree which grew on sandy soil, but were only sporadically seen here. Perhaps the Casuarina trees were destroyed during the time of the military expeditions in 1910.

Fortunately for us, the weather had cleared up. The Arafura sea, also called one of the most dangerous in New Guinea, could be very daunting, but was now remarkably calm.

If limestone, made from burnt shells, was shot at you from a bamboo tube, it meant a declaration of war. When on the warpath large white limestone smudges and stripes covered their bodies. It was quite a gruesome sight to see dark faces with white chalk rings around their eyes coming towards you. Contact with these people was difficult. As an introduction, one party shouted "Omen, omen", after which the other party collectively shouted "Hugh" in chorus. When the other party shouted "Omen, omen", we shouted "Hugh" and finally together "Omen, omen" and together again "Hugh". It was quite a frightening sound when you heard 'Hugh' being shouted by hundreds of men.

When we approached a kampong, the Papuan villagers usually raised their hands to fend off evil. Hands carved from wood were often found at entrances of these wild kampongs. The wooden artefacts found here were more beautiful than any other in New Guinea. It seemed unusual to see the primitiveness of life combined with the romanticism of their myths.
When entering their own kampongs, the inhabitants also raised their hands which dated back to an ancient ritual called Papish.

Buepisj resident on the Casuarina Coast

Our strategy was as follows. We sail up the river in proas or with an outboard motor until we reach a kampong. We would try to win the trust of the Papuans, so the whole village could be vaccinated. Then we would set off for the next village.

We waited at the mouth of the Fajit River until the water rose again. Our patrol boat 'hung' in a seemingly endless plane of dirty grey mud. Slowly, as if searching for balance, the Tasman began to rise again.

While waiting for the water to rise hundreds of 20-centimetre-long whitefish, 'blanaks' jumped along both sides of the vessel and the Papuan crew caught the fish.

The next day we left early in the morning to take advantage of the high tide. We sailed across the Fajit River again to Kampong Basjiem. The people of Basjiem had made a platform for Doctor Visser to work on. There were at least five hundred people in the kampong, but it remained to be seen whether all of them could be reached.

The clothing of these people was extremely simple. All the men were completely naked. A few wore string necklaces around their necks of human vertebras. Their noses were also pierced and decorated with ornately carved pieces of bone or bamboo. Pieces of shell were worn on their forehead and chest. In their hair, they wore hair extensions. These were usually made of reeds, however sometimes the extensions were made of clay balls or human hair. The men's faces and chests were painted orange and occasionally painted black or white. Unmarried women walked around naked, married women wore reed skirts, which were pulled together between their legs. The women's faces and chests were usually painted orange. Some had nose decorations like the men.

All the kampongs on the Casuarina Coast were visited by this expedition, and lots of the camp residents were vaccinated against Framboesia. In Kepi, we were relatively close to the Casuarina Coast, which was as the crow flies, but the journey over land was not easy. Upon the advice of Father Meuwese, we decided to sail up the Wildeman (Wild man) River, and then over the Eilanden (Island) River to Atsj. This Asmat kampong was a large one on the border of the recently established Administrative Post of Agats and the Casuarina Coast. More than a thousand people lived here together and were a much feared hunting group. Women and children who could barely defend themselves were also killed.

Atsj bordered the Casuarina Coast. Father Van Kessel was stationed here and the inhabitants of Atsj were already somewhat used to contact with Europeans. They were happy and excited about our arrival.

The arrival of a foreign boat usually meant they could get tobacco and maybe even knives. Although a Missionary now lived amidst these people in the kampong, their primitiveness had not changed. It was hardly a year ago when dozens of proas full of painted warriors set out on Eilanden River to undertake a large headhunt in the village upstream. More than a hundred heads were brought back and human flesh was eaten for days. Atsj was built on the right bank of the river. Hundreds of Papuan huts were built in a long row along the water. The soil was peaty and soft. The walls of the houses were made of gabba-gabba and the roofs were atap. All huts stood on stilts. Most of the houses on the Casuarina Coast had a rear exit through which one could escape by running into the forest in case they were pursued by other headhunters. However, in case of a big headhunt, not many people would be able to escape because the kampong would be completely surrounded and therefore the enemy would also be lurking in the forest.

The River Fajit is ahead of us, it was dead quiet in the jungle to our left and right. There was no sign of life. Our arrival had probably already been detected by hidden black eyes and this information had been passed to the Basjiem Kampong, the most powerful village on the Fajit River. We quietly motored our way into the Fajit. The river was at least 120 metres wide, fringed by high forests. The village Basjiem must be three kilometres further in and strategically placed at the bend of the river. At first it seemed as if there was no life in Basjiem. But then suddenly figures jumped out one after another from behind bushes. The Missionary, who stood at the foredeck of our vessel, made the sign of peace, bringing the fingertips of both hands together above his head and then spreading them out to both shoulders. Someone on our ship yelled "Omen, omen" and then the call back echoed over the water out of hundreds of throats, "Hugh". Contact had been made. We could safely go ashore.

In Basjiem there was a great deal of screaming going on. One Papua jumped into the river and pushed his head with black frizzled hair completely under water. Others followed him. They only surfaced for a instant and then dived back into the dark brown water. It was a local ritual to wash off all impurity before greeting the strangers.

A large, twelve-metre long proa, with the familiar bird motif, pulled away from the shore, with a man standing and wielding a three-metre long paddle. In fact, it was not a paddle, it was a spear, with a spherical widening at the end. It was Bietjekam, the 'Kepala Perang', War Chief who made his appearance. He had a large hole in his nose and braided bands around his arms and just below his knees. His hair was braided into little strands. He had sharp, piercing eyes and looked rather intelligent.

Bietjekam recognised the policeman who had, on a previous visit donated the Dutch flag. Bietjekam had been careful with this red-white and blue flag because it flew on a bamboo pole in front of his hut and looked brand new.

In Basjiem, Dr. Visser could only give 30 PAM injections, no more, because the rest of the inhabitants were just not interested and disappeared from the queue. At the end of Dr. Visser's tour, we returned to the village where those who had suffered from the hideous Framboesia and had been injected were now completely cured. Their enthusiasm at seeing the Doctor was so great that they lifted the Doctor up and licked his feet. Dr. Visser did not know how to hide his embarrassment.

During our journey by proa to the next kampong, there was some commotion when in the distance a proa fleet approached us from the direction of Basjiems enemy, Kampong Omadesep. These two kampongs were enemies so spears were brought out. The situation remained critical for a few minutes. Our nervous mood disappeared, when it turned out that these people came with peaceful intentions.

Then we visited the Kampongs Buepisj and Nanö with about 450 inhabitants. We were welcomed with repeated shouts of "Papish, Papish atère, Papish". Both men and women repeated this again and again. Papish was a well-known method, also among the Asmat, to restore the cosmic balance that had been disturbed by a special event. Our arrival at several of these kampongs meant that this was their first contact with whites and this was heralded this Papish cry.

These kampongs were built on mangrove cleared riverbank strips and were several hundred metres long but no more than 35 metres deep.

On both sides, the village was closed off by a guardhouse, through which men armed with bows and arrows kept watch. In the men's houses we saw rope-knotted dance masks, a kind of costume reaching to the waist and fitted with hoods in which there were large holes for eyes, noses and mouths.

Kampong Nanö was on either side of the Joe tributary and also stretched along the Fajit River for a distance of a hundred metres. It was a large kampong with an estimated nine hundred people. We saw lots of coconuts and many pigs. Some houses showed a facade decoration of pig jawbones. The houses were less solidly built than those in the other kampongs. Everything seemed to be derived from the Asmat culture, but less artistically crafted. The decoration of these people was much simpler. A single ochre coloured stripe on foreheads and chests, no wicker bands around ankles or arms. There were no elaborate nose ornaments but bamboo sticks. Their particularly long arms were striking.

After four and a half hours motoring past Nanö, we reached Kampong Baoes. This kampong was new and consisted of six houses with one men's house. The houses were built on poles up to six metres high. The emaciation of all the children, many women and older men was remarkable. They were expelled from their village and there was a shortage of sago, coconuts and bananas. The morgues here were filled with dead bodies, especially those of children.

We motored upstream for another half an hour, but then the river lost itself in Rawahs, swamps, which were no longer navigable by motorboat. It is worth mentioning that a few hundred metres beyond the village of Baoes, in a bend of the river, in the crown of some very tall iron wood trees, a fort had been built with holes in the floor to shoot arrows. This large fort, where at least many dozens could take refuge, was reached by means of ladders made of vines and was at least twenty metres above ground level.

We sailed up the winding Kronkel River. Firstly, we came into contact with people from Bajun, who welcomed us to their kampong, but they told us they were afraid of being killed and eaten by us. Upstream, about an hour and ninety minutes from the mouth, we found the Kampongs Tjimare, with about 600 inhabitants and Biagap with around 250 people. Upon arrival here we saw several men busy making proas. This was not done with stone axes, as might be expected, but with spatula-shaped wooden sticks that had been sharpened at one end. And this was used to beat the tree trunk into shape. The contact with these people was very friendly.

On proas we travelled up the Tjambit Kali, creek, a small tributary that flowed into the Kronkel River a few kilometres before the sea. After about an hour and a half paddling upstream we arrived at Kampong Bajun. Whereas mangroves and swamps had surrounded all previous villages, the landscape here took on a completely different character and reminded us of the Steppe land and Savannah landscape around Merauke. We travelled up the river with the outboard motor. About a quarter of a mile upstream, there was an isolated proa in which ten white-painted men were standing. Despite our powerful Johnson engine we could not catch up with this group. A little later we heard the tifas in the distance. This lasted for about five minutes, after which there was complete silence.

Bietjekam, the head of Kampong Basjiem, who was with us, repeatedly drew our attention to spies on both banks. He even predicted that we would be attacked by arrows before we reached the kampong. After ninety minutes of motoring, through a creek that became narrower and narrower with lots of driftwood, we reached the kampong, which appeared to have been abandoned in a hurry. Nets containing fish as well as utensils still lay on the bank. The kampong consisted of fourteen very large houses, on both banks of the creek, with their longitudinal axis in the direction of the current. Half an hour later we left, leaving behind some tobacco and other gifts.

The Mimika was waiting for us at the mouth of the creek. We now travelled on to the mouth of the Cook River. Here we visited Kampong

Aorket. Bietjekam was not very positive in his appreciation of the Cook Bay tribesmen. He strongly advised us against visiting these people, the presumed descendants of Captain Cook's attackers. He confided in us that the people of Aorket had been head hunting in Basjiem a few months before. Of course, they took heads back from Aorket. When we approached Kampong Aorket we saw Papuans releasing proas from the shore and pushing them into the sea. Before long our boat was surrounded by a large number of proas with Papuan men in them.They screamed excitedly and offered us ethnographic items, beautiful drums were offered to us, shields, spears, stone axes and other items. Their woodcarvings were particularly admirable. The bird motif was evident here as in the Asmat area. There were also snake motives, which were also found on the Marind-Anim in the Merauke sub-division. Many had beautifully carved knives made from human bone.

Warriors in their proas

Suddenly we saw a man with one of our knives in his hands, another with an axe and a third with a plate. It was then clear to us that this was a barter. Apparently, they had heard about our arrival and wealth from neighbouring groups. The village consisted of seven large houses on stilts. We didn't see any corpses here. It was estimated that there were about 400 inhabitants in the village. The enthusiasm of the people was enormous and their appearance was healthy and robust. There was no shortage of food. It was striking that these people showed their excitement with unusual dance movements. They moved their upper legs out and against each other, while their feet remained in one place. The men walked naked, the married women wore fibre skirts and most of them had beautifully coloured parrot feathers in their hair. They also painted themselves in the colours white, orange and black. Here, too, the cry of "Papish" was heard.

In contrast to what Captain Cook had written in his logbook about his landing in this bay in 1770, we did not see a single coconut tree. We did see Banana trees but there were no signs of agriculture. Part of our party spent the night in Kampong Aorket. This almost cost Bietjekam his life. When some Aorket people assumed he was asleep, they sneaked up on Bietjekam with bows and arrows. According to Bietjekam with the intention of killing him. But he was not asleep and when his attackers realised this, they ran away. Bietjekam, was very distraught when he told us his story the next morning. We were amazed and horrified that all this had happened in our presence. That day and the next we saw no trace of the people of Aorket. From now on contact with these people would be much more difficult.

Moving on to the next kampong, armed Papuans were waiting for us. Their Chief shouted an order and a Papuan blew a wooden horn. The medical team began injecting the population. Here, the team could observe the kampong life. We saw a sleeping Papuan using a skull as a pillow. We saw a family in a tree house, who had to come down for injections. We saw a kampong resident with a piece of bone through his nose. There were several elderly villagers here.

I left the team a bit earlier. From an estimated seven to eight thousand inhabitants of the Casuarina Coast, living in sixteen kampongs, I had visited about three thousand two hundred of them.

Poles house, Casuarina coast

## Baliem Valley, the mysterious heart

Boy found the heart of New Guinea mysterious, he was really into the Baliem Valley, finding it mysterious and super beautiful, packed with adventures.

Back in 1938, an American named Richard Archbold flying over in a seaplane spotted the valley by chance. He saw this huge, crowded valley surrounded by rocky bits and filled with green farming terraces. He was on a mission from the American Museum of Natural History and ended up being one of the first outsiders to see this place.

The Baliem Valley, about 80 kilometres long and 20 wide, was tucked away in the middle of Dutch New Guinea. Back in the '50s, it was pretty much off the radar, surrounded by big mountains with the Baliem River winding through it like a snake. The place had such a strong vibe it got nicknamed 'Shangri-La' because it felt kind of magical, like a secret spot that not many people knew about. It was called the 'White Heart' too, partly because it was a big unknown and partly because the highest peaks around it were always covered in snow.

By 1953, people could finally get there through Habbema Lake, on the west side. The area, sitting high up over 3,000 metres in the mountains, was all steep and rugged. Wamena, the only big town in the valley, was up at 1,650 metres by the Baliem River and got its first official setup in 1956.

This valley is where the Dani tribe lives. They're known for not backing down and have a strong fighting spirit. They've got good land and they protect it fiercely, sticking to their way of life even as the world keeps changing around them.

Getting to the Baliem Valley was no walk in the park for the Dani people. They had to push through thick jungles where daylight barely touched the ground. More often than not, they were moving in heavy rain, dealing with leeches, trudging through mud, and crossing creeks and rivers.

In Wamena, there was a Mission Post. The missionaries were among the first outsiders to reach Dutch New Guinea, introducing Catholicism to the Dani, who were considered among the least developed Papuans at that time. Besides the missionaries, there were plenty of Gospel Preachers around Baliem, too. The Dani were really looking forward to meeting Jettu, which is what they called Jesus. Every time there was news about visitors, hundreds of them would show up, hoping Jettu was among the arrivals. They'd even start celebrating at the sight of the seaplane still in the sky, but that joy quickly faded when they realised Jettu hadn't come, leaving them pretty upset and disappointed.

The Dani had a reputation for being the toughest around in Dutch New Guinea. They were well aware that other groups were wary of them. Dani tribes often ended up fighting among themselves, including with those from the western part of the valley, known as the Western Dani or Lani. You could spot a Dani from the way they dressed and adorned themselves: pig teeth through their nose, ears stretched with pig teeth, their curly hair slathered in grease, and their koteka decked out with feathers or just a bit of soil. They were into bright colours, especially feathers, and their spears were sharp and ready for action. They lived much like their ancestors did, way back in history, with their homes up in the trees.

The Dani had a simple but profound belief about where they came from. They thought that people, their ancestors, literally emerged from the ground in various parts of the valley, each bringing something important with them like kotekas, fire, tobacco, pigs, or sweet potatoes. That's how they believed life started. Even by 1955, this was still what they believed. The Dani had rich land at their disposal, making their territories quite valuable.

Standing on the roof of the world

Casuarina coast, sleeping Papuan with family member's skull as pillow

## Arfak mountains in Eastern Bird's Head
## Meeting Erika Mersinden, a notorious war Chief
## and man-eater

*Haagsche Courant*, The Hague newspaper, 9 April 1953
By Claude Belloni

'This was also government work in New Guinea'.

Momi was a charming village in the Oostelijke Vogelkop, Eastern Bird's Head of Dutch New Guinea. Here, early in the morning on the twelfth of March 1939, a group of forty five people was preparing for departure on foot, two white men, an interpreter, twelve policemen and porters from the wild Arfak Mountains. An important meeting was to take place between a white man and the infamous war Chief Erika Mersinden of the man-eating Manikion tribe.

The group consisted of the Governor of Manokwari, A. Lamers, the Controller of Exploration, Meylink who was later tragically killed, the interpreter Lodewijk, the policemen and the porters. They were aware that they had taken on, not only an extremely difficult, but above all a very dangerous mission.

Erika Mersinden, with whom the Governor had agreed through numerous intermediaries to meet at a certain place, had at that time no less than forty three registered murders on his conscience. Erika was a hunted man, the Dutch military and Government patrols had been after him for years. He was also a powerful man, although this power was based on fear. In every kampong he had his enemies. Erika had never been caught, he was too devious for that. People in these areas also attributed magical powers to him. The Manikions were also very much feared. They always had their bamboo spears with them on which they skewered human flesh.

In July 1936, the present Chief of Agricultural Affairs in Hollandia, then Controller Boendermaker, was chasing a group of Manikions. A Manikion boy had climbed into a coconut tree in a neighbouring kampong. He had fallen to his death. This was not natural - at least according to the Manikions - it had to have been the Soeangis, the evil and good spirits that govern the lives of the primitive Papuans, summoned by the inhabitants of the kampong.

It was therefore only fair that these kampong people should be put to death but the Manikions spared women or children. Some of the Soeangis makers were taken alive. What was left of them were heaps of white bones, and the occasional skull. This is what Boendermaker's patrol encountered. They could not catch the Manikions.

## Forced march

It was a forced march that the Lamers' group was going to undertake. That meant a considerable distance to the Anggimeren, Anggi Lakes, situated nineteen hundred metres high.

It would normally take a patrol five days. Lamers and his group were going to walk this march in just over a day. Lamers was a little late for his appointment. But he and his party made it, even though the utmost was demanded of them physically. Climbing, logging and wading through wild roaring streams over the 2,300-metre-high watershed.

Birds of Paradise flew over the patrol like bright yellow sunbeams. Sometimes a crown pigeon swooped very slowly over the heaving men. From time to time they came upon startled boars that gruntingly ran away in front of them.

When they arrived at the designated spot where they had agreed to meet Erika there was no one to be seen. Of course there was. You could feel it. That is why everyone in the patrol had the feeling that they were continuously being watched. It gave the men goose bumps. With difficulty they could shake it off. The presence of the patrol was clearly detected by the Manikions as they could clearly read the screeching calls of yellow-crested cockatoos.

To avoid being suddenly attacked from behind, the patrol halted against a steep cliff, on the boulders of a roaring river. Louis, the interpreter, managed to make contact. He shouted at random, in the direction where he suspected the Manikions were hidden. Yes, he got an answer. "Erika is not there. He has a big leg wound", an invisible speaker yelled out. He asked the patrol to come to the place where Erika would be waiting for the Tuan, Master Administration. This was the only place Erika was prepared to discuss matters. No police were allowed to accompany the patrol, only Kepala Lamers and some porters. The rest of the group had to stay behind. This was a setback. Deeper into the Manikion area, you could be robbed or eaten. But it had to be done. Lamers was going to speak to Erika. Lamers did take the police with him, six men with old Beaumont rifles. They left, praying to God for a safe return.

On the way heavily armed and dauntingly painted Manikions who were on warpath suddenly surrounded the small group. The Lamers group was helpless. Luckily these Manikions left the group unharmed. The closer they got to the place where Erika would be, the greater their fear grew. Minutes seemed like hours as they tried their best to keep walking. Where was Erika, anyway? And then, yes, there was someone. It had to be Erika Mersinden, surrounded by heavily armed bodyguards. It was him, a slender man of medium height. Lamers estimated him to be about fifty years of age. A koepiah on his head, like the Mohammedans wear, but made of a dull, black fabric. A sun with bright rays was tattooed on both his cheeks. On his leg was indeed a large, festering wound. The strangest thing was, that his face and limbs were coloured yellow and he appeared to be Mongolian.

At this moment, Erika was not hostile, although he seemed anxious. He calmed down when Lamers unwrapped the gifts. They were beautiful and strong articles, which Lamers had brought for this special occasion, shiny knives and axes and for Erika in particular a beautiful machete. Erika, however, had to promise Lamers to refrain from murderous activities as he now had to cooperate with the Government. Did he want to do that? Erika nodded yes, when Louis, the interpreter, asked him the question. Erika was willing to do this. Lamers told him he would be punished if he started killing and eating his fellow men again. Then the Tuan Administration would be terribly angry. But no, that was not what Erika wanted. Lamers also handed him a huge Dutch flag, the biggest he could get his hands on in Manokwari. Erika had to hang the flag out whenever an Administration patrol passed by his resort.

Erika also received for the occasion, from the Officer, a specially made uniform with big buttons, and an Ordinance enclosed in a bamboo case. In the Ordinance it stated that Erika had now been appointed Chief of the Manikions in the service of the Government of Dutch New Guinea.

However, Commander Lamers was not satisfied yet. He had to have some proof, which he could offer his Resident in Ambon, the Moluccans, that he had indeed met Erika. So he asked Erika Mersinden for one of his rifles in exchange. "Guns?" laughed Erika, he didn't own any, he said. Why does Tuan Administration think he owns a gun? Yes, Lamers insisted, he did know. After all, everyone around the Anggi Lakes knew that Erika did not move anywhere without his bodyguards armed with guns.

Come on, he couldn't come back to his Resident without something from Erika. The Tuan had to be able to show him that Erika Mersinden did indeed want to cooperate with the Administration, which Erika confirmed by giving Lamers one of his valuable rifles. It caused hilarity among the Manikions. What was that white man thinking now? That Erika, their feared Kepala Perang would give away one of his guns? There was a cacophony of amused voices. But Erika put a resolute stop to it. With the commanding gesture of a Prince, he ordered one of his guns to be picked up for him. "Sir must wait", he said. A little later, Erika handed Commander Lamers a neatly maintained preloaded rifle. It looked dangerous and it could do a lot of harm. And now back, Lamers thought. He would not stay another minute, afraid that Erika would change his mind.

Safe and sound, they reached the rest of the group and went home at breakneck speed. It was the success of the year. Lamers received a special congratulatory telegram from Resident Jansen.

The local newspaper in Hollandia, Dutch New Guinea, published the obituary of Erika Mersinden, the war Chief of the Manikion tribes in the Eastern Bird's Head. The Government in New Guinea had a lot to deal with a very elusive Erika, and this was attributed to the great power he had over the Soeangis, the evil and good spirits.The whites who had seen or met Erika while he was still alive were very few and far between. The first of them was the present Resident of North New Guinea, Mr. A. Lamers. At that time, in 1939, he was still Governor of Manokwari.

## Claude Belloni

Based on the story of Mr. Lamers to my father, Boy wrote and published the above article with the approval of the Resident.

Couple from the Baliem Valley

## Pas Valley
## Aeroplane disaster in the Pas Valley

What started as a fun trip to the Baliem Valley turned tragic when an American transport plane, the Gremlin Special, a Douglas C-47, crashed into a mountain ridge in the Pas Valley, just northeast of Baliem, at around 1600 metres above sea level. It was 13 May, 1945, Mother's Day back in the States, and the flight was meant to be a treat for those not on duty, including officers, soldiers, and members of the Women's Army Corps (WAC).

Out of the 24 people on board, only three survived the crash, while the others were laid to rest right there. The survivors, two injured and all in shock, began a tough journey towards civilisation, hoping for rescue.

When the plane didn't return, a rescue mission kicked off, starting with two medics parachuting in, followed by ten more troops for support. By mid-May, a B-17 bomber pilot spotted the survivors. The next day, they dropped supplies, including a walkie-talkie to establish communication. Pulling off the rescue seemed nearly impossible, but with a military C-47, a glider, and a Philippine-American parachute team, they managed to save the survivors on 1 July, 1945.

Among the survivors was Corporal Margaret Hastings from the Women's Army Corps. She's the one who later dubbed the Baliem Valley *"Shangri-La,"* inspired by the mythical place in James Hilton's "Lost Horizon." She shared enchanting tales about the valley and its people afterward. Lieutenant John McCollom came out without a scratch, and Sergeant Kenneth Decker, though badly hurt, made it through. It wasn't until 1958 that they retrieved the remains of the 21 servicemen who died in the crash.

In *"Lost in Shangri-La,"* Mitchell Zuckoff paints a vivid picture of the crash scene.

"The cabin had shifted more towards the cockpit. The walls of the fuselage had collapsed inwards. Both wings were torn from the fuselage. Like a balsa wood toy, the tail had broken off. Flames shot through the wreckage. Small explosions sounded like gunshots. Black smoke obstructed the light. The stench of burnt metal, leather, rubber, wiring, oil, clothing, hair and flesh increasingly filled the fresh air."

The survivors owed their lives to a last-minute decision by Captain Nicholson. In those final seconds, he likely only had a split second to see the danger ahead and instinctively pulled back on the yoke. This action raised the plane's nose, lessening the crash's severity and giving those not directly in the path of destruction a fighting chance to survive.

## Expedition aircraft wreckage

*Der Spiegel*, 19 November 1958
Claude Belloni

Walking through the mountains, a patrol which my father was a member of searched for the wreckage of a plane. They thought they knew where the wreck is. The question was how Kurilu, the ruler of the entire Baliem Valley and the 'terror of Shangri-La', who did not like white people, would behave.

> In the heavy mountain terrain of the Central Highlands, the 'white heart' of Dutch New Guinea, an Administration patrol, three white men, six Papuan policemen and a number of naked porters, struggled. The thin air visibly bothered Controller Rolph Gonsalves, Administrative Officer Pieter Bongers and the writer of this journal, Boy Belloni. The lack of oxygen at that altitude above two thousand metres made breathing very difficult.
>
> We had long left the governed area of the great Baliem Valley behind us. Now our feet moved with difficulty. We had to consider every step carefully where hardly no other European had walked.
>
> We were on our way to the wreckage of the American plane that had crashed into a ridge in the Pas Valley, Northeast of the Baliem on 13 May 1945, thirteen years ago.

Prepare yourselves for trouble, Controller Gonsalves told us anxiously before we left. He was referring to Kurilu, the most powerful tribal leader in the entire Baliem Valley. The Kepala Perang was certainly no friend of the whites. Only once did he show himself to Gonsalves. He did not like strangers in his area. American Missionaries who entered this area left at great speed. Kurilu was not to be played with. For this reason, the patrol in search of the crashed plane, was well armed.

Controller Gonsalves had previously used a tactic that turned out to be correct. He ignored the great chief. The reasoning was that it is not our place to interfere with him. Maybe then he would leave us alone. But now that we had reached the foot of the mountains and were preparing to climb, a small group of Dani came out of the great crowd of Papuans to meet us. They were unarmed. They did not have their three-metre long spears with them. They had also left their strong bows with the short, vicious arrows at home.

In front of us unbelievable stood Kurilu! This was our first contact with the gentleman, his hair was braided in little strands. It was thickly smeared with pig fat. The contact was rather awkward, until Bongers came up with the bright idea to use his mouth organ. In front of the astonished eyes of Kurilu and his warriors, he played it. The young Civil Servant managed to make up all kinds of sounds. Cosy Dutch tunes seemed to be able to appease the mighty chief. He stretched out his hand. The top two phalanges of each finger of his left hand had been cut off, as well as a few phalanges on his right hand, presumably as a sign of mourning at the death of a family member. In disbelief, he brought the instrument to his mouth and was startled when he, too, managed to produce a sound from it. He laughed. He was roaring with laughter. The ice was broken! Later, through the interpreter, Gonsalves explained the purpose of our trip. The wreck was familiar to Kurilu. "Shall I take the Tuans there?" he asked. Gonsalves accepted the offer with both hands and promised Kurilu a beautiful axe. Suddenly, the great chief was in a hurry. He pointed to the sun, which was indeed already quite high in the sky, and said: "Loe-ok". That meant something like 'Come on, let's go'. We would hear this word many times along the way. Kurilu, until recently still hostile to every white person, was now our friend, our guide. It was unbelievable! But with Kurilu with us, nothing could happen to us. It was Kurilu who, every time we rested from a climb, chased us and told us to move on. He was right. The population at this altitude was sparse and their villages were at great distances from each other.

The patrol must set up camp near a village so the Dani porters would not die of cold. The Dani porters were completely naked except for their koteka. It was as if they did not feel the cold. Or they pretended to be very tough, but I don't believe that. In the villages, there was regularly an empty hut. There was also always water.

Kurilu playing on Gonsalves' mouth harmonica

A ten-year-old boy, who had come along from a village on the way, held out his hand. It was embarrassing, but you accepted it. A little later, you regained some self-esteem when you heard a Papuan policeman was huffing and puffing heavily behind you. A half-rotted tree trunk was the only 'bridge' across a metres-deep cliff. You slid over it sitting down. This is how we struggled further, until we reached a village at around five in the afternoon. With the last bit of energy left in us, we set up a double-roofed tent that would be our shelter for the coming night. We ate rice with some canned roasted minced meat and it tasted like a meal fit for a King. Despite our tiredness on this first day, we felt good.

Dressed in two woollen blankets, a thick jumper and a windbreaker, long live the tropics! We rolled ourselves into a poncho to keep out the cold. Gonsalves held out the altimetre, which read 2,280 metres. "We had just passed the 2,300 metre mark and tomorrow we would have to cross two more watersheds at that height". We just nodded. At eight o'clock, the camp has sunk into a deep tranquillity and in the distance we could hear Dani singing in their village. Fatigue wrapped its painful bands around all our muscles.

All too soon, it was day again. The virgin forest, silent, wet and green, with dew. We broke up camp and the second day was a repeat of the first, climbing, descending, sliding, grabbing at branches and roots as we fell.

In the afternoon of the second day, we reached an enormous gorge in the mountain landscape, the Pas Valley where we expected the wreck of the plane to be. When we had set up camp, Kurilu came up to us, smiling broadly with his face covered in black pig fat. He had been given two pigs as a gift by the village Chief of Agetma, a village with less than a dozen inhabitants.

The village was a stone's throw from our camp. It was a welcome gift for our porters and policemen. Kurilu told us that the village helped the survivors in 1945. One of the Dani must be the man Margaret Hastings called 'Pete' in her stories! "That must be Pete!", one of us said. It was one of the first times that the Yali, who lived here and whose name meant people from over the mountains, had met Dutch people.

We reached the wreck on the third day. It was a climb of no more than fifty minutes but it was extremely tough. Suddenly, one of the Papuan policemen who led the way shouted: "Ada Tuan, There is the wreck!" The Gremlin Special C-47 had broken into three large pieces with the front part of the fuselage completely split open. The rear section was still in pretty good shape and presumably was the part from which the survivors had managed to escape. Another three metres below and another fifteen metres down we found the tail and engine that had broken off.

Split open fuselage part of plane wreckage, Baliem Valley

While we were taking photographs, Kurilu came to warn us about an imminent storm. He pointed to the sky, which was heavily clouded and told us that if we did not hurry, we would not be able to walk along the already slippery road. Moreover, at an altitude of 2,390 metres, the rain would be freezing. We took a few more photos and then returned to our camp. The goal had been achieved. We had found and located the wreckage of the American aircraft.

From an administrative point of view this incident forged a friendly relationship between the Dutch and Kurilu, the ruler of the Baliem Valley. The 'Terror of Shangri La'.

Asmat warriors in their war proa

## Asmat territory
## Expedition 'Search for Michael Rockefeller'

November 1961
By Claude Belloni

The art collector, Michael Rockefeller had gone on an expedition to the Asmat region to collect wood carvings but his boat suddenly had capsized. Boy was part of the expedition that was set up in search for Michael.

Michael Rockefeller, René Wassing and two Papuan guides had left on 18 November 1961 for their second expedition in the Asmat area. The first expedition to the Dani in the Baliem Valley had taken place several months earlier and ended in September 1961.

The aim of their second three-month expedition was to record on film the life and habits of the cannibals along the Southern coast. Michael also wanted to collect ethnological objects, such as shields, painted skulls, figurines and Bisj poles. All objects were intended to be collected for the Museum of Primitive Art in New York, founded by his father Nelson.

Wim van de Waal, an Administrative Officer in Agats, a coastal village of wooden houses on stilts above the mud, sold the men his homemade wooden forty foot catamaran. It was made from two local Proas connected by a platform and powered by an eighteen-horse-power petrol engine. The catamaran was filled with many barter items, like tobacco, knives, iron axes and clothing, among other things.

The Dutch officials were not very enthusiastic about this trip. With the two Papuans accompanying them they sailed for about three hours to Atsj, twenty five miles upstream from the coast. They had to pass the infamous junction where the Eilanden River met the Arafura Sea and where tides in Flamingo Bay were treacherous. Michael and René were warned about this by several people as well as by the Mission post in Agats whom they had visited earlier. The Priests considered the catamaran to be unsafe for making this trip.

Near the mouth of the wide Eilanden River, the sea was choppy. The water came in so hard that bailing out did not help anymore. The outboard motor was swamped and stalled. The heavy waves in the Arafura Sea eventually caused the catamaran to capsize which drifted on as a raft. The two Asmat Papuans were frightened and immediately jumped out of the boat and swam to the marshy shore to get help. Michael and René remained behind on the rounded bottom of the overturned catamaran. During the night they drifted further out to sea. Although both men were good swimmers, René refused to leave the boat. After a day and night Michael decided to swim to shore.

It took another day before the news of the capsized catamaran reached Hollandia and the search began. Everything that could sail or fly was used in the search. Neptunes, seaplanes, helicopters to naval planes were mobilised.

Meanwhile, the overturned boat had drifted far out to sea. A Neptune with pilot Rudolf Idzerda was the first to catch sight of the catamaran. There was only one man on it. A self inflating rubber raft was thrown into sea. René swam to the raft. To his surprise, there were provisions and water on board. There was also safety equipment. He used the torches to mark his position and this information was passed his coordinates on to his rescuers.

Eight hours later, René was picked up by a patrol boat. Michael Rockefeller was still missing. René explained that Michael thought he could swim to reach the coast. He had jumped from the catamaran with two empty red petrol cans as floats. Wassing had him in his sights for a long time but had finally lost sight of him.

Michael's father, Nelson Rockefeller, the then Governor of New York and later 41st Vice President of the United States and Michael's twin sister Mary arrived in Biak by a chartered jet plane and travelled on to Merauke. Along with them, an army of some seventy five journalists, photographers and filmmakers had arrived in the otherwise sleepy town and were accommodated in the Government hotel and in private homes. The Australian Air Force also sent a few helicopters. Help came from all sides. After a few hours' sleep, the two Governors,

Rockefeller and Platteel, Governor of Dutch New Guinea, held a press conference. Nelson and his daughter left the actual search to experienced investigators. They followed the progress of this search from the house of the District Commissioner in Merauke.

The crew of the Dutch navy ship, Snellius found one of the red jerry cans in the sea near Kampong Otsjanep. The petrol can was recognised off the coast and later confirmed by René that this was indeed the can that Rockefeller Jr. had taken with him. There was still no sign of Michael. A high reward for finding Michael was announced. Thousands of Papuans began looking for Michael and rumours grew.

On 28 November Nelson Rockefeller decided to return to New York. There was nothing more the family could do and he warmly thanked the Netherlands for everything that had been done so far. The search for Michael continued for some time but was given up on 22 December 1961.

Nelson Rockefeller sent a personal letter to Claude, thanking him for being part of the expedition that tried to find Michael. People had a lot of theories about what happened to Michael. Some thought he might have been attacked by sharks or crocodiles, or maybe he drowned. But there were also whispers that the local Asmat tribe could have had something to do with his vanishing.

Back in February 1958, there had been a pretty intense clash where four high-ranking Asmat were killed by Dutch colonial forces trying to put an end to headhunting. Some rumours suggested that Asmat had admitted to missionaries Van Kessel and Von Peij that they found Michael exhausted at the shore, took him on a boat, and then killed him with spears. This was said to be a revenge act for those killings in 1958. The missionaries, who knew the Asmat and their language well, were told by Bishop Tillemans not to spread this story.

To the Asmat warriors, taking a head was a significant act, without much thought given to who the person was. Michael, not fully aware of the local dynamics, had previously ordered wood carvings from Kampong Otsjanep, not knowing it was at odds with Omadesep, where his guides were from. Michael Rockefeller's disappearance remains a mystery. All that's clear is that he ended up in a place and a situation far beyond what anyone could have expected, with no definitive answers about his fate even to this day.

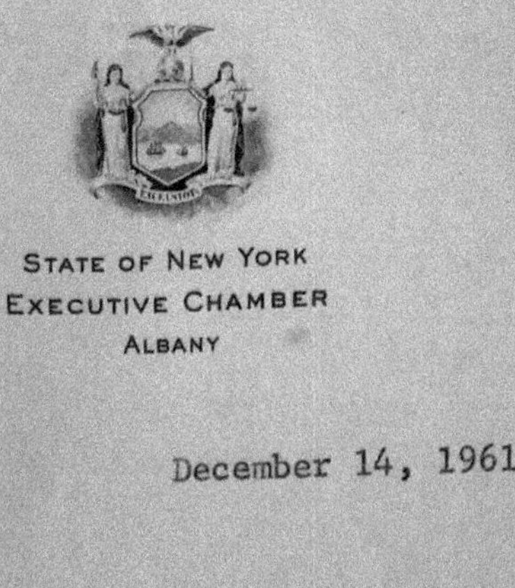



Thank you letter from Nelson Rockefeller to Claude

Anita, Louise, Renée , Scheveningen 1962

# FINALE
## PART VI
## BACK IN HOLLAND
## 6. IN THE COLD

Shivering around the Aladdin

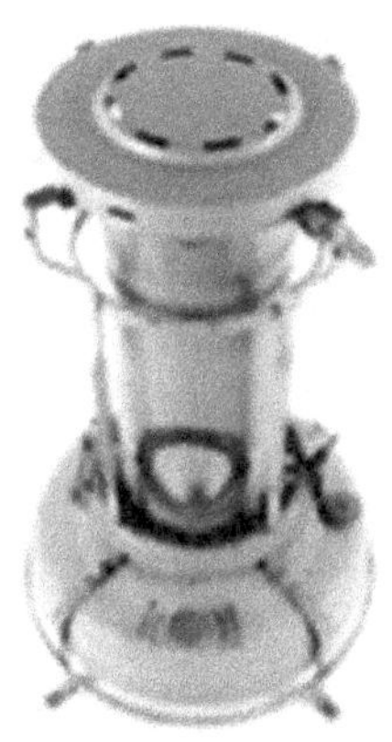

Aladdin petroleum heater

Winter in The Hague, 1962

# 6.1 HAVING HUTSPOT (DUTCH STEW)

Moving from the jungle to the *polder,* reclaimed land, was a huge shift for us. After soaking up the tropical heat for so long, the cold in the Netherlands hit us hard. We were pretty much in the same boat as those Indisch families who made the journey twelve years before us.

*T*hat wet autumn in 1962, my mum, Louise, and I went to pick up my dad from Schiphol Airport near Amsterdam. Boy was freezing the moment he stepped off the plane.

Us three had landed in Rotterdam on the M.S. *Willem Ruys* back in August and headed straight to The Hague. That's where we found ourselves living in a guesthouse on Barentzstraat, squeezed into the first floor like many Indisch families before us. For Boy, and Anita during their short leave before, The Hague was somewhat familiar territory. But for Louise and me, it felt like stepping into an entirely different world.

Walking around in a city that was totally new to me, in a country I wasn't used to, with weather that was anything but warm, was a shock. I missed the 30-degree Celsius warmth. The cold autumn, with its grey skies and biting fog, seemed to go right through me. Our daily walk to the shops took us past bare trees and along damp streets, and winter hadn't even started.

Our new home was up a long staircase with a red carpet, leading to a living room and two tiny bedrooms. Oddly, the shower was this tiny thing on the ground floor, tucked into a cupboard under the stairs. You had to feed coins into a meter for a quick, lukewarm shower — two minutes max. It felt like even folks with an outdoor shower at some old campsite had it better than us.

Cooking in our new place came down to working with just a single burner gas stove. How my mum managed to whip up meals for us on that, I'll never know, but she always pulled it off. She'd switch it up between making fried rice and Dutch dishes like *hutspot*, which is this mix of mashed potatoes, carrots, and onions with a spot for gravy and usually a meatball on top, or *zuurkool*, sauerkraut, mixed with mashed potatoes and chopped pickled cabbage, again making room for gravy and a smoked sausage. Between you and me, I was always more about the rice — whether it was plain white rice or *nasi goreng* (fried rice), that's always been my favourite.

When it got cold, which was pretty much always, we had this small petrol heater called an *Aladdin* to keep us warm. We'd lug it from room to room, trying to chase away the chill. But let's be honest, that heater was a bit of a joke. Cranking it up did make things a bit warmer, but then we'd be dealing with black smoke filling up the room, making it hard to breathe. Our windows were constantly frosted over with what looked like ice flowers. Yeah, it was that cold.

Those days were all about making do with what we had. Despite everything, families like ours found ways to get by. A lot of us felt like outsiders here, even coming up with the term INDO — *In Nederland Door Omstandigheden*, which means "In the Netherlands by Circumstances" to describe our situation. And that's pretty much how it was.

Even by the end of 1962, people from the Dutch Indies in Holland weren't really seen as one of their own. We were often mistaken for Indonesians or Chinese and got treated more like immigrants than Dutch natives. I remember being the only "dark one" in my class, and both my sister Louise and I faced our share of taunts at school. Kids would tease us, saying stuff like '*Pinda pinda, lekka lekka*' (Peanut, peanut, tasty tasty) and 'Indo Peanut Poo Chinese', even pulling at their eyes to mock us. Those moments stick with you. It was clear we were something new to the Dutch kids, something they hadn't quite figured out how to understand yet.

Dealing with teasing was tough for us. We couldn't understand why suddenly we were being called 'poo Chinese'. When we asked our mum about it, she explained it was because we looked different to the kids here, maybe our eyes or our darker skin. Being Indisch meant we stood out, not just by how we looked but how we sounded too. So, we ended up not playing much with other kids around or at school. Louise and I felt pretty left out, even though the Netherlands was supposed to be welcoming to us 'repatriates.'

Then, out of nowhere, the government dropped this heavy bill on us. It was called 'Repayment of national debt.' Even Oma Loes got hit with it. They wanted money back for the trip over here, for clothes, blankets, and furniture we never even got. Oma Loes hadn't received any help or items for herself and her kids, yet she was expected to pay up. With her widow's pension messed up and coming in late, paying this back was a huge struggle. But she did it, every single cent. For Oma Loes, a single mum and an Indisch woman, figuring things out in a not-so-welcoming Netherlands was incredibly hard. She and her family had to live quietly, in near poverty.

That was the reality for a lot of Indisch people here — starting over wasn't easy with no job opportunities, poor housing, and feeling isolated. Back then, there wasn't any support or guidance like there is today. Many Indisch people had to figure things out on their own, which made them turn inward and feel even more like outsiders. They missed the simple things from back home, like the sound of coconut leaves, the alang-alang, Asian long grass swaying, and the scent of *melati* flowers. Sticking close to other Indisch friends and reminiscing about the old days was a comfort, a way to be themselves in a place that felt so alien.

The start of Indisch gatherings and reunions became a thing. These events were built on their shared history, a bond that maybe still ties the second and third generations together. But with this connection to the past, there was also a push to fit into Dutch culture. Indisch people, especially the women, started cooking and eating Dutch foods, trying to blend in as seamlessly as possible.

Integrating into Dutch society was largely a smooth process because the Indos really didn't want to rock the boat — they aimed to merge into the background. My parents were among those who worked hard to adapt, trying their best to become part of the Dutch fabric. In doing so, they felt they had to give up a big part of who they were, losing their Indisch identity to fit into the Dutch way of life. Everything was different — the weather, the houses, the culture, and even the daily routines. Adapting wasn't just a choice; it was survival.

Despite these challenges, the Indisch community brought a lot of their world into the Netherlands, enriching the country with their traditions, food, music, art, dance, sports, literature, and more. Thankfully, many, including my parents, had the strength to push through these tough times. They managed to carve out a decent life for themselves here and made meaningful contributions to Dutch society. Having family already in Holland helped my parents a lot, providing that extra bit of support when they needed it.

Thanks to the Indisch community's welcoming nature and their rich food culture, Indisch *toko's* (shops selling Indisch products and food) and restaurants started popping up all over the Netherlands. They introduced traditional dishes, *rijsttafels* (rice tables), and culinary treats not just to the Dutch palate but also internationally. Indisch cuisine became something special here, with dishes like nasi goreng, *bami goreng* (fried noodles), satay, peanut sauce, prawn crackers, and *spekkoek,* layered cake, becoming beloved treats across the country.

"The Hague, The Hague, you are the widow of the Dutch East Indies," sings aunt Lien, or *tante Lien,* in a famous song by Wieteke van Dort. It captures the sentiment of loss and nostalgia for the Dutch East Indies, a sentiment deeply felt in The Hague. This city became known as the "Indisch city of the world," a place where the Indisch community could find a taste of home. You could find authentic Indisch meals at eateries and restaurants like *Garuda* and *Warung Soeboer,* to name just a couple. Indisch cuisine turned trendy, with people trying out recipes in their own kitchens.

Anita, like many, would sometimes pick up food from *Toko Toet* or *Soeboer* on *Koningstraat,* King street. She'd bring home *nasi rames,* a dish of white rice served with various sides like *rendang* (a spicy beef coconut curry), *sambal goreng boontjes* (green beans in spicy sambal sauce), and *sambal goreng telor* (fried eggs in sambal sauce). We loved *tempeh kering* (fried fermented soybeans) and *abon* (dried pulled meat), too. Sharing these treats in the evening was a real treat for us, a small celebration of our heritage.

The Hague also played a big role in the history of Indo music, especially with the rise of Indo rock bands. Andy Tielman, known as the "godfather" of Indo rock, led the way. The Hague and the rest of the Netherlands saw many Indo rock bands, with the Blue Diamonds, known as the Dutch Everly Brothers, becoming world-famous for their song "Ramona." Other notable bands included the Tielman Brothers with "Carioca" and The Crazy Rockers with "Amapola." But Indo music isn't just about rock; it has influenced a wide range of musical styles.

The Indisch culture in the Netherlands has fostered many creative talents, from musicians to writers. Cultural centres and events like the Pasar Malam offered a platform for these artists to showcase their skills and celebrate their heritage. The Indisch cultural events and gatherings, or *'kumpulans'*, attracted not just Indisch people but also Dutch folks and others. Boy and Anita were regulars at these events, enjoying live music from bands like The Crazy Rockers with Eddy Chatelin, The Valiants with Peter Layton, The Blue Comets, and many more. Sometimes, I tagged along. There was always someone to chat with, have a drink or an Indisch meal with — maybe a *lumpur*, those tasty steamed rice rolls filled with spicy chicken, or a sweet pastry — and hit the dance floor.

Louise and I were big fans of the Tielman Brothers, especially Andy and Reggy, with their killer guitar solos. My go-to tracks were *'Return to me'* and *'That's my life'*. But my music taste wasn't just about Indo rock; I was into a bunch of different stuff. The upbeat tunes always lifted my spirits. I jammed out to Golden Earring's *'Radar Love'*, Fleetwood Mac's *'Black Magic Woman'*, Carlos Santana's *'Maria Maria'*, and dug into jazz legends like Stan Getz. Claude was also into Stan's stuff, along with Chet Baker, Nat King Cole, Tony Bennett, Oscar Peterson, Miles Davis, Duke Ellington, and Louis Armstrong.

I even hit up the annual North Sea Jazz Festival in The Hague and later in Rotterdam, catching acts like Hans and Candy Dulfer, Herby Hancock,

Ella Fitzgerald, Norah Jones, Al Jarreau, and George Benson live. Music just does something special for me, like it wires my brain differently.

We'd also catch performances by Opa Bell on his violin and aunt Dési's soprano voice, sometimes at Dierenpark Wassenaar and other venues. aunt Dési even sang '*Ave Maria*' by Franz Schubert at Louise's and my first weddings. To put it simply, it was magical!

Boy's bookshelf was like a mini museum of stories from back in the Dutch East Indies days. One of the big hitters on that shelf was 'Max Havelaar' by Multatuli, published back in 1860. This book wasn't just a story; it was a big middle finger to how things were run in the colonies, coming from someone who'd seen it all firsthand.

Then, you've got Louis Couperus, who was part Dutch, part Indisch, writing about what life was like over there in books like 'The Silent Force' and 'Of Old People, The Things That Pass'. These weren't just any old novels; they were stories that hit close to home for a lot of people.

Hella Haasse was a heavyweight in Dutch literature, snagging all sorts of awards and even sitting down with the queen on TV. She always said she was an Indisch girl at heart, and her books, like 'Oeroeg' and 'Gentlemen of the Tea', really show what that world was like.

As for Claude, he was all over the map with his reading. He liked writers from everywhere: Wilbur Smith's adventures, Nelson Demille's thrillers, and classics from Shakespeare, Ian Fleming's spy novels, and Tolkien's fantasy worlds. It was a mix that showed he wasn't just stuck in one place or one kind of story.

# 6.2 AT THE BOTTOM OF THE LADDER

Starting from scratch in the Netherlands was a common story for many Indos. Some managed to hit the books again, while others got lucky and landed jobs right off the bat.

*F*or my father, it wasn't easy to find work that fit him. He sent out a lot of job applications but didn't get much luck. I think he wasn't really all in with those job hunts. It's understandable, though. After having a good position in New Guinea, starting from the bottom in the Netherlands, even with his skills, was rough.

He finally got a job at *Novib*, an organisation focused on international aid, and later moved to the Ministry of Social Affairs and Public Health. That ministry was the first to start putting out info commercials on TV. My dad worked on getting government information out through radio and TV, which was a pretty new thing back then.

He was involved with *Postbus* (P.O. Box) *51*, this place where people could ask the government questions. He helped create those *OQ* "Also YOU" ads. With his team, he brainstormed, wrote, and fine-tuned these TV spots. They made commercials about health, safety, and even how to stop smoking. These ads got people's attention and were quite popular, setting a trend that other countries picked up on.

One of the OQ ads that got pretty famous was about keeping clean, especially for kids who were super active all day. It pointed out how a lot of young people would just throw their pyjamas on over the same sweaty underwear they'd been wearing all day, hit the sack, and then do it all over again the next day. The ad's punchline was about teaching kids good hygiene habits from the get-go, ending with a nudge to "You too!" and a shoutout to Postbus 51 for more info.

OQ team members with incoming OQ mail at Ministry of Public Health and Environmental Protection, Leidschendam, the Netherlands

My father's job also involved keeping up with the news, both Dutch and international. He'd sift through newspapers, looking for stuff relevant to the Ministry. Whenever I popped into his office in the mornings, his desk was practically buried under piles of newspaper clippings in all sorts of languages. Reading everything quickly and efficiently was key, and he had trained himself to read way faster than average. But it required serious focus to avoid getting sidetracked.

Being multilingual, including fluent in Malay, was a big plus for my father in his work. At home, he and my mum would sometimes switch to Malay, especially when they wanted to keep things from Louise and me.

We weren't fans of being left in the dark, but we picked up enough Malay words over time to get the gist of their conversations every now and then.

His steady job meant we could finally look for a better place to live. My parents found an apartment in Leidschendam, not far from where the Social Affairs and Public Health office was. We were all ready to leave the guesthouse and its endless battle with the grime from the Aladdin heater — grease on everything from the furniture to the curtains. Despite my mum's best efforts with green soap, that place never felt clean. Our first place in Leidschendam didn't have central heating, but by July 1968, we moved into another flat that did, making a big difference in our comfort.

## Get-togethers, food and dancing

Even with our place lacking central heat, it somehow became the go-to spot for all sorts of meet-ups. We'd have movie nights, family catch-ups, and other get-togethers pretty often. Sometimes, we'd spend evenings reminiscing about life back in the Dutch East Indies and New Guinea. Dad would pull out his old films and slides from his travels and family moments, narrating them himself. You could tell it hit him hard sometimes; his voice would get all choked up, and he'd need a minute to push down the lump of homesickness before he could keep going.

Everyone seemed to love coming over, being together, having a laugh or maybe because of the Indisch snacks like pasties and *lumpur* we'd serve up, or maybe because our house, no matter how small, always felt welcoming. It wasn't unusual for our guests to bring along some home-made goodies too.

That kind of warmth, that's pretty standard in Indisch families. It's in our DNA to make sure everyone who walks through the door gets a warm welcome, usually with a plateful of something tasty straight away. In our books, food isn't just food; it's how we show we care, how we celebrate, and how we comfort. "Have you eaten yet?" isn't just a question; it's a way of saying, "I care about you." Food, in all its forms, is our way of spreading love.

Across the Netherlands, Indisch clubs started popping up, places where you could dive into our food, relive old times, and share that ache for what was left behind. My parents, Anita and Boy, joined a few of these clubs, driving out even to places like *Beverwijk*, just to be part of that community. These gatherings were about more than just hanging out; they were a source of strength, helping everyone keep a piece of home alive in this new land. Live music often upped the vibe, with bands like The Hell Cats and The Time Breakers playing, and my parents, they really got into the dancing, especially the jiving. They had moves!

Whenever a rock tune like *'Jailhouse Rock'* or *'Around The Clock'* kicked in, it was like a switch flipped for them. They couldn't help but jump up and hit the dance floor. Dancing was in their souls, and their feet just knew what to do. They'd pull off these slick steps, keeping their knees close, throwing in some kicks, all while their arms swung in rhythm. Boy had this move where he'd draw my mum in close, spin her around, and then smoothly step back. Sure, it took a bit out of them, and after a couple of dances, they'd need to catch their breath and grab a drink. My dad got nicknamed 'Blue Suede Shoes' because of how into it he was. Watching them go at it on the dance floor, mixing smooth moves with wild energy, was something special.

Boy didn't just dance; he was also the chair of ROKI for over five years. ROKI's this group where people who used to play netball back in the East Indies got together to keep active and socialise. They weren't just about netball though; they had bowling, bridge, tennis, shuffleboard, and regular meet-ups. Boy and Anita, along with Anita's sister Puck and her husband Harry, brother Hans and his wife Joyce, were all about getting into tennis, bowling, and shuffleboard at these gatherings.

Claude, 1994

Minister Irene Vorrink with Claude at the Ministry of Public Health and Environmental Protection in Leidschendam

# 6.3 Knight in the Order of Orange-Nassau

Claude getting a royal decoration was unexpected, but a real nod to all he had done. He was pretty proud of that orange ribbon and only brought it out for special occasions.

Claude worked as a legal secretary at the Ministry of Public Health and Environment Health in Leidschendam.

Jumping to 1976, that marked 40 years of Claude serving the government, counting his time in the Dutch East Indies and New Guinea. It was then that he got knighted in the Order of Orange-Nassau by Minister Irene Vorrink, mainly for his groundbreaking work in New Guinea. What he did there wasn't just a big deal over there but got recognised back in the Netherlands too. He was one of the few to get such honour, even though there were probably others who did just as much to deserve it.

Order of Orange-Nassau

Later on, in 1982, Boy had to have open-heart surgery, which was a lot scarier back then than it is today. He had four bypasses and a valve fixed up at the Academic Hospital in Leiden. Thankfully, everything turned out alright, but it was a slow road back to doing normal stuff again. It was a few months before he felt like himself and half a year before he could play tennis again. Eventually, he got back to fishing, which was a big thing for him. He'd head out with his son-in-law Ed and brother-in-law Hans to catch pike in the winter and carp in the summer. Unlike in New Guinea, though, they'd always throw the fish back in the water after catching them.

Later in life, Boy started feeling the toll of his past, especially the years he spent as a prisoner of war. He'd kept all those tough experiences bottled up, and now, both physically and mentally, it was like they were fighting to get out. There was no running from these battles. I regret never asking him about the nightmares that kept him up at night. A friend guessed it might've been because, with more time on his hands, he reflected more on his past and realised he didn't have much time left. He had a few close friends he'd open up to about what he'd been through.

"

Silent sorrow

So well hidden,

Sometimes tangible

but mostly not.

Silent grief

sometimes seems to disappear,

really disappear

it does not.

Author Unknown

# 6.4 Their very last adventure

No medicine could make a difference.


*I*t was deep into winter, the night stretching from 5 to 6 December in 1995. We'd just had a good time celebrating Anita's birthday, staying up later than usual. It was freezing outside, the kind of cold that made everything slick and tricky to navigate. Around 1 a.m., Dad suddenly started feeling really bad, hit by severe cramps and struggling to breathe. A quick pill under the tongue didn't cut it; his condition just kept getting worse, the pain in his chest ramping up. My mum didn't waste any time and called the emergency doctor, who got an ambulance out to them right away.

The ambulance crew got him onto a stretcher for a quick check — they saw right off he was having a tough time breathing and running a fever. He needed to be in the hospital. They wanted Mum to follow the ambulance, but she was scared to drive on the icy roads, worried about the slippery drive. She tried to give them one of his coats to cover Claude, thinking he might be cold in just his sleeveless shirt and pyjama set, but they assured her he'd be fine under the blanket they had for him.

Come morning, Mum gave me a call over in Hoofddorp, filling me in on everything. We decided I'd come by after work to head to the hospital together. When we got there, we found him in a Medium Care ward, all hooked up to a respirator and surrounded by machines, stuck in his own world where he couldn't even talk to us. He had all kind of wires on his body to be monitored. They also had cameras in his room so the nurses could keep an eye on him.

The very next day, my mum checked in with the hospital first thing. "He made it through the night okay," they told her over the phone. But later that day, while I was tied up in a meeting at work, my assistant came to pull me out — the hospital was on the line.

When I got the call that things were looking bad for my dad, they told me to head straight to the hospital in The Hague. I quickly wrapped things up with my colleagues, grabbed my stuff, and jumped in the car. Trying to reach Mum didn't work out; turns out a neighbour had already taken her to the hospital, and she'd asked for aunt Dési to be there too.

Driving there, my mind was racing. I kept thinking, "Dad, please hang on." I was scared of being too late, especially since I'd been through something similar when Oma Loes passed away while I was coming over from Australia. The hospital parking lot was packed, but I managed to find a spot not too far off so I could make a quick dash to the Medium Care unit.

A nurse met me as soon as I got there, but it was already too late; my dad had passed. They let me into his room, where I just sat next to his bed, holding his hand, crying, and telling him I loved him, even though he couldn't hear me anymore. It felt awful, saying goodbye like that, not being able to ask him anything ever again.

My mum was in another room with aunt Dési, just crying. In just two days, she'd lost her 'jong,' her Boy, forever.

Later, I had to make the tough call to Louise in Sydney to break the news. Thankfully, her husband Erik answered, and he said he'd tell Louise. It was one of the hardest things I had to do.

Afterwards, the doctor told us that my dad had caught a really bad case of pneumonia and basically suffocated. That hit all of us like a ton of bricks. There was no getting around it this time; my Dad couldn't bounce back. The light that always seemed to be in his eyes had gone out, leaving a deep sadness with our family, relatives, and friends. Dad was a man known for his big heart and positive outlook, someone who'd seen a lot of ups and downs in the Dutch Indies, New Guinea, and then some tough times in the Netherlands.

Losing him was especially hard on Mum. They'd been together for nearly fifty years, and suddenly she was without her other half. She really regretted not following the ambulance that night, feeling like she missed her chance to say goodbye. The pain of losing him brought back a flood of memories, including their time spent in captivity together. It was like she was trapped by her past all over again, unable to shake the trauma that now seemed to define her life.

My mum, overcome with grief, made it a weekly ritual to visit father's grave in The Hague. She'd bring flowers and water, carefully tending to his resting place. She'd clean the grave, pick out twigs and leaves piece by piece, that had fallen between the rose quartz stones., and refresh the flowers. Sometimes she'd just stand there, crying. After tidying up, she'd go to the cemetery's chapel to light two candles — one for Boy and one for everyone else she cared about, whether they were still here or had passed on. It was her way of keeping the connection alive, even in such deep sorrow. Sitting in that chapel, Mum found some comfort in her prayers. She told me it helped her. When I came along, I could see a kind of peace settle over her as she sat by the grave or inside the chapel. It seemed to give her a bit of solace. She even confessed to me once during her prayers that she asked to be taken too, to join Dad. But those prayers weren't answered quickly; she lived on for another sixteen years.

I was in Bali with my husband Eric, my sister Louise, and her son Gregory, celebrating Louise's 60th birthday. Francesca, Louise's daughter, and her husband Ryan were still on their way from Brisbane, Australia. We couldn't take our mum with us to Bali; she wasn't up for the long flight and she also couldn't stand the heat anymore. Just a day into our stay in Jimbaran, we got hit by the devastating news from uncle Hans, Mum's brother — our mum, Oma and their sister, had passed away. She was found next to her car at the supermarket, groceries half-loaded, probably having collapsed while out on her own. It seemed like a sudden brain haemorrhage took her, possibly triggered by frustration over forgetting something at the store. That moment marked the end for Anita too, her prayers finally finding their answer.

Getting flights back to Amsterdam was a nightmare; everything was booked solid. After what felt like endless back-and-forth with the airlines, we finally managed to secure seats to the Netherlands. Francesca didn't even get to Bali; she went straight to Amsterdam. That's when we could finally say our goodbyes to Mum and Oma.

Louise and I are forever grateful to our parents for the upbringing they gave us. Despite the financial hardships, they always made sure we were well-cared for. We always went to school in nice, clean dresses, our shoes in good condition, and big, brightly coloured bows in our hair that matched our outfits. Even when my hair was short, I still had a bow. Their love and care were evident in every aspect of our lives.

Louise and I picked up a lot from our parents — values like perseverance, respect, and compassion were big for them, and they passed those down to us children.

They showed us how to face life's hurdles head-on. We're forever thankful for their love, which was always there, no questions asked, for everyone in the family, their friends, and especially us. We've got a treasure trove of memories and stories from them, stuff that ties us not just to our own family history but to the bigger story of people who lived through those times, and to anyone curious about the East Indies and its colonial history.

My parents thought they'd found their forever home a couple of times — first in the Dutch East Indies, then in New Guinea. But like many Indo-Europeans, they often said, 'We are and remain INDOS', a nod to ending up in the Netherlands because of how history unfolded. That feeling, of being in the Netherlands by circumstance, it's something that stuck in our family and amongst most Indos. It always echoed within our families.

Anita and Claude Belloni. Voorschoten, 1993

Winter in The Hague, 1962

# 7. Finally

The stories and memories of our parents are now set down like this, so they won't fade away.

*A*s for figuring out our father's story, Louise and I have had a long journey with that. We've always wondered if he managed to fully let go of the tough times he saw in Japan, to really feel free. Dad remembered everything, good and bad, with crystal clarity. But despite everything, he didn't hold on to any bitterness towards the Japanese or Indonesians. Whatever happened in the past, it shaped not just him and Mum, but us too, in ways we're still discovering.

Anita, Louise, Renée

U.S.S. *Chenango*, Public Domain

# 8. Poem of campmate Ben From the diary of Claude (Boy)

Claude's life was shaped by two deep feelings: a sense of nostalgia for a world that had vanished and would never return, and a yearning for a better, brighter future, a better world.

*L*ike I've mentioned, my father was a big fan of books and poetry, especially material in English. That's why the quotes I've picked for this book are in the style he liked. He once wrote about how, in September 1945, after being released from being prisoners of war, everyone started heading home from Nagasaki. Before splitting up, his good buddy Ben Drewery shared a short poem with him — a poem that stuck with him forever because it captured their feelings so perfectly. Ben, who had a bit of an Oxford English accent, gave these words to my father as a parting gift.

This poem, according to Dad, beautifully captured both his past and that moment in time when longing for a better, freer world was everything.

*"*

And when the stream which overflowed my soul

Was passed away,

A consciousness remained that it had left

Deposited upon the silent shore

Of memory, images and precious thoughts

That shall not die and cannot be destroyed

With thanks to
Ben Drewery, friend and fellow prisoner of war,
Fukuoka 14B, Nagasaki, Japan

Claude (Boy) Belloni

Renée and Louise (on the right)

# 9. ACCOUNTABILITY

*B*elloni family archive, managed by Louise and Renée Belloni, Brisbane, Australia.

Many thanks to the following who gave me permission to use the illustrations and poems in this book.

Belloni, Louise, photo sunset

Doorenmaalen, W.A.L. van, heirs; map New Guinea

Drewery, B., heirs; Poem for Claude Belloni

Heijden Van der; Map Hollandia; School atlas of New Guinea by Drs. H. Eggink, W. Versluys NV, Amsterdam, 1956

Historiek: quonset housing

Indischhistorisch.nl; Model Fukuoka 14B

Internet: photo Men's houses Baliem Valley; public domain

Mansell R., heirs, Palo Alto, CA., U.S.A.; Partial name list Fukuoka 14B

Murakami Hari: Publisher: Penguin Random House LLC (US); Various quotations

Oorlogsverhalen.com; Map of Dutch New Guinea

Siddiqui U.; Poem sunset and sunrise

Stichting Monument Nagasaki; Maquette Fukuoka 14B

U.S.: National Archives And Records Administration: Aerial photograph Fukuoka 14B

Below are the sources I consulted. These can also be used by those who are looking for more depth and want to read more.

KITLV, het Koninklijk Instituut voor Taal-, Land- en Volkenkunde. The Royal Institute for Language, Agriculture and Ethnology

Nationaal Archief. National Archives

NIMH, het Nederlands Instituut voor Miliaire Historie.the Netherlands Institute for Military History

NIOD, Instituut voor Oorlogs-, Holocaust- en Genoicidestudies.Institute for War, Holocaust and Genocide Studies

Stichting Papua Erfgoed. Papua Heritage Foundation

West Papua het vergeten volk. West Papua the forgotten people

Abdoelgani, R., *Heroes Day and the Indonesian Revolution*, 1964

Bergamini, D., *Japan's Imperial Conspiracy*, 1971

Brunsveld-Van Hulten, P., *Het onbeloofde land.* The Unpromised Land, Leeuwarden, 2018

Bruyn de, J.V. Dr., *Het verdwenen volk*, verraad aan en ondergang van een volk. The vanished people, betrayal and downfall of a people, 1978

Bussemaker, H.Th., *Bersiap!*, Zutphen, 2012

Cribb, R., *Gangsters and revolutionaries:* The Jakarta peoples militia and the Indonesian revolution 1945-1945, Singapore, 2008

Delden Van, M., *De Republikeinse kampen in Nederlands-Indië, oktober 1945-mei 1947.* The Republican camps in the Dutch East Indies, October 1945-May 1947, Nijmegen, 2007

Frederick William H., *Visions and Heat: The making of the Indonesian Revolution,* Ohio University Press, 1989

Padmodiwiryo S., *Revolution in the City of Heroes*, 2016

Reid, A., edited by Akira, O., *The Japanese Experience in Indonesia, Selected Memoirs of 1942-1945*, 1986

Schäfer, R., *Terug naar Fukuoka 14.* Back to Fukuoka 14, Ede, 1985

Stellingwerff, J., *Fat Man in Nagasaki*, Franeker, 1980; *Diepe wateren in Nagasaki.* Deep waters in Nagasaki, Franeker, 1983

Vincent, G., *De man die Nagasaki overleefde.* The man who survived Nagasaki: Dick Büchel van Steenbergen *ex-POW Fukuoka 14B*, Meppel, 2019

Willems, W., *Nederlanders door de ogen van de wetenschap* .Dutchmen through the eyes of science, Leiden, 1990

Willems, W., Lucassen, L., *Het onbekende Vaderland*: De repatriëring van de Indische mensen. The unknown fatherland: The repatriation of the Dutch Indisch people. 1946-1964, 's-Gravenhage, 1994

Willems, W., Moor de, J., *Het einde van Indië*: Indische Nederlanders tijdens de Japanse bezetting en de dekolonisatie. The end of the Dutch East Indies, Dutch Indisch during the Japanese occupation and the decolonisation, The Hague, 1995

Zuckoff, M., *Lost in Shangri-La,* HarperPress, New York City, 2011

After I finished writing this book, some new books about the Dutch East Indies came out. I didn't get a chance to read them or include their insights in my work because of my schedules.

I appreciate the accessibility of information from the following websites.

## Websites:

Archief van Tranen. Archive of tears, Pia Media B.V.

Atomic Archive

Buitenkampkinderen. Outer-camp children

De Jongenskamer; voor uiteenzetting van Indische woorden en namen. The Boys room; for explanation of Indisch words and names

Free West Papua

Fukuoka 14B

Indië 1945-1950, The Dutch East Indisch 1945-1950

Indisch anders. Indisch differently

Indisch historisch. Indisch historical

Indische kamparchieven. Indisch camp archives

Japanse krijgsgevangenkampen. Japanese POW-camps

Oorlogsverhalen. War stories

Papua erfgoed. Papuan heritage

Stichting Indische Documenten. Foundation of Indisch documents

Wikipedia

# Interviews

The people I talked to for this book, have been kind enough to let me share their stories. Most of the family, friends, and relatives of survivors I interviewed chose to stay anonymous. Of course, I totally respect their wishes.

F.V., The Hague
J.D., The Hague
B.V., Amstelveen
J.K., Rijswijk
G.C., The Hague
J.M., Delft
L.K., Capelle a/d IJssel
J.J., The Hague
P.D., Utrecht

# Author Notes

## Thank You

Writing this book, *The Sun in His Eyes*, about my father has been a journey filled with warmth. I truly hope that as you read, you found yourself drawn into the remarkable adventures of a man who means the world to me.

My dad was my hero, just as much as my mum was. They both faced their share of challenges head-on, ensuring that my older sister Louise and I never lacked for anything.

There are some incredibly special people in my life who hold a deep place in my heart. I want to highlight two of them here: Louise and my husband, Eric.

Louise, having you as my sister is a blessing beyond words. Working alongside you on this project, with your keen eye for detail, your talent for photo editing, and your creative input on the book's title, has been nothing short of wonderful.

Eric, you've shown me boundless patience, always allowing me the space to prioritise my research and writing, even when it meant putting you second.

This book wouldn't have been possible without the help of several insightful, critically-minded individuals who brought their expertise and understanding of both the subject matter and the English language. Your support was crucial. Thank you for your empathy, constructive feedback, suggestions, tips, and patience. I'm honoured and proud to have crossed paths with each of you on this writing journey.

# "Your story is your strength," Someone once told me.

In this book, I, Renée, the youngest daughter, have shared the life story of my father, Claude (Boy) Belloni, and his family. A significant event disrupted the peaceful life of my father when he was just nineteen, drastically changing his direction. Drafted into the KNIL, the Royal Dutch East Indies Army, his tranquil existence was shattered when the Japanese took control, and he became a prisoner of war.

Yet, despite the adversity he faced, the light of hope never faded from his eyes. His resilience and determination saw him through tough times. Each time he stumbled, he found a way to rise again and continue forward. This optimistic outlook kept the sun shining in his eyes, alongside the joyous moments life brought his way — love, engaging work, and adventures into the unknown.

## Archive of my father

To tell this story, I leaned on a rich archive: Claude's diaries spanning from 1943 to 1948, his articles, documentation, and reports up until 1962, along with later stories shared by him and my mum, Anita. Additionally, I used other important documents detailing his experiences in the East Indies, Japan, the Netherlands, and New Guinea.

Most of what's in the book comes from what Claude told me. But naturally, he didn't share everything. Where there were gaps, I've tried to fill them in as accurately as possible, drawing on information gathered later from family, friends, books, the Internet, and responses from my family and other survivors' families.

## Indo-European connection

It was clear that Claude possessed two remarkable gifts. He was a natural-born journalist, capable of capturing the essence of his experiences with a keen eye for detail and atmosphere. He was also deeply reflective, maintaining a diary over the years, whether daily, weekly, or monthly, and meticulously archiving his life's events. So, the stories I've shared here come from a direct source — I've had the privilege of knowing them firsthand.

The decision to write about my father didn't come easily. It was only after my mother's passing that I began to see how deeply intertwined Anita's history was with Claude's, and in turn, how both of their pasts have shaped mine, making me who I am today. That realisation pushed me to embark on this journey. Having firsthand information was a blessing, but piecing everything together was still a monumental task.

And yes, the connection to my Indo-European heritage matters deeply to me. It's said to resonate within all Dutch people who've had any link to the East Indies, estimated to be around two million. This connection isn't just a part of history; it's a living, breathing aspect of our identities, weaving through the fabric of our lives and stories.


## Life stories

Writing about Claude for the Nagasaki Monument Foundation's website gave me a huge boost. I dug through his diaries and his articles about Nagasaki. Reading his story, along with those of other POWs, moved me deeply and pushed me to dive even deeper into Dad's life. I wanted to capture his journey, write it all down, and share it with the world. My hope was to connect our story to our readers, to reflect, inspire, or even offer new insights into life, depending on where you're coming from.

This is my dad's story, through and through, and I've done my best to make it as open and engaging as possible for anyone who's interested. Thankfully, there are similar stories out there, some turned into books, others kept within families. These narratives deserve to be remembered, which is why I decided to get this book out there. Writing it has been a journey of learning and healing for me. I've felt Dad's discomfort, his pain from standing under the relentless sun, but also his unstoppable positivity. I've seen that light in his eyes — the same light that must have carried him through the toughest of times, giving me glimpses into his life. His story wasn't just his source of strength; it's become mine, too.

Renée Belloni

# About Renée
# Bushgirl, Citygirl, Bushgirl

*T*he life story of my father Claude (Boy) Belloni and family is my debut as a writer. With all my heart I trust that I have managed to convey my father's feelings in this book.

Not all the stories of the past have been told and not all the memories have been collected yet. And yet these stories connect cultures and can touch people's hearts. That is why I hope with all my heart that this story will open doors and hearts. That is why I encourage everyone to write down their stories with memories and experiences of family and friends from the past, so that they are well preserved. And not forgotten, not taken to the grave.

I carry my Indisch roots in my heart with love and cherish them. I am proud of my roots and proud that I may be part of its broad culture and history. Where possible, I propagate this. I think it is important that the knowledge about this and certainly all the feelings involved are preserved and passed on.

What therefore concerns me is how we can make the Indisch culture live on, safeguard it and vitalise it for the future, so that the generations after us understand our culture and want to propagate it in their education and ways of thinking. That is why I am interested in genealogy and for years I have been digging up three family trees that shed more light on family history, work and life. Fortunately, the amount of information online has made my research a lot easier and regarding the Belloni family I now go back as far as 1711.

About my work, I can tell you that I first worked at KLM, Royal Dutch Airlines with my last role as Distribution Manager and also at Air Miles, the loyalty programme of Loyalty Management Netherlands, where I worked from the start as a member of the management team and Contact Centre Manager. After that, I facilitated organisations from my own company on the cutting edge of innovation, customer loyalty and change processes. I am a certified Project Manager, a Customer Relationship Management Professional and an English teacher for foreigners. My last job is Vice President for Sales in the APAC region assisting various industries to combat money laundering, financial crime and countering financing of terrorism through an intelligent based solution.

With my husband Eric, I have been travelling through Australia by truck and camper for the last eight years. I write about our experiences and capture them in photographs and videos. During our travels we like to work, selflessly, on farms or wherever our help and knowledge can be used.

Furthermore, I like to occupy myself with my spiritual life, among other things as a Reiki Master. I like to set the bar high, courses, lectures, books, bring me ever closer to myself. About myself I can say, that I prefer to wear high heels, my nails are painted red and my lips have the same colour. That is how people know me. 'Bushgirl, Citygirl, Bushgirl' might well be the title of one of my own stories. But probably after my book, an anthology of my father's diary, stories and tours, among other things. You can find out more about Claude on my website: www.claudebelloni.com.

Anita, Zoetermeer, the Netherlands, 2002

# APPENDIX

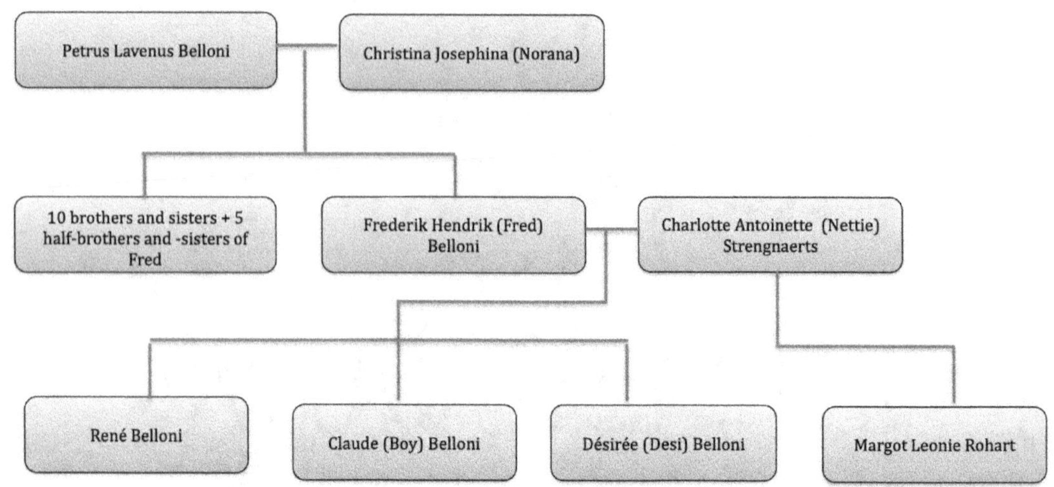

Shortened family tree of Family Belloni

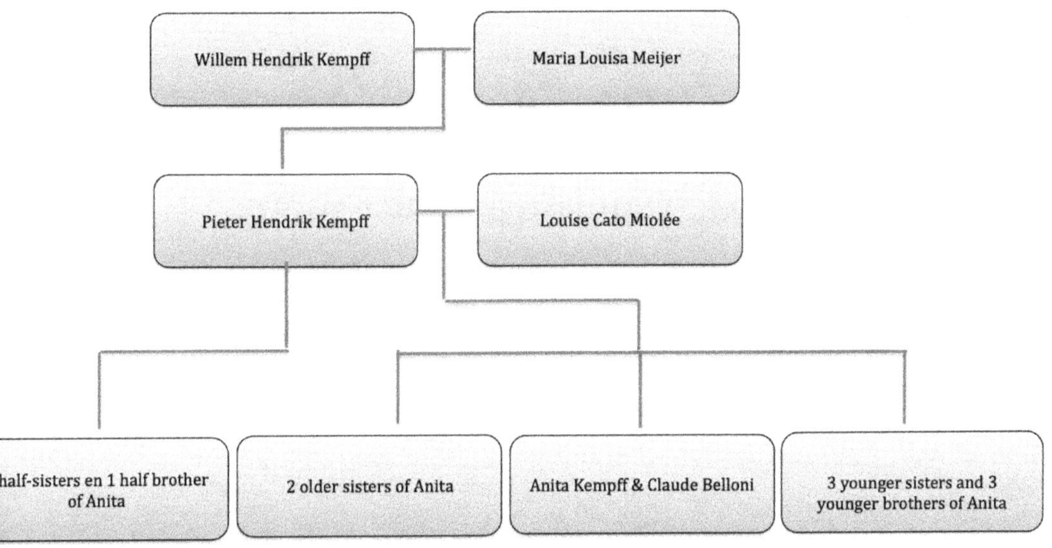


Shortened family tree of Family Kempff

# SUNRISE AND SUNSET

"

May each sunrise promise more,

And each sunset bring more peace.

With thanks to:
Author: Umair Siddiqui

Lest we forget.
Not to forget our past.

Sunset | © Louise Belloni